The Complete Idiot's Refe

Product Innovation Char

Use this form to help establish new product goals and guidelines for your business.

I. Goal(s) for Product Innovation
  A. Target arena(s) into which new product program will take business.
    1. Defined by product type.
    2. Defined by function or end-user activity.
    3. Defined by technology.
    4. Defined by customer/consumer group.
  B. Position within arena(s) that the firm wishes to achieve.
    1. Defined by market share goal.
    2. Defined by market leadership goal.
    3. Defined by dollar goal.
        a. Volume
        b. Profit level
        c. Total dollars
        d. ROI
        e. Payback percent on sales
  C. Special goal(s) peculiar to the firm's unique situation.
    1. Image—maintaining or redefining
    2. Diversification
    3. Other

II. Strategies to achieve goal(s) defined in I.
  A. Strengths to exploit.
    1. R&D-related strengths.
    2. Manufacturing-related strengths.
    3. Marketing-related strengths.
  B. Weaknesses to avoid.
    1. R&D-related weaknesses.
    2. Manufacturing-related weaknesses.
    3. Marketing-related weaknesses.
  C. Source(s) of new products.
    1. Internal
    2. External
        a. Acquisition of companies
        b. Acquisition of licenses
        c. Joint venturing
  D. Degree of innovativeness sought.
    1. Inventive—technological leadership.
    2. Innovative—use established technology in new ways.
    3. Adaptive/economic—let others lead, but be the low-cost producer.
  E. Special Considerations—such as:
    1. Acceptable risk level.
    2. Patentability.
    3. Market size or growth factors.
    4. Line completeness.
    5. Avoiding certain competitors.
    6. Avoiding regulatory or other legal/social pressures.

Market Attractiveness Worksheet

Use this form to help evaluate the attractiveness of a new market.

Market Attractiveness:

	Current			+5 years		
	Hi	Med	Lo	Hi	Med	Lo
I. Market Factors						
A. Size						
B. Growth rate						
C. Diversity						
D. Life-cycle stage						
E. Cyclicality/seasonality						
F. Pricing sensitivity/stability						
II. Service Requirements						
A. Level of technology						
B. Functional substitution possible?						
C. Captive customers						
D. Customer concentration						
E. Customer bargaining power						
F. Stability in recessions						
III. Competitive Factors						
A. Degree of concentration						
B. Attitude: Passive? Aggressive?						
C. Changes in type/mix						
D. Leader's position						
E. Sensitivity of market share						
F. Extent of "captive" business						
G. Vertical opportunities/threats						
IV. Financial/Economic Factors						
A. Industry profitability						
B. Leveraging potential						
C. Investment intensity						
D. Industry capacity utilization						
E. Raw material availability						
F. Barriers to entry						
G. Threats and risks						
V. Social/Political Factors						
A. Social attitudes/trends						
B. Environmental factors						
C. Regulatory constraints						
D. Union constraints						
VI. Technology						
A. Maturity						
B. Volatility						
C. Complexity						
D. Patent protection						

alpha
books

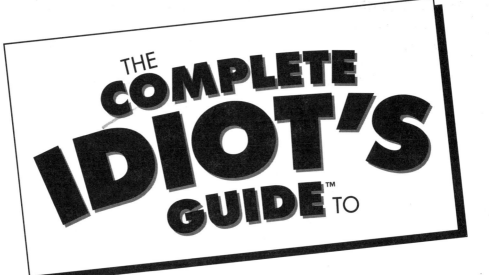

THE
COMPLETE
IDIOT'S
GUIDE™ TO

New Product
Development

by Edwin E. Bobrow, CMC

**alpha
books**

A Division of Macmillan General Reference
A Simon & Schuster Macmillan Company
1633 Broadway, New York, NY 10019

RAP 406 8971V

Copyright©1997 Edwin E. Bobrow

International Standard Book Number: 0-02-861489-5
Library of Congress Catalog Card Number: 97-070166

99 98 97   8 7 6 5 4 3 2 1

Interpretation of the printing code: the rightmost number of the first series of numbers is the year of the book's printing; the rightmost number of the second series of numbers is the number of the book's printing. For example, a printing code of 97-1 shows that the first printing occurred in 1997.

Printed in the United States of America

Note: Reasonable care has been taken in the preparation of the text to ensure its clarity and accuracy. This book is sold with the understanding that the author and the publisher are not engaged in rendering legal, accounting, or other professional service. Laws vary from state to state, and readers with specific financial questions should seek the services of a professional advisor.

Publisher
Theresa Murtha

Editorial Manager
Gretchen Henderson

Editor
Nancy Warner

Production Editor
Michael Thomas

Copy Editor
Michael Thomas

Cover Designer
Mike Freeland

Illustrator
Judd Winick

Designer
Glenn Larsen

Indexer
Chris Wilcox

Production Team
Angela Calvert
Mary Hunt
Malinda Kuhn
Megan Wade

Contents at a Glance

vi

Contents

6 Nurturing New Ideas   55

7 What's a Plan Without a Strategy?   65

Foreword

I had lunch a short time ago with a very successful Japanese businessman. His daughter wanted to major in business in the United States, and eventually wanted to get an MBA.

He was puzzled.

"How can you teach business? It's so broad. There's so much to learn."

In America, I explained, we turn out so-called "business experts" like the Japanese turn out Toyotas. Very quickly. Very efficiently. And they all seem to have one proprietary new product system or another.

Since I've been developing products and positionings for the top companies in the United States, I have watched many alleged "perfect systems" come and go. In one slightly weird methodology, one new product consultant even developed a box with a series of pins for different aspects of the new product development process. When all the holes were filled, he said, the product was a winner. Like most new product schemes (or scams, possibly), it didn't work. There is no black box for new product development. That's why the new product failure rate has hovered at about 90 percent for at least twenty years. Nobody sets out to create a failure. It just happens.

But this book has the answer to developing successful new products. It's a reverse from the usual mindset that says "Make a product and pray to the marketing gods that you can find someone to buy it." Author Edwin E. Bobrow says, "Find things (people) need to buy and then make them."

However, most companies continue to develop products that they want to sell, rather than what the consumer wants to buy. This is especially disheartening in the case of smaller entrepreneurs and companies. They spend their life savings (or R&D budgets) developing a product that hasn't even a glimmer of a chance at success when they could have saved their money and their sanity by spending some money on up-front ground-work and research.

This book can be a life raft to these people. It's a virtual compendium of steps and tasks that managers and entrepreneurs must take to ensure new product success. You can pick and choose the tools that are right for your particular need. Virtually every key part of the new product process is clearly laid out. The book includes "How-Tos" for brainstorming, research, working with management, and even getting space at the retailer level. Mr. Bobrow doesn't know it, but I'm going to "borrow" some of his brainstorming techniques for my own ideation sessions.

This book is comprehensive without being weighty and it's a fun read. The "The Least You Need to Know" sections are worth the price of admission because they quickly explain the do's and don'ts of the new product development process.

As Mr. Bobrow says, "Man has few needs, but many desires." This book talks about fulfilling these desires—the heart of any new product development program.

If developing a successful new product is on your agenda, this book will provide you with the tools for new product success. Mr. Bobrow lays out a realistic approach to making things happen.

Barry Feig

Barry Feig (Newmex@aol.com) has been troubleshooting for marketing companies for over twenty years, developing new marketing concepts, products, and marketing opportunities for corporate giants such as American Express, First Brands, Colgate-Palmolive, American Cyanamid, Pepsico, etc. In 1986, he founded Barry Feig's Center for Product Success (formerly New Products Workshop), where he guides companies through the labyrinth of developing and marketing successful products, using his non-traditional "the consumer drives the market" approach. Barry Feig is also author of *The New Products Workshop: Hands-On Tools for Developing Winners* (McGraw Hill), and *Marketing Straight to the Heart* (Amacom).

Introduction

In the beginning...*everything* was a new product. Today, most businesses rely on new products and services for more than a third of their sales revenue. Now, look around the room you happen to be in. How many of the products around you have been introduced within the past five years? (I don't have the answer—it's *your* room, office, or house, not mine—but, unless you're reading this book in a cave, I bet you can count more than a few new products that have become a regular part of your life.)

Innovation is a fixture of our civilization. It's not some exotic activity of an ivory tower R&D department. And while genius is always welcome, the fact is that mere mortals do the lion's share of new product development—just as they do most of the selling, the tabulating, the planning, and the building that are the everyday activities of business life.

So this is a book for anyone who is directly or indirectly involved in innovation. Or anyone who *wants* to be involved. Or—these days—for anyone who finds that he or she has no choice but to *get* involved in the creation, development, and marketing of new products.

Because new product development soars above all of the artificial barriers that cookie-cut the business world—the thin but stubborn cubicle walls that separate R&D from marketing and marketing from engineering and engineering from sales and sales from manufacturing—no single book can cover every aspect of the subject. But this book will guide you through this exciting and vital field.

Part 1: Poof!...You're a New Product leads you into the world of innovation, telling you what it takes to create, develop, and market new products.

Part 2: Where Babies Come From is about taking charge of inspiration and harnessing creativity in order to generate—on a regular and dependable basis—viable new product ideas.

Part 3: Will the World Like It? takes you beyond your own head and out into the marketplace. You may like your idea, and so may your friends and colleagues. But what about the rest of the world? Here is a discussion of how to set goals and objectives for new product development; how to approach market research; and how to conduct quick, cheap, and accurate tests before committing big dollars and major time to extensive development work.

Part 4: Is It Worth It? fleshes out the all-important transition from good idea to profitable merchandise by showing how to translate the product concept and your picture of what the market wants and needs into a product that is technologically and economically feasible. Chapters here cover the stage-gate system for expediting and controlling new product development, the creation of a fully comprehensive business evaluation, the best strategies for identifying appropriate markets, and identifying the available options for distributing the new product.

Part 5: Made in the Shade prepares you to face the real-world challenges of patents, copyrights, and trademarks, as well as financing new-product ventures. The section concludes with strategies for ensuring that the product you create will embody the high degree of quality that is absolutely essential to enduring new product success.

Part 6: Can You Do It Again? is a blueprint for a sustained success with new products. In order to compete in a business environment that derives fully a third of its revenues from innovation, you need to rely on new product success as the rule rather than the exception. Here are ways to make that happen.

Extras

In addition to advice, guidance, explanations, and examples, this book offers other types of information to point you in the direction of getting the job you want, that define buzzwords and jargon, that furnish facts and figures, that give you tips for going the extra mile, that point out pitfalls to be avoided, that list procedures and processes step by step, and that give brief case histories and extended examples. Look for these easy-to-recognize signposts in boxes:

Prototype

What's new to you is old hat to others. Here are examples of the new product experiences of others.

Buzzword
New product development uses a lot of new words, jargon, catch phrases, euphemisms, and hot-button words. These boxes will tip you off to the most important ones.

Jump Start
These are tips about better ways to get things done and nuggets of knowledge that will help put your thinking about new products in perspective.

False Start
Some new product moves are better avoided. These boxes highlight the pitfalls.

Special Thanks from the Publisher to the Technical Reviewer

The Complete Idiot's Guide to New Product Development was reviewed by an expert who not only checked the technical accuracy of what you'll learn in this book, but also provided invaluable insight and suggestions.

Our special thanks are extended to Elko J. Kleinschmidt, Ph.D., a leading expert on the process of new product development and international factors' influence on new product outcome. Dr. Kleinschmidt is a professor of Marketing and International Business and Director of the Engineering and Management Program at McMaster University. He is a recognized researcher in the field of new product development, innovativeness, and the impact of the international dimension on new products. He has over 30 publications including articles and booklets.

Dr. Kleinschmidt has international working experience in Europe, North America, Australia, and Africa. He has given numerous seminars to companies in North America, Europe, Asia (China), and Australia/New Zealand primarily in the area of new product development and marketing.

His consulting activities have included market forecasts, new product aspects, and developing new product processes for companies.

Dr. Kleinschmidt holds a mechanical engineering degree, as well as an MBA and Ph.D. in Business Administration. His practical work experience includes engineering tasks, investment analysis for technical projects, and technical marketing.

Part 1
Poof!...You're a New Product

Although many companies maintain separate "product development departments" and "new product groups," the trend in new product development is toward a team approach that cuts across departments, specialities, and job titles. Increasingly, staff in all departments are being called on to contribute to the development of new products.

This is an exciting, if perhaps intimidating, trend. The three chapters that follow will give you a leg up into the world of creating and developing new products.

Anyone and Everyone Can Create New Products and Services

In This Chapter

➤ Why innovate?

➤ Innovation versus invention

➤ Available positions on the innovation team

➤ The benefits of failure

The couch you're sitting on, the light you're reading by, and even the book you're reading, all were invented by someone. The fact is that just about anyone and everyone *can* come up with new products and services. You don't have to be part of an R&D team, or a genius inventor, or a marketing specialist. And, in a little while, I'm going to talk to you about nurturing and cultivating ideas—about how to develop them and about where to find them in the first place.

Now, the preceding paragraph was your pep talk. The rest of this chapter is about reality.

Most people think new product development is *all* about coming up with new ideas. Period. Then, *poof!...you're a new product!* Most people are—in a word—mistaken. Inventing new ideas is only a single step in the process of new product development. There is a lot more. And, as I've just said, I'm going to be level with you: Some of that "lot more" is discouraging. But here's the bottom-most bottom line: Discouraging or not, if your company doesn't bother to come up with the new ideas, or comes up with them but fails to follow through with the "lot more," your company will wither and, sooner or later, die.

Now, *somebody* better do something. Why not you?

Travel with me back to 1985. We were all younger then and full of hope. At least we were young and hopeful enough to introduce some 10,000 new products into the American marketplace. By the beginning of the 1990s, we were five years older—and, some of us, about a hundred years less hopeful. By the 1990s, around 8,000 of those new products had been discontinued and withdrawn after millions of dollars and millions of hours had been plowed into their development and marketing.

The Me-Too Approach

Wouldn't you be better off just putting this book back on the shelf—maybe you haven't even left the bookstore yet!—and sinking some dough into mutual funds, a nice bond portfolio, or even U.S. Savings Bonds? As for innovation…well, no one knows better than you that there's a lot of competition out there. Why not just wait for the other fella to take the dumb risks, bring out a new product or service, and, if by some fluke the thing catches on, pounce on it and copy, copy, copy.

Jump Start
According to new-product consultant A. L. Page, for every 11 "serious" new product ideas or concepts, 3 enter development, 1.3 are launched, and 1 succeeds.

The me-too approach *can* and *does* work, at least in the short term. If the market for a new product grows fast enough and gets big enough, there is plenty of room for me-too competitors. But that's the short term. In the long run, most me-too firms die, some more quickly than others.

Are there exceptions to this prognosis? Sure—but far fewer than you think. Let's look at a dramatic example. IBM introduced the personal computer on August 12, 1981. Talk about a successful new product! In the initial months of its release, demand far outstripped supply. By all indications, IBM was on its way to owning the world.

But that didn't happen. In fact, today, IBM is a greatly downsized corporation with a very modest share of the PC market. What happened? By the middle 1980s, a horde of manufacturers—the majority of them small start-up companies—copied IBM's innovation. Michael Dell, CEO of Dell Computers, one of the most successful of those companies, frankly, if uncharitably, observed that "any idiot with a screwdriver" could manufacture a PC.

So here's an example of the innovator taking all the risk, and a flock of imitators cashing in on most of the rewards. Right?

Not quite.

There are a few good lessons to be learned from this example. First, innovation in and of itself is not enough. Your company must follow through with great marketing, distribution, manufacturing, appropriate patent protection, and continual refinement and improvement of the product in response to (as well as in anticipation of) market needs and desires. IBM fell short of the mark in a number of these areas and was overtaken by hungrier, less muscle-bound, and more agile competitors. However, relatively few of those competitors survived for long. It's not as if a heap of upstart companies got together and beat up exclusively on IBM. They beat up on each other, too, and most fell, dazed, by the wayside.

Finally—and this is key—the "me-too" companies that survived knew what to *copy* and what to *innovate*. Some pioneered improved designs, better displays (i.e., video systems), and faster processing speeds. In effect, they produced new products. But design innovation is not the only element that can make for a new product. Other firms introduced innovative pricing and distribution strategies, including direct sales. Some innovated by including special offers of "bundled" software. Some skillfully marketed innovations in customer service and technical support. All of these represent new product development.

The point is this: Innovation does not always require reinventing the wheel. Many companies have achieved long-term success by knowing how to combine a me-too approach with product innovation.

From The Wheel To "Beam Me Up, Scotty"

Speaking of inventing the wheel, let's go further back in history. Take a lesson from the ancient Greeks. Ancient Greek civilization thrived gloriously for more than three centuries of innovative thought and a continual quest for knowledge. Then, as Athens became encrusted with bureaucracy, inertia became the rule, and Greek civilization suffered from a spiritual and intellectual hardening of the arteries that rendered it incapable of mastering events or even responding to them effectively. The result was that Greek civilization was supplanted by an upstart competitor—Rome—which innovated widely, commercialized its innovations, and ultimately spread its influence over a third of the world. Historians, especially those who are passionate about Greek civilization, eagerly point out that most of Rome's so-called innovations were borrowed (stolen?) from the Greeks. True enough. But the Romans were great refiners of what they borrowed, and they used the me-too approach as the basis for genuine innovation, introducing to the broadest possible market ideas ranging from glass making, to brass smelting, to credit financing, to military strategy, to concepts of justice and government.

By and by, the Romans likewise became complacent and stopped innovating. Over a thousand-year period, Roman civilization declined and fell. Its demise was followed by a long and dreary era known as the Dark Ages, in which innovation, departure from the status quo, was actively discouraged—often by the keen edge of the headsman's ax or the burning flames that dance around a stake. The Renaissance, with its rebirth of learning and a restless desire to explore the world, reintroduced innovation as a valued cultural norm, and, since then, the cycles of innovation/followed by inertia/followed by innovation have grown shorter and shorter.

> **Buzzword**
>
> In physics, *inertia* describes the tendency of a body to resist acceleration, to remain at rest (or, if already in motion, to stay in motion in a straight line) unless acted on by an outside force. In business and other human affairs, the word describes resistance or disinclination to motion, action, or change. Whether in physics or business, *inertia* operates with the force of natural law and is difficult to overcome.

Futurist Alvin Toffler described this in his 1970 book, *Future Shock*, pointing out that from 6000 B.C. to 1600 B.C., the fastest available long-distance transportation was the camel caravan, which moved at about eight miles per hour. In 1600 B.C., the chariot was introduced, and speeds approaching twenty miles per hour became possible. Yet, almost 3,500 years later, an English mail coach averaged only ten miles per hour. A mere 100 years after this, steam locomotives were traveling nearly 100 miles per hour. Within 60 years of the introduction of advanced steam locomotives, an aircraft exceeded 400 miles per hour. Twenty years after this, pilots were traveling at double this rate—faster than the speed of sound itself. Within about 10 years of this landmark, human beings were crouched in space capsules, hurtling along at 18,000 miles per hour.

Inertia kills businesses just as sure as it kills civilizations. In the distant past, it was possible to live without innovation—if you can call slogging through the Dark Ages living—but the course of history has increasingly tended toward innovation, so that, today, standing still is no longer an option. Through the middle of this century, when you spoke of a generation, you meant roughly a twenty-year period. Any number of "solid" companies made their bread-and-butter money on products that easily endured ten, even twenty years without innovation. As marketers and innovation specialists see the world, a generation is now no more than seven years, and the company that fails to reduce product cycles from a matter of years to a matter of months may well shrivel and die.

> **Jump Start**
>
> Forty-six percent of the money allocated by U.S. firms to new product development is spent on products that fail—that are either canceled or never yield an adequate financial return—according to a study by the Booz-Allen & Hamilton consulting firm.

Why play the new product game?

➤ *It can be profitable.* For your firm, it can mean whole new markets. For you personally, it can mean professional—and financial—advancement.

➤ *It can be fun.* Living in Greece at the high tide of its civilization must have been a blast, especially compared to the place when it was on its dull, downward slide. And England under Queen Elizabeth I was probably a lot more exciting than when it was ruled by Aethelred the Unready. If you've got something against having fun—well, why not just say that innovating is more intellectually rewarding, spiritually satisfying, and emotionally fulfilling than doggedly following the leader.

➤ Finally: *You no longer have a choice.* You can mark time and waste away on the sidelines. Or you can assess the field, do what you can to weight the odds in your favor, play the game, and take your shot at winning.

What If I Don't Have a Brand New Idea?

Maybe all of this energizes you. Or maybe it makes you feel like you're up against a wall. Relax. Inertia, remember, cuts two ways. It may make it difficult to get going, but, once a thing is going, inertia makes it hard to stop. Innovation is not only moving ahead these days, it's accelerating. Why? Because new products beget new products.

Let's go back to the wheel. Maybe it started out as a kind of roller made out of a log. Perhaps it evolved into a solid, round stone with an axle hole through it. As time went on, innovation after innovation was added to the basic wheel: new materials, tires, bearings. Then there were innovations called for by additional new products: a fast mail coach required different wheels from an ox-drawn freight wagon; steam locomotives required one kind of specialized wheel, while diesel locos needed another; the automobile called for additional wheel innovations, and different kinds of automobiles required different wheel and tire combinations.

The personal computer, though based on a host of existing products, comes close to being a genuine invention—startlingly new when it was introduced. Since its introduction, it has created markets for a dazzling array of additional "peripheral" products: improved video accessories, improved audio accessories, printers, scanners, modems, disk drives, and so on.

Jump Start
A new product does not have to be an entirely new invention. In fact, the overwhelming majority of new products are innovations based on existing products.

The beauty of new product begetting new product is that the process makes room for you to play any number of positions in the game. You don't *have* to be an inventor. The new product team can also use innovators, technological innovators, entrepreneurs, and technological entrepreneurs, in addition to inventors.

➤ *Innovators* think of ways to apply (and modify as required) existing products, processes, or services in new markets/environments.

➤ *Technological innovators* think of new products, processes, or services for present markets.

➤ *Entrepreneurs* think of businesses to build around new products.

➤ *Technological entrepreneurs* think of ways to commercialize inventions and innovations via (usually) small businesses.

➤ *Inventors* think of new products, processes, or services.

Buzzword

An *entrepreneur* is someone who organizes, operates, and assumes the risk for a business venture. Characteristically, this is done in the context of a small, independent business. An *intrapreneur* is a person working within a large corporation who takes personal responsibility for turning an idea into a profitable finished product. Like the entrepreneur, he or she does this through assertive risk-taking and a relentless drive toward innovation.

And there is even more to this team roster. I've used the phrase "thinks of" to describe what each of these players does. That phrase actually encompasses activities usually carried out by a *variety* of individuals: different folks who specialize in research, design, fabrication, marketing, selling, and so on. The word *entrepreneur* is also not fully adequate. While entrepreneurs are usually associated with small companies, big business has learned the value of entrepreneurial individuals in the corporate environment. *Intrapreneurs* operate within a large organization to take responsibility for turning an idea into a profitable finished product through the kind of assertive innovation and risk-taking that characterize the activity of the entrepreneur.

A Baby Only a Mother Can Love

A team requires a captain. Many people believe that this is a job for the *entrepreneur* or *intrapreneur*. Often, it is this individual who quarterbacks the new product process. However, any member of the team can serve as the *champion* of a project, the person who really kicks it along, who keeps it alive, who gets it done. Big organizations try over and over to institutionalize the process of innovation—and, later in the book, we will discuss ways to do just that—but, however the process is gussied up with bureaucratic titles and functions, innovation usually comes down to a champion leading a team (sometimes the team is a "skunk works," a small, loosely structured research and development unit).

However your organization handles new product creation, at some point the process comes down to you, an individual either giving birth to or nurturing an idea. Make no mistake, this can be a dangerous position. What if your new product fails to find a market? What if you raise a baby that only a mother could love? The odds are that this is precisely what will happen.

Later, we'll discuss strategies for insulating your company—and yourself—against the consequences of failure (see Chapter 15, "Opening the Gates"). But let's take a final moment here to analyze what is meant by "failure." In the worst-case scenario, you champion a new product—birth it, feed it, teach it to walk. And it fails to return anything resembling a profit. What have you lost? Money? Well, of course…

…unless you recognize that the very process of pioneering a product *energizes* a company—even if that particular product fails to produce an immediate cash profit. New product development can create team morale and purpose; create or maintain an environment receptive to growth and change; and stimulate creativity, motivation, enthusiasm, and the *will* to win.

Buzzword
Skunk Works, a small, informal research and development unit within a larger corporation, is a term that was coined from Al Capp's comic strip *Li'l Abner*, in which Big Barnsmell runs the Skonk Works, which produces moonshine "Kickapoo Joy Juice."

And that, dear reader, is the failure. In case of success, in addition to doing all of these good things, a new product creates a new market or new possibilities within an existing market. It generates profits. It stakes out, for you and your company, a piece of the future.

The Least You Need to Know

➤ Developing new products is a risky enterprise, but it is *certainly* necessary for the growth of your business and *probably* essential to its survival.

➤ Most new products are not *inventions* (wholly new to the world), but *innovations* (extensions and enhancements of existing products).

➤ Developing new products is generally a team effort that offers opportunities for a variety of people with a variety of interests, talents, and skills.

When Is a New Product New?

New products are not necessarily new inventions. In fact, few are. First, no law says that even brilliant inventions will succeed as new products. Thomas Alva Edison, perhaps the greatest and certainly the most famous of America's inventors, began his inventing career by building an electric vote counter, which he intended to sell to the U.S. Congress. The Congressmen examined the invention and were duly impressed. But they did not buy it. The fact was that the *last* thing they wanted was their votes instantly and accurately tallied. The delays inherent in a system of voice vote and roll call allowed individual members of Congress time to strategize together and persuade one another in order to swing the vote. Only temporarily discouraged, Edison declared that, from then on, he would first find out if people *wanted* a product before he went ahead and invented it.

Second, most new products are really *innovations upon* inventions. The innovations make the invention more usable and acceptable in the marketplace.

So, What's New?

You understand now that your company does not *have* to develop a sheaf of patents and new inventions in order to introduce new products. Does that mean you should throw unlimited resources at new product development? Of course not.

It is not sufficient to come up with new products willy-nilly. That's like doing target practice without defining your target. Maybe you'll hit something. Maybe you won't. And maybe somebody will end up getting hurt. Once you make the commitment to new product development as a corporate goal, your company needs to create a program of *strategic innovation*. Now, let's look at the noun root of that adjective *strategic*. In classical Greek military organization, a *strategos* was a general, and the word *strategy* is derived from a related Greek word meaning "the art of the general." At its most basic, the art of the general consists of the following:

1. Defining objectives and goals in the military/political arena

2. Assessing the army's resources and advantages

3. Formulating a plan in which resources and advantages are deployed in order to surprise and surpass the enemy and achieve defined objectives and goals

Buzzword

Objective and *goal* are not synonyms, though they have allied meanings. An objective describes something you want to achieve in the short term, whereas a goal is something you want to achieve over the long term. Usually, it's best to define a goal, and then to define the objectives necessary to reach that goal.

At its most basic, the art of the general differs little from the art of the manager, who must:

1. Define objectives and goals in the marketplace

2. Assess her firm's resources and advantages

3. Formulate a plan whereby resources and advantages are managed (deployed) in order to surprise and surpass competitors and achieve defined objectives and goals

We will explore and discuss strategic innovation throughout this book; however, now is the time to take the first step in the strategic innovation process: to understand what a new product is in the real world.

A Bouquet of New

A new product can be:

➤ An example of new technology—i.e., an invention: Edison's incandescent electric light, for example.

➤ A new innovation—which makes an invention appealing to a given market: Apple's graphical user interface made personal computing more palatable to more people.

Prototype

A new innovation is typically a deliberate attempt to reinvent the wheel—to take a very basic invention and renew it in compelling ways. The wristwatch had been around a long time by the 1930s when Mickey Mouse was added to it, and a long-familiar adult timepiece was suddenly transformed into a gotta-have children's accessory, which ultimately entered the pantheon of American pop culture icons.

Wristwatches have been innovated upon as self-winding mechanical devices; as super-accurate, battery-driven quartz timekeepers; as digital timekeepers; as devices that combine multiple functions, including pulse rate and miles walked; and as personal information managers. The Timex-Microsoft "Data Link" watch, for example, can download alarms, phone numbers, and to-do lists from the wearer's personal computer—all without physical connection to the computer. The watch is held up to the computer monitor screen, which transmits the data to the watch via patterns of light.

By the 1940s, the popular *Dick Tracy* comic strip had equipped the square-jawed detective with a "two-way wrist radio." Today's technology has made cellular telephones small enough to fit unobtrusively into a shirt pocket or on an armband—a *wearable* phone. Perhaps the next wristwatch innovation will be a watch-phone combination.

➤ An improvement or addition to an existing product—handled correctly, this has the impact of introducing a new product without carrying all the risks: Software manufacturers are particularly adept at introducing periodic "upgrades" to existing products and persuading users that the upgrade is desirable to own.

➤ Something new to the market—a familiar product is introduced into a new arena: L'eggs takes women's hosiery out of the department store and into the supermarket.

➤ Something new to the market segment—not as radical as a product that is new to a market: A hardware manufacturer stops distributing his goods through a distributor, and instead sells directly to hardware retailers.

➤ Something new to a country—translating a product that is already successful in one country into another country's marketplace: Japanese cars sold well in Japan, and they have been marketed very successfully in the United States.

➤ Something that represents a new category for a company—a firm identified with one type of product also begins to offer an apparently unrelated type of product: Black and Decker, known for its line of electric hand tools, buys General Electric's small appliance division.

➤ Something is added to an existing product line—line extensions are new products that nevertheless represent a *logical* development from existing products; they are evolutionary rather than revolutionary: The folks at Mystic Tape introduce a wide assortment of "designer colors" to their adhesive tape line.

➤ A new brand is introduced—a company brings out multiple brands in competition with one another: Detergent and cigarette companies routinely do this.

➤ Something is repositioned—think of this as CPR for a failed or failing product, which brings it back to life: Sears, long perceived as a place to go for tools and home appliances, introduces its "softer side of Sears" campaign to reposition itself as a source of reasonably priced women's clothing and accessories as well as table saws and lawn mowers.

➤ Something is repackaged—often, this is part of a repositioning effort; new packaging can make the product appear new, exciting, innovative: A maker of a PC video accelerator card (a circuit board to improve the performance of the PC video display) packages his product in a brightly colored box, suggesting his product is not only the key to new levels of graphic artistry on the computer, but also user friendly, a product for real people and not just computer gurus.

Buzzword

Positioning is how a product or service (or an entire company, for that matter) is perceived by the best potential customer for that product or service (or company). If the way a product or service (or company) is perceived does not produce sales, an effort is made to *reposition* it—that is, to change the way consumers perceive it.

Whatever particular flower you pluck from this "bouquet of new," it—the product—should appear *in some significant degree* new and desirable to the consumer or end user. In this novelty lies both the potential for profits from a new market or market segment, as well as the pitfalls of challenging what consumers are accustomed to.

New to the Consumer or End User

What do consumers want? Wow. You'll have to read the rest of this book to find out. And, I promise, you'll find out a lot—but it won't be nearly enough. There is no substitute for intelligent analysis, testing, *and* market instinct—imagination that starts from the seat of the pants. However, some sorting is in order here and now so that we can think about what newness means to the consumer.

To any consumer, a product or service is new if it has never before been seen, heard of, or used. No argument there. But very few new products take the country by storm. Usually, a certain group of consumers—we can call them "purchase leaders"—try the new product. For a variety of reasons, ranging from socioeconomic background, education, and (probably) genetics, these people are willing to change their behavior and quickly learn to accept or even learn how to use a new product or service. In the meantime, the mass of consumers—let's call them "purchase followers"—wait until the purchase leaders try the product and report liking it.

By the time a large market materializes for the new product, it's often hard to call the product "new" anymore. That's a good thing as well as a not-so-good thing. It's *good* in that a product that has earned the reputation of being tried-and-true is easier to sell in a sustained fashion than a product perceived as new-and-untested. It's *not* so good, however, in that the newness of a product is what gives it much of its push in the marketplace. Newness makes the product worth learning about, at least for a while. It makes it newsworthy, at least for a while. It makes it worth talking about, at least for a while. When the perception of newness fades, the extra push is gone.

Measuring Up

It's often difficult for those planning new products to guess to what degree consumers will perceive their product as new. Sometimes an invention will fail to be perceived as really new, whereas an existing product that is simply improved will be hailed by the buying public as a glorious revolution. However, the closest you can get to an *objective* measure of newness is the degree of behavioral change and learning required to motivate purchase of the product.

Marketing consultant Thomas Robertson attempted to classify new products by how much learning and behavioral change they required. He created three categories:

➤ Continuous innovation: Requires little learning or behavioral change. New car models or packaging changes fall into this category. To the marketer, the advantages of a continuous innovation product are precisely that the consumer need make little effort to adopt the new product. Its disadvantage is that it won't be perceived as being out of the ordinary, exciting, or newsworthy. ("I already have a widget. Why do I need to spend money on a new model?")

➤ Dynamically continuous innovation: Requires a moderate degree of learning and entails some disruption in consumption pattern. The electric toothbrush was hardly a revolution—people had been brushing their teeth for a long time—but it did require a certain change in behavior, a change that was a matter of degree rather than of kind. This area offers a high degree of flexibility to the marketer, who can emphasize product benefits on the one hand, while minimizing the learning curve on the other; however, this type of innovation still may be insufficiently new to generate excitement in the marketplace.

➤ Discontinuous innovation: These products require a high degree of learning and behavior change. VCRs and personal computers are examples. Note that they are exciting products and even now continue to command a lot of press, both advertising and editorial. The disadvantage: they darn well better be exciting—exciting enough to motivate significant changes in consumer behavior.

Don't rely exclusively on so-called objective measurement of concept or product acceptance. This is a good place to start, but it is no substitute for a thoughtful and intuitive exercise of the imagination aimed at assessing the consumer's *subjective* perception of a product's newness. Such a seat-of-the-pants approach may also be guided and tempered by formal market studies and/or consumer questionnaires.

Does the Consumer Want Features or Benefits?

When you think about a product or service, try getting beyond product *features* and think instead about product *benefits*. Features describe product attributes; for example, a certain overnight shipper might describe the principal *feature* of its product as fast, reliable shipping. True enough, but how can this be made to connect dramatically and compellingly with the consumer? Shift from the product feature to the product *benefit*: "Shipping via BrandEx means you never again have to worry about getting your package to its destination on time." The benefit is an emotional perception (here, freedom from worry), a positive feeling derived from using the product.

What Do the Other Kids Say?

In addition to looking at newness from the consumer's perspective, think about the newness of a product from the point of view of the trade. How does the manufacturer, distributor, or retailer perceive the product? Also be aware that, in the case of industrial—as opposed to consumer—products, the end user may view newness either as a consumer would or as the trade would.

From the corporate and trade perspective, a product may be perceived as new if it falls into any of the categories listed under "A Bouquet of New."

New Technology

Because this category requires the greatest change in consumer behavior, new products of this type are the most challenging to market. Moreover, the company that embraces new technology may obsolesce its own existing products—something that not only alarms local CEO types, but also worries dealers and retailers, who may have an inventory to sell off, and upsets industrial consumers, who are concerned that their state-of-the-art equipment may suddenly be outmoded.

On the positive side, new technology can be exciting and can generate huge support within the trade. However, it requires careful planning that balances phase-in and phase-out without taking away from the impact of the product's newness.

New Innovation

The trade will find products in this category more easy to accept than new technology, but also less exciting—unless everyone concerned is convinced that the innovation improves an underlying invention to such a degree that a new market is indeed opened up.

Jump Start
Innovation should not be considered merely for the sake of introducing something new into the marketplace. Innovation should always be directed at making a product more appealing to a current market or opening up additional markets. Support for innovation in the trade should include material (advertising, informational fliers, promotional videos, and so on) that explains how the innovation has increased the marketability of the product.

Improvement or Addition to an Existing Product

Less sweeping than innovation, this category of new product nevertheless also makes the product more appealing. However, beware of creating perceptions in the trade or among consumers that the improvements and additions were necessary because the original product was somehow flawed. On the positive side, personal computer software upgrade programs have demonstrated that, at least with high-tech products, customers will accept the idea of purchasing frequent enhancements and improvements. For high-tech industries, this can be nearly the equivalent to what auto makers enjoyed back in the days when it was routine to trade in last year's model for this year's.

New to the Market

In Meredith Willson's classic musical, one of "The Music Man's" rival hucksters repeatedly scorns the legendary traveling pitchman by singing out: "But he doesn't know the territory!" This is precisely the resistance you must overcome within the trade when you attempt to take a familiar product out of its customary market and introduce it into a new one. Cooperation with the trade is called for. You have, after all, much to learn about the new market. Often, a special sales force, special advertising, innovative displays, new packaging, and creative promotions are required to get the product over the hump.

Prototype

An often-overlooked avenue of innovation is via a special sales force. These are sales personnel who make it their business to open up new markets for existing as well as emerging products. For example, distribution in the publishing industry was once strictly divided into trade (sales through bookstores), direct mail (sales that result from catalog and mail appeals), and special sales. This latter category traditionally consisted of books especially created for special customers.

Just as distribution was divided, so was the type of book produced for each distribution channel. Different books were produced for the trade, for direct mail, and for special sales. Today, however, more and more publishers actively seek ways to distribute the *same* product in multiple channels, and special sales forces are deployed to explore and exploit new channels for books that are also distributed in the trade and through direct mail. Advances in computer-aided publishing have made it relatively easy for a publisher to customize books in unique ways to suit individual customers, and special sales forces often innovate new distribution channels by forging creative partnerships between publishers and special customers.

New to the Market Segment

This is a less ambitious approach than defining a whole new market, because you already have familiarity with (and contacts in) the market. Nevertheless, it is best to exploit the trade's perception that opening up a new market segment is the equivalent of introducing a new product. Again, a special sales force, special advertising, innovative displays, new packaging, and creative promotions are steps to consider.

New to a Country

Media maven Marshal McLuhan introduced the idea of the world as a "global village" back in the 1960s, and, more recently, any number of wide-eyed folks have been claiming that the Internet has rendered political borders and national allegiances obsolete.

Well, try telling this notion to a marketer.

It's true that more products are more global than ever before, but what sells in one country will not necessarily sell in another. If you doubt this for a moment, travel on down to Atlanta, where the Coca-Cola Company has a museum called "The World of Coca-Cola." One of its central features is a bank of spigots that dispense a myriad of Coke products from all over the world. It soon becomes clear that the mango-flavored soft drink that is a top seller in the Philippines is not sold at all in Italy. (Of course, Coca-Cola itself is sold everywhere—the truly global exception that proves the rule.)

Be aware that translating a product from one country to another is not necessarily a shortcut to developing a new product. It requires research, design, and marketing efforts, and then, in response to what these indicate, the product may have to be modified, repackaged, priced innovatively, or promoted in a new way that is literally foreign to its native country.

Buzzword

A *line extension* is a new product that represents a continuous, logical development of the products a company currently offers. For example, Minolta, a maker of conventional cameras, introduced a digital camera, designed to feed electronic images into your personal computer.

Something That Represents a New Category for a Company

If you introduce a new product category to your company, be aware that you will have to deal with new buyers, new customers, new distribution systems, new types of packaging, and new positioning for a different type of consumer. Moreover, something that represents a new category for the company may not be new at all for a market in which competitors are well established. Whoa! Some headache.

On the other hand, all these new people represent new opportunities for revenue. After all, you're not in business to take it easy.

Something Is Added to an Existing Product Line

"Reputation, reputation, reputation! O, I ha' lost my reputation, I ha' lost the immortal part of myself, and what remains is bestial!" Thus said Cassio in Shakespeare's *Othello*. Marketers responsible for promoting a new addition to their firm's product line understand Cassio 100 percent. The inherent logic of line extensions is a great way to gain acceptance for these new products within the trade—provided the *existing* line has a good reputation, reputation, reputation.

Repositioning

The trade may welcome your efforts to revive a flagging product by repositioning it for a new consumer. Repositioning, however, involves *educating* dealers, wholesalers, and retailers. Don't depend on them to "get it" on their own. Also, be sensitive to trade resistance to a repositioning effort; it might tell you that your strategy is askew or even that you should leave well enough alone.

Prototype

Repositioning can be a dramatic move. The makers of Arm and Hammer baking soda had a long-familiar product suffering from a shrinking market. Fewer and fewer people could find time to bake from scratch, and a host of elaborate antacid products had long since displaced baking soda as a remedy for sour stomach. True, Arm and Hammer had few competitors. But where was the market? The answer was to reposition the product as a deodorant for your refrigerator, and an extensive ad blitz was designed to execute the repositioning.

Aspirin is another all-too-familiar product, which, over the past twenty-five years, has been under assault from a variety of competing pain relievers, many of which claim to be safer, more effective, or simply *newer* than aspirin. The Bayer company owned the lion's share of the aspirin market, but, like Arm and Hammer, was faced with shrinking demand. When medical research suggested that aspirin had an unexpected benefit—significantly reducing the risk of a second heart attack in persons who had suffered a heart attack—the company launched an ad campaign to reposition the product as more than a headache remedy. It was now a potential life saver. The medical research gave added meaning to Bayer's leading copy line for its aspirin product—"The Wonder Drug that Works Wonders"—and the aspirin market, after years of decline, opened up once again.

New Brands

The packaged-goods trade is accustomed to dealing with multiple competing brands from the same company. For example, there are very few cigarette manufacturers in this country, but dozens of cigarette brands. Much of the competition in the tobacco industry takes place between brands offered by the *same* company: Philip Morris offers Philip Morris, Alpine, Benson & Hedges, Bristol, Cambridge, Chesterfield, Marlboro, Merit, Parliament, Players, and Virginia Slims cigarette brands. In other industries, however, multiple brands may at best meet with resistance and, at worst, may be regarded as evidence of lunacy.

The Perfect New Product—Ha!

Understanding the varieties of new products is critical to establishing strategic innovation— that is, to establishing an effective framework supporting balanced new-product development. This understanding is basic to assessing risk versus reward and your investment versus the return you may reasonably expect from it.

In a 1982 study, management consultant Booz-Allen & Hamilton concluded the following:

➤ New-to-the-world products, which create entirely new markets, accounted for about 10 percent of total product introductions.

➤ New product lines, by which a firm newly enters an established market, accounted for about 20 percent.

➤ Additions to existing product lines accounted for 26 percent.

➤ Improved products (Booz-Allen specifically studied cost reductions, products that provide similar performance at a lower cost) made up 11 percent of new introductions.

➤ Repositioning or targeting existing products to new market segments accounted for 7 percent.

Here's another thought-provoking statistic: 30 percent of the "new-to-the-world" product and "new product line" categories accounted for 60 percent of the new products viewed as most successful, although non-innovative new product lines and new items in existing product lines were least successful.

Despite the risks, then, the rewards are obviously present, and a company is as ill-advised to devote too many resources to developing "safe" new product categories (such as line extensions and repositioning) as it is to going whole hog on new technology or new innovation. Balance striving for the big hits with upgrading bread-and-butter projects.

Want help defining new products for your firm? Start by answering the following questions:

1. How does the consumer or end user perceive your product?

2. Have you measured the degree of learning and behavioral change necessary on the part of the consumer by using the three classifications spelled out earlier in this chapter?

3. Have you tried to determine the consumer's perception of what is new as it applies to your product?

4. What does the trade or industry consider a new product to be?

5. Do your executives agree as to what is a new product for the company and your trade?

6. Have you measured the new product against corporate and trade classifications offered in this chapter?

7. Has your company developed a system unique to its own needs for measuring and categorizing new products?

8. Have you made the connection between what is defined as a new product and how you will begin to think about marketing the product?

9. Have you begun to think of the different strategies necessary for the different categories of newness?

10. Does your system help organize new products so it helps you see how you can best market them?

11. Is your new product category framework used in developing corporate strategy?

12. Does your new product program have a balanced allocation of resources among categories?

Once you've answered the above questions, you should have a rough picture of just how prepared your company is for innovation, as well as what kind of innovation best suits the environment of your business.

The Least You Need to Know

➤ New products are not necessarily new inventions; most new products are innovations developed from existing products and should be directed at making a product more appealing to a current market or opening up additional markets.

➤ As a rule, the newer the product, the greater the reward—but the greater the risk. However, rewards diminish more sharply than risks for companies that try to "play it safe" by avoiding "new-to-the-world" and "new product line" innovation.

➤ *Highly* innovative and *slightly* innovative products do better than those with a moderate degree of innovation.

➤ Companies need to make sure they diversify their product lines with safe new categories as well as new technology and innovation.

Who Wants Something New Anyway?

We saw at the beginning of the last chapter what Edison learned the hard way: people don't always want something new. The U.S. Congress had a set of needs that definitely would not have been served by acquiring an efficient electrical means of counting members' votes. In inventing his electric vote tabulator, Edison made an assumption based on a general truth: efficiency is better than inefficiency. Like many general truths, however, the one Edison depended on turned out to be unreliable in a particular case. He would have been better off paraphrasing Abraham Lincoln: All of the people want new things some of the time, and some of the people want new things all of the time, but not all of the people want new things all of the time. And then he should have set about defining just who and what that "some" was. This is the essence of new product research.

New Is Not Always Better

Or maybe it is. I don't know, and that's not really important anyway. The point is that there is no guarantee that *consumers* will share your enthusiasm. If *they* don't think new is always better, then you can't depend on invention and innovation alone to sell your product. A 1981 study by the *Journal of Marketing* suggests a complex relationship between degrees of a product's perceived newness and its success in the marketplace.

New Product Success Probability

	Success Ratio	% Successes	% of Cases
The synergistic "close to home" product	1.39	72%	12.82
The innovative superior product with no synergy	1.35	70%	10.26
The old but simple money saver	1.35	70%	15.38
The synergistic product that was new to the firm	1.29	67%	10.76
The innovative high-technology product	1.23	64%	14.35
The close-to-home, "me too" product	1.08	56%	8.20
The better mousetrap with no marketing	0.69	36%	7.17
The "me too" product with no technical production synergy	0.27	14%	10.76
The innovative mousetrap that really wasn't better	0.00	0%	10.26
Mean	1.00	52%	
Total			100.0%

SOURCE: Edwin E. Bobrow and Dennis W. Shafer, Pioneering New Products: A Market Survival Guide *(Dow Jones-Irwin, 1987).*

Let's think about this. The new product with the rosiest prospects for success blends synergy with familiarity. *Synergy* is the combination of known or familiar product elements in new ways. So the synergy is new, but the elements of that synergy are old, and the product itself is familiar. In other words, the *new* product most likely to succeed has only one really new element—synergy—whereas everything else about it is "old." "Build a better mousetrap," Ralph Waldo Emerson said, "and the world will beat a path to your door." Had Emerson substituted, say, "transuranic de-emulsifier" (whatever that might be) for "mousetrap," we would not be quoting him.

Now, only a little less rosy are the prospects for a wholly new product, a product without synergy—but a product that is perceived to be clearly superior to existing products. Yet tied for success-rate honors is the "old but simple money saver" product! Whatever else the consumer wants, he wants to save money.

Was Edison a Failure?

By the late 1870s, when Thomas Edison began working on the incandescent electric lamp, he was already famous and was frequently visited by members of the press. One of them, eager for word on the progress of the lamp, asked for a report and learned that the inventor had spent months testing thousands of materials to use as a filament. None was satisfactory. The reporter sympathized with Edison, remarking that he must be disappointed at his lack of success. The inventor glared at him and then flatly denied that he had been unsuccessful. On the contrary, he said, he now knew of thousands of materials that would *not* work as a filament for an incandescent lamp.

Why New Products Fail

We can learn a great deal from why new products fail. Back in 1979, R. Calantone and R. G. Cooper published an article in the *Journal of the Academy of Marketing Science* categorizing new product failure. Here's what they found:

➤ Twenty-eight percent of the cases they studied were "the better mousetrap that nobody wanted." Technology is a powerful engine. But it *is* an *engine* only—and

Buzzword
Synergy, as applied to a new product, describes a product in which two or more known product elements are associated a new way that results in a whole greater than the sum of the parts. For example, concrete is a building material that was known to the ancient Romans. In 1854, an Englishman reinforced concrete with iron bars. The new product, ferroconcrete, is one of the most successful examples of synergy.

False Start
Wait a minute. Produce a genuinely new product and you have a 70 percent chance of success!? Not quite. According to a Booz-Allen & Hamilton study, 97.5 percent of new consumer products are dropped *before* going to market (and, presumably, after varying amounts of dollars have been spent on developing and testing them). Perhaps 70 percent of *the remaining 2.5 percent* are commercially successful.

shouldn't be put in the driver's seat. Just as Ford Motor Company has never lived down the Edsel fiasco, so IBM will forever be branded by the black mark of the PC Jr. Introduced in the 1980s, it was very innovative and included not only a cordless keyboard, but a brand new internal architecture. IBM's engineers loved it. Consumers? Well, the new technology was fine and dandy, but they hated the child-proportioned keyboard (users cursed its "Chiclets" keys), and the new architecture precluded expansion, which made it a bad investment. One hundred million dollars evaporated.

➤ Okay, if new technology fails, what about a "me too" product? Twenty-four percent of Calantone and Cooper's failure cases flopped because they were conscious attempts to cash in on a market some competitor had opened up. It's a primordial impulse. You see a pie cooling aromatically on the windowsill, and you gotta have a piece—your fair share. But a market is not a pie, and neither you nor anyone else is entitled to a "fair" share. Me-too is not enough. Your new product must give consumers a reason to switch from the competitor's product to yours. For example, any number of PC manufacturers rushed to imitate IBM's original PC. What many of them produced was no better, but it was cheaper—and that gave consumers a reason to buy from the me-too competitors.

➤ As if the nature of the marketplace didn't offer up enough problems, there's the hard, cold facts of physical reality. Fifteen percent of Calantone and Cooper's failures were "technical dogs." Maybe the design is inherently flawed. More often, especially in high-tech items, such as new software, minor bugs flare into major disasters that forever tarnish the reputation of the product—if not the entire company. An example of this was the original version of the Apple Newton "palmtop" computer—a great idea that didn't quite work.

➤ *Technical* dogs? Well, it's also a dog-eat-dog *world*, and 13 percent of the failures studied were due to a competitor deliberately setting out to torpedo a product by slashing his prices, offering a great promotion, or in some other way stealing thunder from the upstart innovator.

➤ Then there is the "price crunch." Thirteen percent of Calantone and Cooper's new product cases failed because of price resistance. This may be true of any new product—breakfast cereal, kitchen cleanser, or a passenger aircraft. For example, the Lockheed L-1011 was one of the best passenger aircraft ever produced. But it's not manufactured anymore because it cost too much.

➤ Calantone and Cooper lumped the remaining 7 percent of new product failures they looked at into a category they call "plain and simple ignorance." Bad marketing, a sudden rush of competition, changes in government regulations—you name it—can hatch the fly in your brand-new ointment.

The Other Side of Failure

Wallow with me a moment longer in this slough of failure. Why? Because we want to get to the other side.

And what *is* the other side of failure?

Success.

If we understand what causes new product failure, we can make sure we do the opposite when it's our turn. (Of course, that's not enough to ensure success. We must study failure and success together.) Here's some sure-fire ways to fail:

➤ **Don't bother to analyze the market:** This is a very good way to fall on your face. Spend all of your money on developing a product—that's fun—and leave nothing to spend on finding out whether folks want it or not.

➤ **Rush to market with a defective product:** The product dies, your company's reputation is wounded, and maybe you and your friends brainstorm together on the unemployment line.

➤ **Let wishful thinking drive development projections:** Costs almost always end up higher than anticipated. In fact, strike the word "almost." Make up those costs in a higher retail price point, and you may just price your new product out of the market.

➤ **Don't bother with timing:** A good new product is good any time, right? The answer is *sometimes*. And therein lies the rub. Bringing out the right product at the wrong time can be as devastating as bringing out the wrong product at the right time.

➤ **Just ignore your competition:** And maybe they'll go away. Or maybe they'll slash the price on a competitive product and slash your new entry out of existence. Analysis of competition is part of any thorough market analysis.

False Start
The *just do it* approach is also known as *Ready! Fire! Aim!* It involves actions based on the seat of the pants, and, typically, requires after-the-fact rethinking and damage control.

➤ **Millions for R&D but not one cent for marketing!** If you don't communicate the product effectively to consumers, it will fail. Money must be spent on marketing during development. Similarly, once a marketing strategy is determined, be certain there is funding support for the sales effort.

➤ **A small market is better than none:** Unless it's *too* small. If you're not in the handicrafts business, mass production is still the name of the game, and nothing reduces costs more effectively than economy of scale.

➤ *Positioning!* **What's that?** We told you in Chapter 2. It's how your best potential customer perceives your product. Position your product as the solution to a problem, the fulfillment of a desire, or, better yet, the answer to a prayer.

What I've Got Does the Job

"Hey! It's *New!*"

"Hey!...So what?"

"Hey! It's *New!*"

The answer is still *So what?*

You see, your product may be new to you and your company, but distribution may not accept it as new or the consumer might not adopt the product. Even more common, other products or services might already be satisfying consumer or end user needs. The consumer, therefore, is not moved to purchase your product.

I Didn't Know I Needed That

There is no limit to the amount of money you can spend on studying the market—unless, of course, you need to make a profit somewhere along the line. Perhaps, as part of a new-product development program, it would be better to devote some of that money to creating markets. Some new products really do succeed according to the build-a-better-mousetrap formula: *If you build it, they will come.* But many require educating the market.

Prototype

Early sales of personal computers soared, then reached a plateau for a time. It's hard to recall nowadays, but people actually started to ask themselves, *What will I do with it? Why should I spend a couple or three thousand dollars to balance my checkbook or write a letter?* At this point, makers of PCs and PC software started to educate the market, showing consumers in myriad ways that they had an unacknowledged *need* for a computer in their home.

I Didn't Know I Wanted That

Then there is the kind of new product marketing that depends more heavily on the traditional objectives of salesmanship. Do you remember *AIDA*? No, not the Giuseppe Verdi opera, but the rosary of veteran salespeople:

A: Get your prospect's *A*ttention.

I: Develop your prospect's *I*nterest.

D: Build your prospect's *D*esire.

A: Move your prospect to *A*ction.

It's wonderful when a new product slots itself right into a marketplace need. But, as the old saw goes, *Man has few needs, but many desires.* The right product promoted by the right marketing program can make consumers aware of a hitherto undiscovered desire. You may have to promote a new product with special emphasis on the third letter of the AIDA formula.

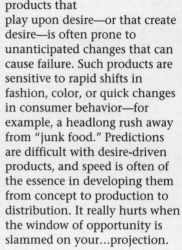

False Start
The market for new products that play upon desire—or that create desire—is often prone to unanticipated changes that can cause failure. Such products are sensitive to rapid shifts in fashion, color, or quick changes in consumer behavior—for example, a headlong rush away from "junk food." Predictions are difficult with desire-driven products, and speed is often of the essence in developing them from concept to production to distribution. It really hurts when the window of opportunity is slammed on your...projection.

"And Yet it Moves..."

In 1632, Galileo Galilei published his *Dialogue Concerning the Two Chief World Systems*. The book promoted a new product: the idea that the earth moved around the sun. The product was received poorly in at least one market. The Church summoned Galileo to Rome for trial by the Inquisition and, in June 1633, the astronomer was condemned to life imprisonment for "vehement suspicion of heresy." To free himself, Galileo withdrew his new product from the market; that is, he formally recanted his theory—though (it is said) not without muttering under his breath "and yet it moves."

With all the risks, why pioneer new products?

Because, like the earth, your business, your customers, and your competitors do not stand still. As Galileo found, new ideas are risky, but they are also inevitable. Whatever the risk, new products will emerge, and some of them will make the profits that not only mean success, but survival.

If Galileo found the market initially unreceptive, he and others soon transformed that market, educating it until it *was* receptive. Some ideas, some new products are worth that kind of effort. While it's also important to realize that some new products are *not* worth that effort, it is far more important to focus on the ones that *are*. Not only can a new product produce direct profit, a *program* of new product development enhances a company's image as an innovation leader. But the benefits go well beyond even that. The mindset as well as the specific activities involved in new product development tend to diffuse throughout an organization, improving the speed and efficiency with which all a company's resources are deployed. The spirit of pioneering may or may not build a better mousetrap, but, more than likely, it will build a better company.

The Least You Need to Know

➤ Understanding why new products fail is as important as understanding why they succeed.

➤ If we understand what causes new product failure, we can make sure we do the opposite when it's our turn.

➤ By identifying the varieties of market resistance to new products, the resistance can be overcome.

➤ With all of its risks, developing new products offers rewards that can be *measured* in sales dollars as well as *felt* in a continually reinvigorated corporate spirit.

Part 2
Where Babies Come From

All new products start out as ideas, and while it's true that some ideas hit you like the proverbial "bolt out of the blue," pinning your career on a passive hope for inspiration is a very precarious proposition. The chapters in this section suggest ways to super-charge serendipity with methods and techniques for generating ideas. In addition, you'll find guidelines for creating corporate environments that foster rather than stifle creative thought.

Don't Just Sit There Waiting for Godot

Fans of television's urbane sitcom *Seinfeld* may remember the episode in which Jerry Seinfeld and his friend George Costanza sit down to develop a pilot for a TV comedy series and end up scripting "a show about nothing." Well, the playwright Samuel Beckett beat them to this by about forty years with his *Waiting for Godot*. What's that play about? Two tramps, Vladimir and Estragon, await a mysterious fellow named Godot. He never arrives. End of play.

Literary critics and philosophical pundits have pondered the meaning of Beckett's play, and they even gave him a Nobel Prize. Are they just stupid? Maybe not about this. Because Beckett described life—or, at least, what all too many of us do in life: sit, shoot the breeze, hold meetings, conduct studies, hire consultants, and, basically, wait. Wait for the Big Idea, the Ultimate Product, what software developers call the "Killer App"—the killer application that *everyone* will want to own. The thing is, the Big Idea is usually like Godot. It never arrives. End of play.

We Are All Creative (Even You!)

Now, I've brought you through the first part of this book, where I've tried to suggest to you that, risky as new product development is, you need to develop new products in order to grow both corporately and personally. In fact, in the context of today's compressed cycles of innovation and obsolescence, the issue is not so much one of growth as it is survival. Craftsmanship is a timeless quality, but I know of no company in business today that prides itself on the fine quality of its buggy whips. Nor does Wall Street offer much stock in firms wholly devoted to the manufacture of typewriters.

I've brought you here. Now where are you?

You are confronting the big hurdle—this thing called creativity. Without it, you won't develop new products and services. It's that simple.

Now, what do you do if you ain't got it?

The glib answer is: You *get* it. But there is a more accurate answer: You *got* it. You just gotta get *to* it.

You don't think you *got* it?

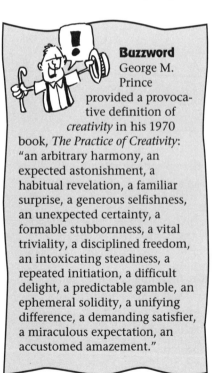

Buzzword
George M. Prince provided a provocative definition of *creativity* in his 1970 book, *The Practice of Creativity*: "an arbitrary harmony, an expected astonishment, a habitual revelation, a familiar surprise, a generous selfishness, an unexpected certainty, a formable stubbornness, a vital triviality, a disciplined freedom, an intoxicating steadiness, a repeated initiation, a difficult delight, a predictable gamble, an ephemeral solidity, a unifying difference, a demanding satisfier, a miraculous expectation, an accustomed amazement."

If you are earning a living or have ever earned a living, if you have managed to survive so far, if you have *ever* gotten *anything* you want—you are creative. Thomas Edison (*yes*, Edison again!) once said that genius is "1 percent inspiration and 99 percent perspiration." Romantic musical historians talk about how Mozart's creative genius drove the composer miraculously and mercilessly, so that he produced some six hundred masterpieces in his brief thirty-five years of life. The fact was that Mozart and his wife, Constanza, lived so extravagantly that he had to work around the clock to support their lifestyle and keep one step ahead of his creditors in an age when debt meant a prison sentence. There are few old sayings older than "Necessity is the mother of invention." But the fact is, you do what you have to do. And you do it every day. And, most of the time, you don't even think about it.

This isn't to say you can't *start* thinking about it. You can *learn* to be even more creative than you are at present. More accurately, you can learn to access more of the creativity you already have, and to turn it on when you need it.

Brainstorming

Brainstorming is not itself a new product. The idea that creativity could be induced in others and systematically developed got its start back in the 1930s when Alex Osborne of the advertising agency Batten, Barton, Durstine, and Osborne developed the "brainstorming" technique. Osborne developed an unstructured process in which judgment (*"Are you crazy? It will never work!"*) is deferred while a group of brainstormers focus exclusively on generating a *quantity* of ideas.

In the classic brainstorming session, six to twelve individuals sit down to a freewheeling and deliberately fast-paced session. Neither comment nor criticism is permitted. The only objective is to generate as many "wild" ideas as possible.

Prepare for brainstorming by clearly stating the problem that is the focus of the session. Make the ground rules clear: no judgments, no grimaces, no cringing, no tsk-tsks, just a lot of ideas, with none being branded too ridiculous for inclusion. A good leader will warm up the participants by getting them in the "wild" spirit. Laughter is by no means a bad way to warm up. Somebody should be delegated to take careful written notes.

Variations on the Brainstorming Theme

Many brainstorming variations have been developed. You may want to sample some of them:

➤ Do *not* tell the problem to the group, but direct the conversation toward the problem without divulging it.

➤ Try "reverse brainstorming." Have the group list all the possible weaknesses of a new product idea. Then, after the listing phase of the session is complete, address each weakness in order to eliminate or improve it.

Jump Start

While brainstorming, a strong group leader is needed to put a lid on judgments and criticism, which will kill the flow of ideas. The leader also keeps up the pace of the exchange. The most important function of the leader is to encourage each person to listen to the others' ideas and to move each idea ahead by adding to it.

False Start

Avoid relying on a tape recorder. You will end up with a lot of unproductive conversation to review. Even worse, most people censor themselves when they feel that what they say is being recorded for posterity.

Jump Start

A short time limit during trigger response, like eight to ten minutes, seems awfully stingy, but that's the point. The time limit will create a feeling of pressure and urgency that will encourage quick solutions.

➤ Break the group into subgroups, each of which brainstorms for short, intensive periods. These are often called "buzz groups." Reconvene the larger group and ask someone in each buzz group to report on their activities.

Trigger Response

Trigger response is a distinctive variation on brainstorming developed by George Muller, director of design at Ford Motor Company. Groups of eight to twelve people are set up. Each group defines the problem it will work on. The groups may work on the same problem or on separate problems. Once the problem is defined, the group must agree on the desired solution. This done, the next step is to generate as many ideas as possible to achieve that solution. Here's how it works:

1. Each group draws two lines down a piece of paper, producing three columns.

2. Each group lists in the first column all the solutions to the problem group members can think of.

3. Each group gets eight to ten minutes to write down solutions.

4. Someone is picked at random from one of the groups to read the list.

5. All other groups strike out duplications. At the same time, they write down in column two any new ideas that are triggered by the reading of the list.

6. The process is repeated to fill column three.

7. After each group has completed the process, the lists are collected and discussed with all participants to see if any other thoughts occur. These are recorded.

8. The final lists are then given to an interdisciplinary group of executives to discuss and evaluate.

Going Solo

Brainstorming is by definition a group activity. However, it is possible to borrow from the brainstorming spirit in order to generate ideas on your own. Give yourself *permission* to list wild ideas without self-censorship or evaluation. Jot them down—or use a tape recorder, if you prefer. (This will be a private and confidential tape, so have no fear.) Before you begin, set an arbitrary time limit—say a half-hour—and set an alarm clock to signal the expiration of the time. Don't go beyond the time limit.

Checklisting

Did you know it is possible to create a checklist that will generate ideas? Checklisting is a method of extending the intuitive idea supply by:

1. Providing solution possibilities

2. Stimulating the production of new ideas beyond the list itself

The checklist is a series of questions that help focus intuitive, creative thought, encouraging the creation of combinations of ideas that are not immediately apparent or habitual.

You, as part of a brainstorming group, are presented with a current product or a current product category and asked to make something new out of it. You begin the process by running down a checklist of questions:

Put to other uses	In what new ways can the present product be used?
Modify	What happens if you change meaning, color, motion, sound, odor, form, shape?
Adapt	What else is like this? What other place or thing does this product suggest?
Magnify	Make it bigger? Stronger? Higher? Longer? Thicker? Add something? Multiply?
Minimize	Make it smaller? Lower? Shorter? Thinner? Split it up? Reduce quantity? Understate?
Substitute	What else instead? *Who* else instead? (Different customer/end user?)
Rearrange	Interchange components? Change layout? Change sequence? Transpose cause and effect?
Reverse	Transpose opposites? Turn it backward? Upside down? Inside out?
Combine	Blend? Assortment? Combine units? Purposes? Appeals?

Attribute Listing

This is a technique for focusing brainstorming sessions by *first* listing the basic characteristics or attributes of a product and *then* brainstorming to generate new ideas relating to these attributes. Here's how it works:

1. List the attributes or characteristics of the product in question. (Alternatively, you may want to focus on such things as specifications or even limitations of the product.)

2. Brainstorm on this list in order to develop a list of modifications, changes, variations, additions, subtractions, and innovations that would make the product more desirable.

3. Evaluate the resulting suggestions after the brainstorming session is concluded.

Here is an example of an attribute listing for a specific product and the ideas it generated:

CAMERA

Component	Attribute	Ideas
Body	Weight?	Make super light
	Shape?	Wafer-size and shape
	Style/color?	Imitate clothing, accessories
Lens	Interchangeable?	All-in-one zoom
	Filters?	Built-in filters
	Lens hood?	Built-in
Film	Type?	Preloaded film backs
Viewfinder	Type?	Ease of focus; use bright, contrasting colors for focus
Case	Purpose?	Protect camera; more useful if integral with camera; waterproof, shockproof
	Appeal?	Imitate clothing, accessories; like a pocketbook
	Added value?	Contains a miniature tripod
Strap	Flexibility?	Multiple length; variable functions: wrist, arm, neck
	Added value?	Theft-resistant, personally identifiable
	Appeal?	Imitates clothing, accessories

Morphological Analysis

If you like, you can make attribute listing a whole lot more complicated by designing creative sessions to visualize and analyze all possible combinations of variables relating to a product concept. The idea is to combine two or more variables in multiple ways, then look at the results to see if any viable new product ideas have emerged. Let's say you're trying to come up with new wall-paneling products. You would list at least three variables:

1. *Material:* hardboard, plywood, wallboard, plastic

2. *Color:* birch, oak, walnut, maple

3. *Surface:* knotty, large open-grained, close-grained, flecked

These variables alone will generate 64 combinations!

The Synetic Solution

Synetics has been around for more than thirty years as a problem-solving, idea-generating technique. It was developed in 1961 by William J.J. Gorden, who coined the term from the Greek, meaning the joining of different and apparently irrelevant elements. To use synetics most effectively, it is helpful to have a skilled group leader who has been trained in the technique. However, the four key concepts of the technique are useful to consider for any group idea-generating effort:

1. *Listen:* Business—especially American business, alas—is in love with meetings. Most of us soon learn to sit quietly and politely through these, letting our minds blissfully wander. Synetics develops *active listening.*

2. *Spectrum policy:* Whereas the object in brainstorming is not to judge ideas as good or bad, but simply to generate them, *spectrum policy* frankly admits that most ideas are "bad" (that is, not useful for addressing the problem at hand). However, even these "bad" ideas contain good elements and may be moved from the negative to the positive end of the spectrum by identifying and building on the good points until an acceptable solution is reached.

3. *Common understanding:* This is a role-playing technique and can facilitate reaching a common understanding of the central issues involved in a problem or new-product goal. Someone in the group plays the part of the "client" with a problem or need. He or she holds dialogue with the group (the "company") in an effort to explain, define, and appreciate the problem or need.

Jump Start
Because of the number of variations possible as a result of morphological analysis, it would probably save time to use a computer program to assemble the combinations of attributes. Alternatively, each attribute could be reproduced several times on index cards and the cards combined in different ways in order to promote the visualization of new product ideas.

Buzzword
Active listening, in the context of a creative session, requires a moderator who monitors discussion, writing the key concepts and leading ideas on a flip chart. This reinforces the listening process and ensures that nothing important is lost.

4. *Group leader:* A skilled leader can make the difference between a productive group effort and one that degenerates into a session of posturing, grandstanding, and jockeying for dominance.

Tanks a Lot

There is another approach to group creativity, and that is to go outside of your organization by taking the plunge into a "think tank." A think tank is, in effect, a group consultant, a panel of outside experts your company hires to brainstorm a problem or concept. Usually, a company hires a consultant for expert advice on some particular issue. A think tank, however, is hired to think, to perform brainstorming by proxy. The advantage of bringing in hired brains is that the think tank group typically includes experts your company doesn't have.

Prototype

A think tank called Innotech once provided a brainstorming group to a construction equipment company. Mixed in with the engineers on the panel was an entomologist—a biologist specializing in the study of insects. He provided an analysis of strength-to-weight ratios in ants that ultimately resulted in ideas for the development of a new earth mover.

The Three Esses

No, ladies and gentlemen, this is not a Yiddish pronunciation of a word beginning with *A*. I really do mean three *esses*:

➤ Serendipity

➤ Synergy

➤ Sensitivity

These are the three esses of creativity. No matter what formal techniques you use to stimulate creativity and promote the generation of ideas, major breakthroughs often "just happen" as a result of one or more of the three esses.

Serendipity relies on an awareness of relevance in apparently accidental happenings. The classic example is Sir Isaac Newton formulating his gravitational theories after he was thumped on the head by falling apple. Thomas—you guessed it!—Edison was experimenting with a way to record telegraph messages by reproducing the dots and dashes of Morse code on waxed paper, when he noticed that the paper produced a hum when it was passed rapidly beneath a needle. Edison noodled with the needle and created the phonograph. If Newton, Edison, and others were guided by tunnel vision that closed them off to what was happening around them—the myriad phenomena most folks simply disregard as irrelevant—they would have produced no new ideas.

Buzzword
Serendipity is the faculty for making fortunate discoveries.

Synergy is the association of two or more relatively familiar elements in a new way such that the result is greater than the sum of the parts. Creative individuals become accustomed to combining the familiar to create something new.

Sensitivity is an openness to experience with the object of spotting opportunities and needs. The foundation of genius is sensitivity. Are you born with it? Some people are. If you weren't born with it, are you out of luck? Not necessarily.

➤ You can consciously work at developing sensitivity by honing your perceptions.

➤ Read—especially in your field—as much as you can.

➤ Look for trends.

➤ Refuse to become comfortable with your biases. Question them. Question what you base your conclusions on day to day.

➤ Beware of the vocabulary that blocks creativity. "It won't work!" "Get real!" "Are you kidding!?" "Let's form a committee." "We've never done it before." "It isn't budgeted." "That's not for our market." "Has it worked for anyone else?" "We're not ready for it." Expunge such phrases from your personal lexicon.

Fostering the Fuzzy Front End

Specialists who make it their business to develop new products and services call the initial idea-generating phase of the process the "fuzzy front end." Unfortunately, many businesses don't devote much effort to this creative phase. After all, it's *fuzzy*—and how do you put "fuzzy" in a P&L or a quarterly report or The Strategic Business Plan? You may well have to look elsewhere than to your institution for support of the fuzzy front end. Just never let anyone above (or below) you persuade you that the fuzzy front end is a luxury, an extra, something you don't have time for. It is the seedbed in which new products take root.

Here are some things to do to foster the fuzzy front end and leap over mental blocks:

1. Give yourself dream space. Don't let anyone tell you that *just thinking* is non-productive.

2. Enhance your environment to promote creativity. Look for variety at home and at work.

3. Seek out idea-oriented people in the workplace and in your social life.

4. Encourage creativity in others at every opportunity. Listen. Don't judge.

5. Deliberately break out of everyday routines.

6. Impose creative deadlines on yourself.

7. Make yourself an expert in your area of innovation: read, listen, think about connections.

8. Find out where other "idea people" get there ideas. (We'll talk about idea sources in the next chapter. Stay tuned!)

9. Don't think of problems as *obstacles*, but as *opportunities* to create ideas. Study problems in order to generate ideas.

10. Avoid negative people.

11. If you can't avoid negative people, protect your ideas from them. After all, they are your babies.

The philosopher-historian Jan Huyzinga called human beings not *Homo sapiens* (man the knower) but *Homo ludens* (man the player). The fuzzy front end is, above all, *play* time. Sure, it's play in the service of serious business, but it *is* play nevertheless, and you've got to gather the emotional courage and clear the imaginative space to get yourself down to this serious fun.

The Least You Need to Know

➤ Effective techniques are available for fostering creativity such as brainstorming, checklisting, attribute listing, and synetic solutions.

➤ Read, look for trends, questions your biases, and beware of vocabulary that can block your creativity.

➤ Be prepared to devote time to the "fuzzy front end," even if your company does not formally support this crucial phase of new-product development.

➤ Creative time is relatively cheap, because it comes before large sums of cash are committed to advanced development; nevertheless, you may have to do battle with the powers that be in order to stake out an ample enough "fuzzy front end."

Where Do You Get Those Ideas From, Anyway?

The world is clogged with ideas. The veins of new product notions run deeper and thicker and are more varied than the riches of a Wild West gold rush. The key is to prospect for these nuggets in a targeted way rather than randomly groping the hills or idly waiting for time and the winds of change to expose the ore.

Two major forces motivate new product ideas. Ideas may be *pulled* by marketplace needs, demands, and desires. Or they may be *pushed* by new technology generated by deliberate scientific research or serendipitous discovery. Either way, ideas spark the new-product process, and there is, therefore, a great need for new product ideas. The attrition rate is high, especially in the early stages, so quantity as well as quality are important. The previous chapter suggested some techniques for generating ideas. This chapter offers sources of fuel to "run the generators" and spark productive thought.

Think

Thomas Watson, who founded IBM in 1924, placed on the wall behind his desk a single framed word: THINK. It became the corporate motto of one of the most influential companies of the century. *Think*. The handiest source of new product ideas is your mind, if for no other reason than that you are always carrying it around with you.

You've got a mind. The next step is to open it and keep it open. What you want is to be open to *change*. Management guru Peter Drucker has made the observation that most successful innovations *exploit change*. In his 1985 *Innovation and Entrepreneurship*, Drucker defined seven specific kinds of change that are sources of innovation opportunity:

1. **The unexpected**, including unexpected success, unexpected failure, and unexpected events.

2. **Incongruity** between reality as it actually is and reality as it is assumed to be.

3. **Innovation** based on process need.

4. **Changes in industry structure and market structure**—especially those that catch everyone unaware.

5. **Demographic shifts.**

6. **Changes in perception, mood, and meaning.**

7. **New knowledge**, including the scientific and the nonscientific.

Jump Start
Expand your reading range by getting someone else to do some of the reading for you. Have an assistant, junior staff member, or intern survey, read, and highlight articles of interest. He or she should prepare a brief "executive summary" for you. Making such assignments not only extends your new-idea feelers, it is a welcome creative challenge for entry-level staff, who are accustomed to being burdened exclusively with typing and filing.

Open a Book, Open Your Mind

Or open a magazine, newspaper, business periodical—whatever. And don't limit yourself to the publications in your field; however, by all means, you should be certain that you cover these.

When was the last time you saw an executive sitting at her desk reading a journal, let alone a book? The truth is, most of us are afraid to be "caught" reading on the job. After all, we're supposed to be seen *working*, not reading.

Well, let's define work as doing something with a pen or pencil in your hand. We can safely extend that instrument to a highlighter: one of those transparent yellow or neon pink or soothing blue odorless markers. Put one of these in your hand, *then* read. This will have two benefits:

1. It will make it look as if you are *working* when you are really *reading*.

2. It will allow you to highlight any new-product-producing ideas you happen to find in the course of your reading.

Want to look as if you are doing even *more* work? Start an index-card file in which you jot down the ideas you highlight. Head each card with a key word. Arrange the cards alphabetically—or in any order that seems logical and useful to you. Instead of actual index cards, you may want to enter this information electronically on your PC, using any of the free-form database programs on the market today. Chances are that you already own such a program.

> **Jump Start**
> As an alternative to writing down your ideas and notes from publications, give an intern or assistant more work. Use "Post-It"-style stickers to flag pages on which you have highlighted material and hand the periodical over to someone else who can write up an index card or make a database entry.

Required Reading

Sit down, take out a sheet of paper, write the title *Required Reading* at the top, then use the sheet to prepare a list of "required reading" in your field. If the list is large, try to narrow it down to the publications most likely to spark ideas and, especially, new-product ideas. Don't put this task off. Once you have done it, take the "required" part of the title seriously.

In addition to a "Required Reading" list customized for your special field, the following general publications are essential for taking the pulse of change.

Newspapers:

> *The Economist*
> *The International Herald-Tribune*
> *The New York Times*
> *The Wall Street Journal*
> Your local newspaper

Periodicals:

> *Business Week*
> *Forbes*
> *Fortune*
> *U.S. News & World Report*

> **Jump Start**
> Check out the offerings of the U.S. Government Printing Office, which publishes a wealth of data from the U.S. Department of Commerce and other government agencies. Many larger cities have U.S. Government Bookstores, where you can browse the offerings at your leisure. If you have access to the Internet, check out the FedWorld site on the World Wide Web at http://www.fedworld.gov/.

Quarterly Periodicals:

Society and Innovation (published by Warren, Gorham & Lamont, 210 South Street, Boston, MA 02111)

Economic Outlook, USA (published by Survey Research Center, University of Michigan, P.O. Box 1248, Ann Arbor, MI 48106)

Standard Monthly References:

Economic Indicators (Council of Economic Advisors)
Survey of Current Business (U.S. Department of Commerce)
Business Conditions Digest (U.S. Department of Commerce)
Monthly Labor Review (U.S. Department of Labor)

All of these are available from the U.S. Government Printing Office, Washington, DC 20402. In addition, consult:

International Financial Statistics (IMF, Washington, DC 20402)

OECD Observer and Economic Outlook (OECD Publications Center, 1750 Pennsylvania Avenue, NW, Washington, DC 20006)

Standard Annual References:

U.S. Statistical Abstract (U.S. Department of Commerce)
Economic Report of the President
U.S. Budget

All of these are available from the U.S. Government Printing Office, Washington, DC 20402.

Extra Credit

The kids that always did best in class devoured the extra-credit reading list. Isn't it about time you did the same? Go to the periodicals section of any good public library and look for the following publications. If you can't find them at the library, write to the address below:

➤ *Official Gazette of United States Patent & Trademark Office of Commissioner of Patents and Trademarks*, Washington, DC 20231.

➤ *New Product, New Business Digest*, General Electric Co., 120 Erie Boulevard, Schenectady, NY 12305.

➤ *New Products and Processes, Newsweek*, 444 Madison Avenue, New York, NY 10022.

➤ *New From Us*, Prestwick International Inc., P.O. Box 205, Burnt Hills, New York, NY 12027.

➤ *Technical Survey*, published weekly by Predicasts, 1101 Cedar Avenue, Cleveland, OH 44106.

➤ *NASA Tech Briefs* from National Aeronautics and Space Administration, Director Technology Transfer Division, P.O. Box 8757, Baltimore/Washington International Airport, MD 21240.

➤ *New Product Development Newsletter*, Point Publishing Co., Inc., P.O. Box 1309, Point Pleasant, NJ 08742.

➤ *New Product News*, Dancer Fitzgerald Sample, Inc., 405 Lexington Avenue, New York, NY.

➤ *International Commerce Magazine*, U.S. Department of Commerce.

For more information on foreign patents, write to the Institut National De La Propriete Industrielle, 26 Bis Rue De Leingrad 75008, Paris.

Cruising the Infobahn

These days, not all new product news appears in print on paper. The Internet, particularly the World Wide Web (WWW), is an excellent source of new product news, both domestic and international. Each day, more and more companies are creating "home pages" on the Web. These usually include a wealth of information about new products. You can use one of the many "search engine" software tools now available (such as Excite, Yahoo, InfoSeek, and so on) to locate a company of interest to you. Better yet, begin by jotting down a list of the firms most prominent in your field. Then use a search engine to locate the firm's home page. Once you're at the home page, start digging.

Please Open Before X-Mas

Childhood! Remember how deliciously hard it was *not* to open your presents before Christmas? Well, now that you're all grown up, there's a set of

Buzzword
If you don't know that the *Internet* is the name for a group of worldwide information resources linked together in an electronic network of electronic networks and accessible by anyone with a computer and a modem, then you won't know that a *home page* is an Internet site, created by an individual or organization, that contains "hypertext links" to data relevant to the individual or organization. A home page is like an electronic table of contents, providing orderly access to whatever the individual or organization has to offer.

gift-wrapped packages all around you—and I bet you're hardly showing any interest in them. These are the ideas that are generated in-house. Identify the in-house sources of ideas. These departments usually include:

➤ Research

➤ Engineering

➤ Sales

➤ Marketing

➤ Production

According to a study of 40 companies published back in 1968 by the American Management Association, 33 firms identified research and engineering departments as their primary source of new product ideas. An almost equal number—30—named sales, marketing, and planning. A dozen firms cited production as a source of new product ideas, and ten companies mentioned miscellaneous executives as well as the board of directors. You can expect current statistics to run about the same.

Establish solid networking connections with the movers and shakers in each of these departments.

Ye Olde Suggestion Box

The old, corny, much-abused suggestion box is nevertheless an idea that can generate the germs of brand-new products. But if you're really serious about soliciting ideas from employees, you'll want to consider dressing up the old suggestion box concept, and you'll also need to overcome certain prejudices.

Let's look at the prejudices first:

➤ *Our "people" aren't very creative.* This is never a productive assumption. Do something to encourage the expression of creativity. (More on this below.)

➤ *We'll be flooded with dumb ideas.* Maybe. But you can regulate the flood somewhat by telling your employees what types of ideas you are looking for. There will still be plenty of bad ones to sift through, but who said coming up with good ideas for new products was easy? Besides, quantity is important in gathering new ideas.

➤ *If we reject employees' ideas, they'll get discouraged and morale will suffer.* This won't happen if you regularly express appreciation for all ideas and if you provide timely feedback to the submitters. Express rejection in terms that are as positive as possible. Even employees whose ideas are rejected will feel good about participating in the creative process.

Now, how can you really turbocharge the suggestion box?

➤ *Promote the suggestion program.* Make it a company-wide initiative. Create special posters, e-mail announcements, articles in the company newsletter, all boosting the suggestion program. Don't hold a meeting to generate enthusiasm, throw a party!

➤ *Welcome ideas with open arms.* Do not pass harsh judgment. Never put anyone or anyone's idea down. Remember that, in the earliest stages of idea generation, quantity is as important as quality.

➤ *Provide prompt, meaningful feedback.* Don't let submitters feel that their ideas go into a black hole and are lost forever.

➤ *Make the submission process easy.* When you try to sell something to a customer, you want to make it as easy as possible for him to part with his money. Similarly, make it painless for the employee to part with his idea. Make the submission process crystal clear. Consider developing a "submission kit," which should include a guide defining the kinds of ideas you're looking for, the criteria by which they'll be judged, relevant deadline dates, and so on.

➤ *Provide tangible incentives.* Develop a program of bonuses and other rewards (vacation time, expenses-paid trips, etc.) in return for new product ideas.

Play Time

A number of leading companies—3M Corporation has long been prominent among them—provide what they call "scouting time" to allow employees to work on pet projects and personal ideas for new products. It takes corporate courage to provide such "play time," which may or may not be directly productive and which is outside the direct control of management. But for 3M, the investment resulted in the development of such products as Post-It Notes—a major new-product success story.

The Customer's Always Right...There

Ask any manager if his company values customers, and he'll look at you wide-eyed.

"Of *course* we do!"

But you can be sure that his company doesn't value them enough. Not only are your present customers your best potential future customers, they are also a valuable and vast untapped source of new product ideas. Why pay a high-priced consultant to think up new products when you can ask a customer, who'll tell you—for free—what he wants?

Cultivate Customer Creativity

Invite a group of customers to a brainstorming session. This could be arranged as a pleasant weekend retreat at some desirable resort—mix work with recreation as an expression of gratitude to the customer. Make no mistake, however—while your customer will appreciate the recreation part of the weekend, he will also be flattered and pleased that you value his ideas highly enough to have asked him to participate with management in a brainstorming session. Customer brainstorming retreats help cement profitable business relationships while possibly generating new-product ideas.

Focus!

More formal than the brainstorming session is the focus group. This is a professionally moderated session in which customers focus on specific issues, problems, and needs. Usually, it is your firm's responsibility to present the ideas, concepts, and even prototypes and working models to the focus group for their response and suggestions.

Ask Your Vendors

A good supplier strives to be your business partner. Like you, the vendor is on the lookout for new applications for their products, so it's in the supplier's interest to help you come up with new products. Arrange discussions and visits with vendors. Make connections with their technical and research people. The liaison will benefit both of you—and, if your supplier is a large firm with a well-funded R&D department, it may gain you some free access to bigger facilities than your own.

Covet Thy Competitor

Short of industrial espionage, keep a close eye on your competition. What are they doing? Why? How successfully are they doing it? (You can obtain sales data from published sources, as well as by asking customers, retailers, and wholesalers.)

Routinely purchase your competitors' products. Use them as the focus of internal brainstorming groups. You should do the same with your competitors' advertising and promotional literature.

False Start
Remember that me-too products are rarely very successful. Don't copy your competitor. Learn from him. Let his example *trigger* ideas and *stimulate* thought.

What Trade Shows Are For

You and your competition spend big bucks to set up booths at trade shows for one reason: to capture customers. But, whether you like it or not, you also end up showing your wares to one another.

Better make the best of it. When you attend a trade show, don't spend *all* of your time courting new business. Open your eyes. Walk all the aisles. You should send someone to all of the shows, including those you aren't even exhibiting at. You or your designated observer should take notes and take photos. Study not only the products, but the traffic in and around each booth. What products draw a crowd? Casually sidle up to a few booth visitors as they leave a center of especially intense activity. Try to find out what they liked and what they didn't like.

Inventors

Astoundingly, these folks all too often get lost in the new product shuffle. Depending on your business, the private inventor can be a rich source of new product ideas, including fully developed new products. Most book publishers routinely solicit submissions from prospective authors. Does your company similarly solicit inventions?

Too Hot to Handle

There are two drawbacks to actively soliciting submissions from private inventors. First, you will very rapidly accumulate a slush pile of unworkable ideas. You will need to employ someone to manage the slush pile, to filter out the dross and pass along material with potential. Even more serious are possible legal problems caused by accepting submissions from inventors. The classic sticky wicket is when an idea is submitted that the company has already thought of. Some fine day, you come out with the product and, lo and behold, the inventor— long forgotten (by you)—emerges from the woodwork, subpoena in hand. A second common problem is when the idea submitted ends up not actually belonging to the submitter, thereby triggering claims and counterclaims that can be disastrously expensive to prosecute or defend in court.

Jump Start
Write to local Chambers of Commerce for a schedule of inventors shows. You might also drop a line to the Office of Inventions and Innovations, National Bureau of Standards, Washington, DC 20234.

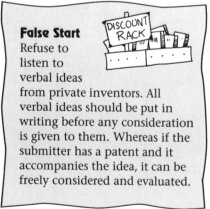

False Start
Refuse to listen to verbal ideas from private inventors. All verbal ideas should be put in writing before any consideration is given to them. Whereas if the submitter has a patent and it accompanies the idea, it can be freely considered and evaluated.

If you are going to invite ideas from the outside, be certain that you have an explicit and legally responsible procedure for handling submissions. Unless you simply refuse to consider any outside unsolicited ideas, you should put in place a system that refers all submissions to your legal department, which then sends a release to the submitter. If the release is not signed, the idea should be returned *without any company executive having seen it*. It is critically important that no one in the company—except for designated legal counsel—take it on himself to answer, correspond, acknowledge new ideas, or seek waivers.

> **Buzzword**
> *Intellectual property* defines the vast field of commercially exploitable concepts that, as with any other kind of property, entail certain rights and privileges for the owner. Many new products involve (often depressingly tangled) issues of intellectual property development and rights.

Back to School

Consider developing working relationships with universities—perhaps your *local* university—and with specific scientists and researchers within the university. In the old days, academics typically had little appreciation for the commercial potential of what they did. This is less and less true today, and many universities have strong corporate relations departments as well as aggressive policies on "intellectual property."

Cutting in the Middleman

The last few years have seen the emergence of a new kind of professional, the idea broker. His or her trade is in intellectual property. He or she acts as an agent, arranging intellectual property deals between firms, between academic institutions and commercial concerns, and between private inventors and corporations. It is in your best interest to get to know a few reputable idea brokers and regularly review their offerings.

> **Jump Start**
> Listen to your family, especially to your children, who are a good, immediate source of contact with current fads, fancies, and enthusiasms. Besides, this is a way to put your kids to work—without violating any child labor laws.

Another outside professional you might consider hiring is a professional clipping service. These outside bureaus are usually employed by publishers, political figures, celebrities, and so on to look for articles and reviews relating to them. However, you can hire such a bureau to clip articles on specific product topics. You can also purchase software programs that scan on-line editions of newspapers, magazines, and journals for the subject areas you specify. Relevant articles are "delivered" to your e-mail address.

A Final Lesson from the Civil War

Probably no military conflict in history swarmed with more spies than the Civil War. Yet, on neither side, Union or Confederate, was military intelligence ever very good. The problem? While there were plenty of spies to go around, neither side ever developed a truly effective apparatus to process and distribute the information the spies gathered. Spies stuck their necks out—sometimes right into a noose—to get the facts, but precious little was done with the information they so perilously collected.

Like Civil War spies, ideas lurk around every corner and at every turn. Now, what are you going to *do* with them? In and of themselves, ideas are of little value. They are the thinnest of thin air. Now that you know where to look for ideas, read on to Chapter 6 to learn about what to do with the ideas you collect.

The Least You Need to Know

➤ Two major forces motivate new product ideas. Ideas may be *pulled* by marketplace needs, demands, and desires. Or they may be *pushed* by new technology generated by deliberate scientific research or serendipitous discovery.

➤ Most new product ideas are born by exploiting change.

➤ Sources of ideas include your imagination; your colleagues and staff; your customers; your suppliers; published works in your field, general journals, periodicals, and reference works; inventors; academic researchers; and others.

➤ Don't run away from problems. *Look* for them. Unsolved problems are a prime generator of new-product need.

➤ Look *everywhere* for ideas, then make certain that they are not merely filed away and lost.

Nurturing New Ideas

Children and water: an example of irresistible attraction. I'm not talking about swimming and wading pools, but about giving a kid a supply of water and some containers, and watching him play. Maybe it's the essential contradiction involved—how water is shapeless, uncontrollable, accidental, yet will take on whatever shape contains it.

Ideas are like that. Their most essential nature is shapeless, uncontrollable, accidental. They are sparked by inspiration and serendipity—two elements that stubbornly resist inclusion in a bean counter's P & L. Try to rationalize all aspects of new product development, and you'll kill the very qualities that produce new ideas in the first place. On the other hand, you *are* running a business, and you quite literally cannot *afford* to rely on shapeless, uncontrollable accident as your sole engine of innovation. If I were writing a management textbook, I'd say that this chapter is about creating organizational structures to promote and manage new product development. But I'm writing a *Complete Idiot's Guide* to new product development, so what I'll say is that this chapter is about making a home for new ideas.

No Right Way

Look out upon the corporate landscape. If you have a reasonably experienced eye, you'll pick out the lofty mountains. Those are the companies that are intensely research-and-development oriented, always pushing toward the creation of new products. Then you'll see the steep valleys, the firms that, in many respects, are well run, but always seem to stumble over new product development because they have never developed an organized approach to innovation. Between these extreme topographical features are the vast majority of companies, which exhibit varying degrees of organizational development in managing their new product processes.

There is no single "right" way to foster and manage new product development. But while the range of options may seem bewildering, you really have six basic management systems to choose from:

1. One person innovates without any formal structure.

2. A new product committee is chiefly responsible for innovation.

3. A new product department is established.

4. The company uses a product manager system.

5. A matrix/venture team/group is used.

6. Outside consultants are brought in.

What Fits

The type of system that's used usually reflects the size of the company. In small companies, it is usually the owner or head of the firm who takes chief responsibility for initiating new product development. The subsequent work involved is generally a company-wide effort. But, as companies grow, they need to formalize a management system that will accomplish two objectives:

1. Drive new product development toward corporate goals.

2. Overcome uncertainties that defeat new product development.

First and foremost, choose a management system that fits your size, and also such variables as:

➤ Whether you are producing a product or service

➤ Whether your customers are industries or consumers

➤ What others in your industry do

➤ How management views allocation of time and dollars

➤ Whether you want to create products that cut costs or lead technology

➤ How you market existing products

Jump Start
It makes sense to get as many *key* people involved in new product development as is possible (within the limits of practicality). The more people who feel that they "own" an idea, the more supporters that idea will have. Investment is a powerful motivator.

The hard fact is that, even if you establish a management system that fits your company comfortably, new product development is always a struggle and sometimes a down-and-dirty fight: new product development people—whoever they may be in your organization— have to *sell* their "children" into the corporate system.

The "C" Word

And it's a *very* nasty word indeed. *Committee* is all too often synonymous with such terms as *ignore, delay, boondoggle*. Committees *can* be a new idea's worst enemy, yet, in most organizations, they are, for better or worse, the way things get done.

Committees get a bad rap because of three failures:

1. Failure to set specific goals for the committee

2. Failure to pick a strong leader

3. Failure to spell out the committee's responsibilities and authority

In addition to the "three failures," committee members may be overly guided by vested interests and a desire to protect their turf; members may use the committee structure to evade and avoid responsibility for failure while staking out a piece of the credit; committee members may simply fail to work well together. The committee must be monitored for performance and modified if necessary. It is no passive panacea.

If you address the above three points successfully, and you give a committee a reasonable chance to exploit its inherent strengths:

➤ The committee gets together those who have the responsibility to make new product development happen.

➤ The committee concentrates and blends ideas and expertise.

➤ The committee can be flexible—can grow or shrink; can be ongoing or organized for a specific project. The committee can take total responsibility for new product development, or it can be assigned to address specific phases, such as concept generation, idea screening, marketing, and so on.

➤ A *committee's* decisions are generally more palatable to top management than the "whims" of an individual. (In fact, the committee often consists of top management.)

Department of New Products

If the size of the company warrants it, a permanent new products department may be more appropriate than a committee. The departmental approach partakes of most of the strengths of a committee while avoiding many of the pitfalls, provided that the department embodies the following qualities:

➤ Has a strong leader—someone who can organize a group effectively, who fully grasps corporate goals, who is willing and able to break into new areas.

➤ Has members with knowledge of the company's operational abilities, activities, strengths, weaknesses.

➤ Harbors no bias toward other departments or individuals.

➤ Represents strong analytical talent.

➤ Has time to develop new products and is free from time-eating functional responsibilities.

➤ Has high visibility within the company.

➤ Is welcomed as a partner in profit.

➤ Is empowered to work with people throughout the organization and to marshal both internal and external resources.

➤ Has a working knowledge of relevant industries and markets and is led by people with "real world" operating experience.

➤ Commands and integrates a variety of skills.

➤ Has project champions as well as devil's advocates.

➤ Is open to ideas from all sources.

Just as the essence of new product development is an often uneasy balance between free-form imagination and disciplined development (Edison's inspiration and perspiration), so the new product department should be independent but, at the same time, *bound*—tied to the goals of the company. Like any other department, it must be managed—but it must not be sat on. It must be allowed to break new ground, but it can never be permitted to become elitist or removed from the realities of the marketplace.

False Start
Be aware that a department should not occupy an ivory tower. This can lead you into the trap of the "NIH Syndrome." If an idea doesn't come from within the department—"Not Invented Here"—the department kills or ignores it.

Product Manager System

The size and diversity of a company may well ratchet up complexity not only beyond the scope of an individual or a committee, but even beyond that of an entire department. Packaged-goods manufacturers and other consumer-products firms offering diverse lines often use a product manager system to ensure the creation of a steady stream of new products while effectively managing existing products. Proctor and Gamble, which developed the prototype of the system at mid-century, calls their product managers "brand managers"—a term that some other companies use as well.

In the product manager system, related products (or brands) are bundled together under the direction of a Group Director, who reports to a Director of Product Management; additional input and direction comes from a New Product Group Director. Reporting in turn to the Group Director are the Product Managers. These individuals concentrate on innovation within their specific brand or product area, which they know intimately. Because they report to overall managers, including a New Product Group Director, their micro view of innovation is given the broader perspective that takes in company-wide strategic objectives. Since the Product Manager is concerned with a relatively narrow field in which to innovate, his contributions are usually focused on repositioning and line extensions, with some innovation. Rarely does a Product Manager spark a new-to-the-world product; that's not the way the system is designed to work.

On the Matrix Team

The product manager system is now more than fifty years old, and while it works well in certain contexts—especially where a large, complex company offers many brands— more recent management trends have favored team-oriented management models over hierarchies. Task force, project team, venture team—all are variants of the matrix team approach.

A largely autonomous team is assembled from representatives of the firm's functioning departments—finance, marketing, manufacturing, design, and so on—and is given the responsibility either for developing a single specific new product or several lines of new products. Because it consists of the people who actually do the work of the company day in and day out, the team continually draws upon the expertise of the functioning departments. It does not develop its own marketing group, for instance, but uses the full facilities of the organization's marketing group when these services are required.

The matrix approach can bring to bear for a specified time the full strength of a company to develop new products. However, it can be awfully hard work. Each member of the team must be able to marshal her department's forces for the project at hand. There is real danger that the matrix team may degenerate into a concentrated microcosm of the power struggles, posturing, and jockeying that are a part of any organization. For a full-time matrix team (in this case usually called a venture management group) to be effective, the individual departments represented on the team must be able to contribute on an ongoing basis to new product development in addition to performing their daily functions. This can become expensive in terms of investment in personnel. Certainly, it demands a great deal from the staff—though the best people welcome the challenge of participating in the development of new products.

The Venture Commitment

If your firm goes the matrix team/venture team/venture group route, management must make a commitment to it that includes the following dimensions:

➤ Empowering a strong group leader—which means supporting her, even when her authority co-opts that of functional department heads.

➤ Allowing team members to devote *all* of their time to the project.

➤ Providing adequate funding, usually from an independent source.

➤ Providing a significant degree of independence from the rest of the company and from company policies.

➤ Accepting a high degree of risk.

It Ain't Over Until It's...Really Started

Doting mothers are reluctant to cast their offspring upon the tender mercies of the world. By the same token, the company should not expect the venture team/group to step out of the new product picture immediately after a new product is hatched. It is usually more effective to allow the group to manage development and marketing until the product is fairly launched. Usually, this point is demarcated by a target dollar volume. Once that figure is reached, management of the product is integrated into the appropriate functional departments, and the venture *team* is disbanded, or the venture *group* moves on to another project.

Get Out of Here

The matrix team approach and its variants require the resources of a fairly large company. Smaller companies (and large ones, too, for that matter) may turn over part—rarely, if ever, *all*—of new product development and market planning to outside consultants. This is hardly an admission of inadequacy. On the contrary, if developing new products is not a full-time objective for your company, why pay for full-time people to do it? Consider consultants to handle all or particular phases of new product development:

➤ Research companies—for concept testing

➤ Concept development groups—can provide a variety of new concepts

➤ Marketing specialists—to coordinate the efforts of your own people to create an effective product that is marketed effectively

➤ Technical experts—to fine tune a product's nuts and bolts

➤ Packaging and design groups—to provide the design expertise you need to create the most effective package

➤ Naming specialists—for coming up with that all-important name for your new product

The Champ

You may assemble a new product development structure within your organization that has the precision of a Swiss watch. It may make a perfectly lovely pattern on a flow chart.

61

But regardless of how you structure the process, new product development begins, is kicked forward, is maintained, and successfully culminates because of the presence and effort of a product champion. Whether your firm is small, with all new product ideas emanating from a single person, or large, with product managers and/or matrix teams, you'll need champions.

Buzzword

Champion, in the context of new product development, is someone willing to fight for the product, pushing it through, over, and around the many organizational and human obstacles that threaten to mire it in the muck of inertia.

Sports fans, let me ask you: Are champions made or are they born? Probably a little bit of both. But one thing's for sure—they have to be welcomed, developed, and nurtured. This means that support has got to come from the top. Top management must be involved in new product development on a regular basis, and the CEO needs to believe that new product development is the lifeblood of the firm. Then he needs to communicate that belief throughout all levels of the organization.

Prototype

In the early 1950s, the U.S. Navy solicited proposals for the development of the Sidewinder missile. The Navy generated a long and stringent list of specifications. What William B. McLean, the physicist in charge of a missile-development team at the Naval Weapons Center, understood, however, is that specifications suffer from a serious drawback: they force both customer and would-be contractor to presume they know the answers before they have any experience with the product. McLean wanted to get the answers first and carried out experiments on his own time. Once he developed a prototype, it failed. Actually, it failed thirteen times—more than enough to kill the project.

But McLean persisted, taking what he had learned from the "failures" to make modifications and launch one more test, on September 11, 1953, which landed right on target. As quickly as it had been officially killed, the Sidewinder was officially reborn, and it remains a key part of the U.S. arsenal—a highly successful product—that owes its existence to the man who championed it.

Yeah, Yeah, Yeah. But Where Do I Go From Here?

It's one thing to set up a corporate structure that can stimulate, foster, and bring to realization new product ideas, but then you're left with the *process* itself. What is its nature, and how can it be managed to promote success? Such is the stuff of the next chapter.

> **False Start**
> Avoid suffocating new product processes with overbearing interference from top management. Top managers should supply direction and support, not daily supervision.

The Least You Need to Know

➤ While there is no single "right" environment in which to develop new products, successful ongoing new-product development requires some type of structure.

➤ Going to outside consultants is not an admission of inadequacy, but can be a wise use of resources.

➤ Whatever structure you choose—and the choice is generally related to the size and diversity of your business—you must be (or find) a new product champion.

Chapter 7

What's a Plan Without a Strategy?

thunk.

In This Chapter

➤ The need for a strategic plan

➤ Dangers of the random approach to new product development

➤ Preparing for and creating a strategic plan

➤ Defining business and new product goals

Are you excited yet? I hope so. But it's not too late to take a deep breath, calm down—and quit.

That's right: *Quit.*

In Chapter 15, "Opening the Gates," you'll find a discussion about something called *stage gates*—checkpoints, guard stations, and toll booths that a new product concept has to get through before it goes on to the next stage of development. Well, we've reached a "stage gate" of our own in this book. You see, there's some things you need to have in place before you just go on trucking. And now's the time to find out if you've got these things or not. Here goes.

Know Where You're Going, or You May Wind Up Somewhere Else

I've a feeling you can't stomach another reference to Thomas Alva Edison, so let me turn to another American hero. General Douglas MacArthur, Supreme Allied Commander of the Pacific during World War II, was known for bold operations that cost remarkably few casualties. Asked to account for this, he replied: "I will not take by sacrifice that which I can take by strategy."

No commander worthy of command would commit his troops to battle without a strategic plan, and the foundation of all strategy is a goal or set of goals: a clear idea of where you want to go. Yet many CEOs—especially (but by no means exclusively) in small companies—send their troops into one random battle after another in an unfocused, aimless quest for new products. Sooner or later—and probably sooner—this approach drains financial as well as managerial resources. Keep introducing line extensions, modifications, new styles, new variations on existing products, and you may end up cannibalizing your current business without creating new customers or new market growth.

Now, I said earlier that new product development not only offers opportunity for greater profits and even greater personal and professional fulfillment, it may well spell the difference between survival and demise for your company, especially in the long term. I'll stand by that statement, and my point here and now is this: Unfocused new product development may so thoroughly sap your resources that you will have nothing left to take up the slack when your present products finally do die.

A Law of Nature?

I happen to be writing this book in an election year. I'm sure you've heard what I'm hearing from the candidates now. When the nation's economy is good, the incumbent takes credit for it. When its economy is bad, the incumbent chalks up the failure to "business cycles."

Before you allow yourself a self-satisfied snicker, think about all the talk you've heard concerning "product life cycles." As random new product development is the bane of many smaller, entrepreneurial companies, so a blind belief in the theory of product life cycles, coupled with abuses in marketing segmentation and product differentiation, leads to unnecessary, resource-wasting product proliferation in larger firms.

Flash! Product life cycles are not a law of nature. Blind faith is no substitute for clearly articulated corporate goals and a new product development program based on strategy.

From Vision to Mission

Having introduced General MacArthur into our discussion, let's bring in another military concept: mission. A mission is nothing more or less than a definition of the boundaries of your activity and your goal(s): what you want to attain and what you may and may not do to attain it.

Mission is a straightforward concept, but, like many apparently simple things, it can be difficult to put into practice. Defining the boundaries and goals of a business requires a CEO or top management team with *vision*—another of those deceptively simple words. In the context of new product development, vision is the quality that allows definition of business boundaries that are neither too narrow (and therefore cause you to overlook opportunities) nor too broad (and therefore invite you to squander resources). Vision must simultaneously stimulate and focus (filter and limit) new product development.

Stimulate and Focus

Thinking in terms of business categories can help make questions of vision, mission, and strategy less nebulous and abstract. Categorizing your business can be an important first step toward defining who you are, as a business. And knowing who you are should make it easier to define your goals. Here are the major categories you might use to think about your business:

➤ *Trade categories:* These are the simplest ways of stating what you do. If you make nuts and bolts, you are in the nut and bolt business. If you want to expand your business, but remain within the trade category, you might describe yourself as being in the fastener business, so that you can now think about turning out such items as, say, sheet-metal screws, which don't take nuts. You might even expand further afield, into the nail business.

Buzzword
At its simplest, a *mission* is an assigned task. In the context of strategic planning for your business, your mission defines the boundaries of your business activity in terms of a specific goal or set of goals.

Buzzword
Vision describes an act of imagination that is guided and informed by discernment and foresight. In developing new products, vision should both reveal possibilities and focus on practical limits.

False Start
Don't think of your firm in terms of trade categories. This way of thinking doesn't stimulate the development of new products. Trade categories can be narrow and nonconceptual—which means that they are restrictive rather than stimulating.

➤ *Power source/material categories:* These categories are based on the source materials of a business. For example, a steel manufacturer creates all sorts of products made out of the source material steel. A steel manufacturer need not think of itself as in the spring business or the I-beam business, but in the steel business. This can be a refreshing way of looking at your business by promoting vertical integration.

Prototype

Vertical integration can leverage the strength of many businesses. Look at the communications industry, for example. Just a few years ago, companies defined themselves as broadcasters, book publishers, magazine publishers, newspaper publishers, telephone service providers, movie studios, and so on. Today, many of these once very separate industries are being vertically integrated into "communications companies."

The basis of the vertical integration may include such "power sources" or "material categories" as ownership of the means of transmission of electronic signals (satellites, telephone lines, and so on) or the idea that, in agreeing to publish a novel, the company is not just buying the rights to a book, but a *copyright* that may be exploited in various media. The copyright is the material and power source and defines the company's business. Vertical integration can be a powerful factor in stimulating as well as focusing new product development.

False Start

Be careful. Like trade categories, even power source/material categories may restrict your thinking unduly. By the 1970s, American steel companies that thought of themselves strictly in terms of steel started to fall by the wayside, beaten down by Japanese competitors, who developed new products defined in terms of expanded and more flexible customer service.

➤ *Distribution categories:* Sometimes, thinking of products in terms of distribution channels can produce a whole new business. L'eggs built a business on the proposition that panty hose could be sold in supermarkets, not just at department store hosiery counters. Dell Computer, Gateway, Micron, and others created a new industry when they started selling computers directly—via mail order—to the end user.

➤ *Market categories:* You may define your company chiefly by the market(s) it serves. In turn, for consumer products, these markets are defined in demographic, psychographic, or lifestyle terms. For industrial, business-to-business products, they are defined by the needs of the business customer. The advantages of targeting your market precisely are that you can gather very specific information about what the market wants and needs, and you can tailor your new product strategy accordingly. You can know your customer intimately. The disadvantage is that you may target too narrowly and, therefore, miss potentially profitable new product opportunities. A manufacturer of bowling shirts might target bowlers exclusively and distribute only through sporting goods stores. However, recognizing that bowling shirts are a fun item of pop culture, the maker might also tap into specialty clothing stores that cater to hip young folks.

➤ *Product categories:* These categories can integrate all of the others to define a business quite narrowly or quite broadly. Does Levi Strauss produce jeans or casual clothing? Does Gerber make baby food or is its business babies?

The Three C's

Categorizing your business is an important step toward defining your mission. To take the strategic planning process further, preparatory to setting business goals, you need to integrate this categorization into an understanding of the three C's of your particular business:

1. *Customers:* Who are your customers now, and what do they need? Who else would you like to acquire as customers? You'll need to look long and hard at your customer base, find out what they like and don't like about your product(s), find out what they think about your company, find out what they need now, and what they might need in the future. We'll talk more about this in Chapter 11, "Needs and Wants."

2. *Competitors:* How do your competitors attack the market? What gaps in the market have your competitors failed to fill? What values do your competitors provide that you do not? What values do they fail to provide that you can supply? How will competitors react to a new product you introduce? More on competition in Chapter 11.

Buzzword
Demographics are the statistical characteristics of human populations; these may include age, income, gender, and so on. *Psychographics,* a word coined specifically for marketing, relates more specifically to attitudes and beliefs—mind-set.

Jump Start
A good way to gain a degree of objectivity in evaluating your own business is to look at it from the point of view of an outside, detached investor. Would you bet your money on your firm? Why? Why not? (And, if not, what would it take to change your mind?) Next, take apart what your company does. Look at your various products or product lines as investment portfolios. Which of these, as a potential investor, would you back? Which would pass up? Why?

3. *Company:* Take an unvarnished and unbiased look at yourself. List your firm's strengths and weaknesses. Think of ways to strengthen the weaknesses, but also find ways to play to your present strengths. More to come in Chapter 8, "Measuring Up."

Now—Go for the Goal!

Once you have categorized your business and come to an understanding of the three C's as they apply to your business, you are ready to set your goals.

Let's begin by exploding two myths about goals:

Myth #1. *I already have a goal*. No, you don't. You think you do. Your goal is to make money. Your goal is to increase sales. Your goal is to survive. These are not *strategic* goals—goals toward which you can build a strategic plan. Goals must be carefully thought out; then they must be *written* out.

Myth #2. *Expletive deleted! I don't have a goal after all—and, and, and* everybody else *does!!!* No, you're not alone. Remarkably few companies have genuinely strategic, clearly stated goals.

What is a strategic goal? The short answer is that a strategic goal is a carefully, clearly defined statement of what you want your company to be, to do, and to achieve in the relative long term (usually three to five years). Goals differ from objectives primarily in scope and time span. Objectives are the building blocks that make up goals; that is, goals can be broken down into a set of constituent objectives. The important thing is to establish realistic objectives that contribute toward achieving your strategic goal(s).

Business Goals

Before we go on to a discussion of the process of defining strategic goals, we should get some idea of what such goals are supposed to look like. I've already pointed out that broad goals such as "make more money" are too vast and vague to serve as *strategic* goals. Of course, General MacArthur wanted to *win* the war in the Pacific. But he didn't set that as his strategic goal. Instead, he worked with other Allied commanders to create a strategy of "island hopping"—retaking one Japanese-held Pacific island after another—with the goal of invading Japan. (In this strategic plan, each island was an objective, building toward the invasion of Japan.) Similarly, it is a given that you want to make more money. But how?

Let's say you've looked at your current business and your current customers. As a result of this study and self-examination, you've concluded the following about your company:

1. Acme Widget is the leader and innovator in the widget industry.

2. Acme has invented a better way to do X.

3. Acme products provide quality and value.

4. Acme has good name recognition; many consumers think of Acme when they think of widgets.

5. High production costs cut into Acme's margins.

6. Competitor A is beginning to achieve comparable name recognition in the widget market.

Based on these conclusions—which you might call a "Market Position Statement"—you can formulate a list of genuinely strategic business goals:

1. Become a higher-volume manufacturer that generates greater profit margins through production efficiencies.

2. Leverage down the cost of sales as volume increases.

3. Exploit the Acme reputation for innovation by continuing to be *the* innovator, developing and marketing new products.

4. Become the dominant company in the widget industry.

Publish such *goals* within your company, and your managers will have a clearer idea of the *objectives* they must in turn define and attain for their departments in order for the company as a whole to reach its goals.

Translating Goals into the Language of Business

Strategic business goals are expressed in words—a kind of wish list tempered by reality. Sooner or later, however, you'll have to translate the words into the language of business, and that language is dollars. New product development strategy should not only include a Market Position Statement (a self-portrait of your company—a snapshot of where you are) and a Statement of business goals (a word picture of where you want to go), but a Statement of Financial Goals expressed in target dollars per year. Such a statement can be quite complex, filling many spreadsheet pages, but its essence boils down to four basic elements:

1. Dollar figures for financial goals over a certain period—say the next three to five years

2. Target growth rate expressed as an annual percentage

3. Volume from current products/businesses, expressed in dollars

4. Gap-volume required from new product development, expressed in dollars

The "gap-volume" is the dollar amount of revenue required to close the gap between what current products and businesses are actually projected to generate and the percent of growth you've set as a goal. Of course, some portion of the gap-volume can be achieved by means in addition to new product development, including acquisition, cost cutting measures, and so on, but I assume that, because you're reading this book, you're most interested in closing the gap with new products.

Here is an example of a simple statement of financial goals. Business volume is expressed in millions of dollars:

Table 7.1 A Statement of Financial Goals

	Yr 1	Yr 2	Yr 3	Yr 4
Financial goal	$120	$136	$150	$16 2
Growth rate		13%	10%	8%
Volume from current business	$109	$113	$118	$123
Gap-volume required	$11	$23	$32	$39

Playing the Game

Now that you have some idea of what a goal looks like, how, exactly, do you go about creating a suitable set of them?

If yours is a small firm and you are the boss, you may perform all of the necessary business analysis and determine the goals yourself. Or you may want to bring in a consultant to help with this process.

In larger firms, the process of establishing goals might go something like this:

1. A team leader is appointed. This could be the CEO or her designated deputy, or you might use an outside consultant.

2. The team leader solicits from the heads of every department (that is, the key decision makers in the organization) a simple, single-page statement of corporate goals. You might specify an emphasis on new product goals and how these fit into the corporate goal picture.

3. The team leader additionally solicits from each key person a two-column list, company strengths on one side, weaknesses on the other.

4. Each key person should then write three *concise* statements:

   a. Where has the company been?

   b. Where is it now?

   c. Where will it be in three to five years?

5. The leader has each person submit a mission statement for the company and a mission statement for new product development/new product marketing.

6. The leader asks each key person to suggest the management system most effective to achieve the new product development and marketing goals as reflected in the mission statement.

Nothing is more difficult than thought, and this exercise is a process of intense thought. However, key management team personnel should welcome the hard work as an opportunity to make themselves heard in a direct, crystal clear manner. Once the various statements are completed, the team leader compiles them into a single summary document, which is distributed to the key people for further consideration. Based on these documents, the process is essentially repeated. Each key management person revises and submits a new set of statements and returns them to the leader. With these revisions in hand, the leader convenes a meeting or series of meetings in which the revisions are revised once again and consolidated into a draft of a statement of corporate and new product goals.

Jump Start
A good consultant will work with you the way a physician works with his patient. He will examine, probe, and poke in an effort to discover your firm's hopes, dreams, aspirations, previous marketing activities, current capabilities, likely prospects, and general business history. With this information as background, the consultant will help you to establish practical goals.

False Start
Avoid carving your statement of corporate and new product goals into stone tablets to be carried down from the penthouse suite. The draft is a *draft*. It is a working document that is subject to more revision as business strategies are developed. To some extent, goals and strategies evolve together. Indeed, some academics as well as practicing business professionals argue about whether goals really do precede strategy or vice versa. 'Tis ye olde chicken and egg conundrum.

73

The Wheel: You Don't Have to Reinvent It

Let's pause here a moment. While it is quite true that many—perhaps most—companies muddle through without a strategic plan, yours is not the first organization to work up such a plan. It *has* been done before.

I once overheard a backstage conversation between a starstruck concertgoer and a piano recitalist. "I just can't understand how you can look at all those notes on the page and figure out where to put your fingers so fast!" the fan exclaimed. The pianist replied: "Well, the notes do occur in familiar clusters."

The trained musician does not read individual musical notes, but chords and phrases—just as we read a book by recognizing familiar words and phrases rather than picking out individual letters. Similarly, while you must formulate a strategy that works for your particular organization in your particular markets and at the particular time you happen to occupy in the history of the world, the elements of all business strategies do occur in familiar clusters. As you can categorize your business, so you can categorize business strategies. Review the section called "A Bouquet of New" in Chapter 2. This is essentially a list of the "familiar clusters" that go into a new product strategy. Your *particular* strategy might consist of adopting one or more of these new product options in order to distinguish your product from that of your competitors—as viewed by your customers.

Season to Taste

Not that the list in Chapter 2 is a shake-and-bake one-taste-pleases-all recipe for new product strategy. You need to look not only at *your* company's resources, strengths, and weaknesses, but at the marketplace—*your* marketplace, *your* customers, *your* reality. Look especially hard for the *changes* that spell opportunity:

➤ Changes in the size of the market

➤ Changes in relevant external factors, such as economic conditions, government regulations, lifestyle trends, technological innovation, and so on

➤ New uses for a product

➤ New users of a product

➤ Demand for new products or product differentiations

➤ Product-line gaps that might be filled

➤ Distribution gaps that might be filled

➤ Usage gaps that might be filled (through strategies to stimulate nonusers into buying and light users into buying more)

➤ Competitive gaps that might be closed—for example, by strategies aimed at penetrating the competitor's market

And Look Homeward, Angel

Before you take flight into new product programs, don't confine your gaze to the world beyond your walls. Look inward, too. Consider such factors as the following, which represent your company's internal resources:

➤ Management's philosophy, attitude, mind-set

➤ Management's personal objectives and goals—and how they relate to those of the company

➤ Available skills

➤ Available resources

➤ Physical plant

➤ Location

➤ Method of distribution

➤ Productivity

➤ Cost factors

➤ Company's self-image—how it sees itself

Then look ahead. In this chapter, we've seen that clearly defined corporate goals and a strategic plan are oft-overlooked business necessities, and we've examined an approach to setting goals and to creating a plan to attain them. In the next chapter, we'll look at ways to develop new product objectives—the actual elements that go into the realization of the larger new product goals and the even larger corporate goals.

The Least You Need to Know

➤ Strategy is a concept borrowed from the military and is all about determining how best to deploy your resources in order to achieve your goals.

➤ Be honest in your corporate self-assessment.

➤ Creating strategy involves at least two major steps: recognizing your resources and your market, and taking action (if necessary) to modify your resources and market.

➤ It is critically important to define goals that simultaneously expand your horizons and focus your resources.

Part 3
Will the World Like It?

You like your idea. The folks at the water cooler like your idea. Your spouse even likes your idea.

But what about the rest of the world?

One way to find out, of course, is to take a chance, drop some big bucks, produce the product, and see if a market develops. But few companies can afford to roll the dice like that. Fortunately, there are alternatives to such a crap shoot. The chapters in this section outline procedures for creating goals and objectives for new product development; define the scope and limitations of market research; and suggest options for quick, cheap, and reasonably accurate predevelopment market research.

Measuring Up

Having achieved a firm grasp on corporate goals born of a hard-won knowledge of what you are and what you want to become, you can turn to developing objectives for your company's new products and new product lines. To a military general, strategy is meaningless if it is not followed. If goals and objectives are laid out only to have the various subordinate officers run off and fight their own battles, the war is unlikely to be won. Similarly, new product objectives must be developed in a way that contributes to the corporate mission and fits the company's strategic goals.

The step from overall strategic goals to new product objectives can be a daunting leap. This chapter will suggest ways to bridge the chasm.

False Start
Watch out! Disciplining top management to focus on new products that contribute to corporate goals is not always easy. As in the case of the little boy or girl who comes through the door with a stray puppy that "just followed me home," it can be hard to say no to a pet project. Depending on just whose pet it is, it may be impossible to say no. But pets can be very expensive to feed and care for. And sometimes they end up making a terrible, smelly mess.

Buzzword
A *superior product* can be many things in many different contexts to many different customers. But a superior product may always be defined by the following characteristics: offers unique features that differentiate it from other currently available products; satisfies customers more than the competitors' stuff does; is of high quality and represents good value; solves customers' problems with competitive products; reduces customers' costs; is innovative.

Remember Failure?

You might take a moment to glance back at "Why New Products Fail" in Chapter 3. I'm not going to rehash the many reasons for new product failure here, but I want to suggest that most of the causes of such unpleasantness discussed back in Chapter 3 may be reduced or eliminated by developing corporate goals and a strategic plan, then creating product objectives in step with these goals, and, finally, employing the necessary discipline to stick to the product objectives.

The Sweet Smell

Failure stinks. Let's move on to success.

If you are depressed by the many reasons for new product failure, be heartened by the many, many reasons for new product success. I can't list them all, but here are some surefire causes of triumph:

➤ Your product is superior

➤ Your product is market driven

➤ Your product is the result of diligent homework

➤ Your product is the result of clear definition

➤ Your product is well launched

➤ Your product is the child of a good home

➤ Your product thrives on synergy

➤ Your product has an attractive market

➤ Your product is well executed

➤ Your product has been developed, launched, manufactured, and marketed quickly

➤ Your product is well supported

Superiority Complex

The new product—whether it is an invention, innovation, redesign, repackaging, whatever—should really offer *something new* to the consumer, and, equally important, the consumer must be able to recognize that newness. I'm not talking about new for the sake of new, but a newness that offers:

➤ Previously unavailable features and benefits

➤ Features and benefits that meet the consumer's needs more effectively than the existing products of your competitors

➤ New levels of quality and value

➤ New solutions to current problems—especially problems with competitive products

➤ New levels of cost reduction for the consumer

➤ And, okay: *newness*. While novelty alone is an awfully shaky foundation on which to build new product success, it *does* contribute to success.

Put the Market in the Driver's Seat

Strongly related to product superiority is a knowledge of—and a focus on—the market. It is possible to do very complex market analysis, which, undertaken intelligently, can be effective. On the other hand, such analysis can infinitely delay new product development by fostering indecision that would make Shakespeare's Hamlet look happy-go-lucky. At minimum, however, you need to take two steps toward understanding your market—and then add a dash of verification:

Step #1: *Start by determining consumer/user needs and wants.* Depending on the nature of your business, "market research" can be elaborate and comprehensive (as well as expensive), or it can consist of a number of phone calls, informal questionnaires, and casual questions. In either case, let the customer contribute to the design of the product.

Step #2: *Study your competitors' products.* Appreciate the strengths of what they have to offer, but look for the weaknesses. What can be improved? How can your product solve problems either unsolved by—or created by—competing products?

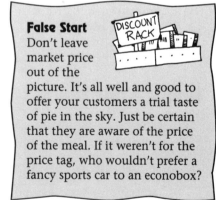

False Start
Don't leave market price out of the picture. It's all well and good to offer your customers a trial taste of pie in the sky. Just be certain that they are aware of the price of the meal. If it weren't for the price tag, who wouldn't prefer a fancy sports car to an econobox?

81

Once you have defined a new product concept, specs, or set of features, go back to your customers. Does what you propose satisfy them?

Finish Your Homework Before You Play

Most management experts agree: properly conducted, the so-called "predevelopment phase" of new product development usually enhances the prospects for success significantly. However, predevelopment can become an endless excuse for delaying new product development unless, like the development process proper, it follows a specific schedule and a prescribed series of steps. The appropriate steps vary from product to product, but usually include:

1. Screening—discussed in Chapter 9

2. Market study—discussed in Chapter 17

3. Assessment of technical feasibility (*"Oh, yeah…Can we really make this thing?"*)—also discussed in Chapter 17

4. Building the business case—discussed in chapters 12 and 16

Building the business case includes answering the following questions:

➤ Will the proposed product make a profit? Will it sell in sufficient volume and with an adequate margin?

➤ Who is our target customer? Can we position the product to reach this target?

➤ Does the proposed product fit into our business? Is it worth changing our business to fit the proposed product?

➤ Can we build into the product the features, benefits, and performance necessary to make it a winner?

➤ Can the product be developed at the right cost?

Know What You're Doing

Before significant funding and effort are invested in development, be certain that the new product has been fully and clearly defined. This includes:

➤ Definition of the target market. Who'll buy this thing?

➤ Definition of the product concept. What benefits will the product deliver?

➤ A full laundry list of product features, requirements, and specs. What is the division of the "must have" and "would be nice to have" categories?

"...3, 2, 1. Ignition. Lift Off!"

There is a widespread and utterly misguided belief that good products sell themselves. While it's hard to sell bad products no matter what you do, all products, even very good ones, need help. Their benefits must be communicated and marketed.

A good launch is critical to the success of a new product, and an intelligent marketing plan is critical to a successful launch. See Chapter 22, "Execution's the Thing," for a discussion of launch-related topics.

New product success is greatly enhanced in organizations that promote a lot of give and take between R&D and marketing departments. Communicate. Cooperate. Interact.

Jump Start
Think of the marketing plan as a *component part* of the new product, as real as an IC chip or a toggle switch. Make it integral to the new product development process as early in that process as possible.

The Energy of Synergy

Most mornings, you can't walk into the office without stumbling across this word by about nine o'clock. I've defined it in the "New Is Not Always Better" section of Chapter 3, but it bears repeat consideration here. Synergy leverages *present* strengths, resources, and product experience into a *new* product. To the degree that the proposed new product differs from your current business, it loses the advantage of synergy.

Synergies to exploit in new product development include:

➤ *Available resources:* Personnel and equipment are present in house.

➤ *Experience:* It's new, but you've done something like it before. Unpleasant surprises can be costly.

➤ *Technological synergy:* The new product will be born of technology you currently possess.

➤ *Marketing synergy:* You have in place the sales force, distribution channels, advertising, and other market resources necessary to handle this new product.

False Start
Beware of "step-out" projects (new products unrelated to current business). These are by no means doomed to fail, but they are harder to pull off, because they cannot draw on current momentum and expertise.

It is always better to create new products for attractive rather than unattractive markets. An *attractive market* is one that offers high potential (is large and growing, consisting of customers who need the product and for whom purchase of it is important) and that is not burdened by intense competition (not clogged by competitors who offer strong products of high quality and low relative price, and whose sales force, distribution, and support services are highly rated).

Do It Right

To a certain extent (more so, certainly, than any of us would like), new product development is a roll of the dice. But a lot of the process *is* controllable, and no part of it is more controllable than the execution. Speed is important in new product development, but carelessness is unforgivable. It is not unforgivable just for some highfalutin moral reason, but because consumers will not forgive new products that are flawed in design or in quality. Most people spend much of their lives trying not to look like fools. Consumers are no different. They won't take a chance on a new product that has a flawed reputation.

Do It Fast

Speed is increasingly of the essence in new product development. The idea is to get to market fast. But how do you "do it right" *and* "do it fast"? Well, just because you might do something slowly doesn't mean you'll do it right, and it's also true that speedy execution does not preclude high quality of execution. No two ways about it, though, it *does* make the task more challenging.

The single most effective way to speed up the process is not to make mistakes. Instead of cutting corners, build in quality at every step, so that you do it right the first time and don't have to waste time doing it over again.

Beyond this, ensure that following happens:

➤ Invest time in defining the new product at the outset, so that you won't squander time on unfocused and unnecessary activity.

➤ Avoid running a relay race. Ever since Henry Ford made the assembly line practical, American business has been obsessed with sequential processing: do this, finish it, then do this, finish it, then go on to this, and so forth. To whatever degree possible, abandon *sequential* processing for *parallel* processing, in which more activities take place simultaneously. Divide the task at hand into separate parallel steps, but maintain constant intercommunication.

➤ Through clear definition of corporate goals and strategic plan, prioritize proposed new projects. Which ones are important to work on *now*? Which can be back-burnered? Which can be scrapped? Make the hard choices, then get to work on them.

Back It Up

As every parent learns, there does come a time when you must send your children out into the world. But that doesn't mean that you abandon them. Be certain that all departments of your operation—R&D, marketing, advertising, and especially customer service/ tech support—are there to monitor the new product, to support it, to support the customers who use it, and to listen to what the customers say about it.

Fit to Be Tried

We've looked at the general factors that contribute to the success of any new product. No matter who you are and what your company does, these are elements that are usually critical to success. Beyond these are the factors that help you decide whether or not a new product will work *for your company*.

Developing a good set of product objectives flows from your corporate goals and mission. In fact, such objectives can be incorporated directly into the strategic plan. Dun & Bradstreet created a set of overall new product objectives back in the 1980s. It's a good example of what a list of objectives looks like:

➤ The idea is compatible with our corporate image.

➤ The product can be standardized.

➤ The idea has significant sales and profit potential.

➤ The market has repetitive functional need for more of the product.

➤ The product relies on managerial skills we have or can develop.

➤ The idea has a unique, distinctive benefit.

➤ The idea offers rapid startup to high velocity sales and early payback.

➤ There are no known legal or social (governmental) limitations.

➤ Developmental costs are not excessive.

➤ The product will not require intensive servicing.

➤ The product can be derived, at least in part, from existing production capability.

➤ The product should be sold by a sales force.

What, exactly, should go into creating new product criteria? Jack Loechner, president of The Associates Group, a consulting company specializing in new product marketing and development, proposed the following components. In effect, they are a list of criteria for new products:

85

1. General program objectives in terms of number of items or lines, opportunities from which to select, size of opportunity sought.

2. Revenue or unit volume objectives within express period of time following commercialization.

3. Return on investment expressed in terms of dedicated assets employed.

4. Limitations on capital investment.

5. Profitability objective in keeping with corporate standards and goals.

6. Development time for design, engineering, manufacturing, marketing plans.

7. Leveraging company assets: brand name, manufacturing, marketing, and so on.

8. Investment limitations in terms of development costs, tooling, inventory, distribution.

9. Technical or physical characteristics and/or limitations.

10. Marketing and distribution considerations: sales organization, customer base, served markets.

11. Specific introduction dates desired. Trade show requirements.

12. Proprietary or patent requirements for invention.

13. Overall corporate fit with current lines, services, business philosophy, integration plans.

14. Unit economics expressed in terms of base price, value added, price/volume relationship, labor versus material intensity.

Does every product objective have to fit all of these criteria? Not necessarily. Choose the ones that are right for you.

Take Your PIC

A somewhat more specialized and detailed approach to listing new product objectives is the product innovation charter—or PIC—a concept developed by marketing student Merle Crawford. The PIC is a detailed and clear statement of new product objectives. It includes the following:

A. *The goal or objectives* for the product innovation activities.

   1. The *target business arena* that product innovation is to take the firm into, or keep it in. These arenas are defined in different ways, examples of which are:

a. By product type (e.g., specialty chemicals, or cars and trucks)

b. By end-user activity or function (e.g., data processing or food)

c. By technology (e.g., fluidics or xerography)

d. By customer or consumer group (e.g., service stations or state lotteries)

2. The position *within those arenas* which the firm wishes to achieve. This position is usually stated in more than one way:

a. Market share goal, or a position of relative leadership.

b. Dollar goal, either sales volume, or profit level, total dollars, ROI, payback percent on sales, short-term/long-term.

3. Special goals, objectives, or conditions peculiar to the firm's unique situation. Examples are:

a. Image, to maintain or to seek.

b. Smoothing out of various irregularities.

c. Diversification.

B. *The program of activities* chosen to achieve the above goals.

1. *Strengths to exploit:* Many exist, though usually one of three types:

a. An *R&D* skill or capability, (e.g., glass technology).

b. A *manufacturing* facility, process, skill, or material (e.g., food processing, or wood chips).

c. A *marketing advantage* (e.g., strong sales force, an image, or a trade franchise).

2. *Weaknesses to avoid:* Usually one or more of the same list as above, e.g., avoid relying on an R&D for a new product, or avoid new products that require unavailable market contacts.

3. *Source of the innovation.* That is, will the new product's points of differentiation be developed:

a. *Internally* (by R&D, marketing, etc.), or

b. *Externally* (by acquiring companies, products, or processes), or by

c. A deliberate *combination* of both, one variation of which is the joint venture.

4. *Degree of innovativeness sought, if any.* Alternatives can include:

a. *Inventive.* Technological leadership, whether product, package, service, positioning, or whatever. Be "first to market" with it.

b. *Adaptive.* Lie back, let others lead; adapt or modify; use "innovative imitation," be "second, but best."

c. *Innovative applications.* Utilize established technology but apply it creatively to new uses. Essentially a special combination of the two above.

d. *Economic.* Build strength by producing what others have created, but doing it more economically. The low-cost producer.

5. *Special restrictions or directions.* Highly situational, but not miscellaneous or casual. Some examples are:

a. *Level of risk* that is acceptable.

b. *Sense of urgency* or criticalness.

c. *Product quality level*—usually a stipulation of high quality, for protecting an image, or for trading one up.

d. *Patentability*—sometimes absolutely critical.

e. *Size or growth trends* in markets being considered, coming from the strategic planning matrices.

f. *Line completeness.*

g. *Number of new items per year,* either a minimum or a maximum.

h. *Avoidance of certain competitors.*

i. *Avoidance of environmental problems, or other social pressure.*

Giving Good Weight

Criteria defining product objectives are important, but relatively few of these criteria can be considered black or white, *no-go* or *go*. The next step beyond creating the product objectives is to develop an evaluation system that measures these objectives. This might be a very simple system indeed, with the key objectives labeled as "vital," "desirable," "indifferent," or "unnecessary." If you prefer, these adjectives can be translated into numerical scores, so that you can add up the "vitals" and "desirables" and subtract the "indifferents" and "unnecessaries," then come up with a *go/no-go* score.

The actual steps for establishing new product criteria are simple enough to describe:

1. Select primary evaluative criteria—as part of the strategic business plan, a PIC, or even a simple list.

2. Weight the criteria by relative importance.

3. Establish the range of the rating scale.

4. Determine the evaluators of the new product proposal.

5. Calculate the overall index of the new product proposal.

But where do the "weights" come from? In most larger companies, weighting is determined through a team approach, led by a divisional manager or CEO. Then the consensus of top management is sought, and the weighting scale is finalized. Admittedly, much of this procedure is subjective. But the process does quantify or describe the collective subjectivity of experts, and in this way enables new product developers to communicate with some precision and some degree of objective understanding of corporate goals, of top management's vision, and of one another. Weighting objectives is a kind of language, and, like any language, it is imperfect and imprecise. But it is certainly better than no language at all.

Can This Be Any Harder?

This is supposed to be a *Complete Idiot's Guide*, and, like an idiot, I've guided you into a dark and twisted thicket. Don't give up. And don't let go of the original energy that propels new products in the first place. What we've reviewed here are methods for conserving time, effort, and money by rationalizing *some* aspects of new product development. Stay sane by reminding yourself that the methods outlined in this chapter are not ends in themselves. They are instruments only—means to an end. Now, let's go on to researching the market.

Jump Start
The nature of the rating system you use is less important than ensuring that everyone who uses the system understands it and applies it consistently.

The Least You Need to Know

➤ It's important to develop new product criteria that are relevant to the company's situation and its goals.

➤ Establish some system for evaluating and rating new product criteria, so that rational judgments can be made and so that communication is effective among all those involved in developing new products.

➤ Whatever goals you set, be certain that a concept of superiority governs them all.

Chapter 9

Do Do That Voodoo? The Challenge of Market Research

In This Chapter

➤ Potential and pitfalls of market research

➤ Market research: when to use it and when to leave it alone

➤ Market research rules of thumb

➤ Varieties of market research and when to use each

Creativity is fun. Let's not forget that. Of course, when you've got hundreds of thousands, maybe millions, of dollars riding on a new product—in fact, when you've got your job and the jobs of others along for that ride as well—no doubt about it, creativity can get a little hairy.

No wonder you want to sit on something other than the seat of your pants. You want to stack the deck, load the dice. That's where market research comes in. Certainly, the concept makes sense: *ask* people what they want. And some market research can be just that simple. But most isn't. In fact, market research has become as complex as any field of science. The problem is, it's not a science. It *can* lead to dramatic discoveries, but, despite the seemingly scientific stacks of numbers and statistics and graphs, it can also lead to many wrong answers and misguided interpretations. As early as 1963, advertising pioneer

David Oglivy remarked in his memoir, *Confessions of an Advertising Man*, that marketing executives "are coming to rely too much on research, and they use it as a drunkard uses a lamppost, for support rather than for illumination."

This chapter is meant to sober us all up.

Research First, Last, and Always...Maybe

Marketing professor Robert G. Cooper, in his 1993 *Winning at New Products,* pointed to a set of extensive Conference Board studies of the reasons for new product failure and underscored the number one reason: poor marketing research. Managers most frequently chalked up new product flops to a "lack of thoroughness in identifying real needs in the marketplace." An executive in one industrial firm confessed, "We decided what our marketplace wanted in this [unsuccessful] new product without really asking that market what its priorities were."

The experts seem to agree, then, that market research is critical. Let's roll up our sleeves and dive into the first of two chapters that tell you how to do it.

And I'd do just that, if it weren't for the lessons of history. *Historically*, breakthrough products have seldom been identified through anything resembling market research.

False Start
Don't make the mistake of assuming that just because a new product is the apple of R&D's collective eye, consumers will necessarily love it, too.

Wheels have been found on children's toys from pre-Columbian Mexico, yet there is no evidence that wheels were put to practical use by these pre-Columbian cultures. The saddle appeared some 700 years before the stirrup—a product that offers the great advantage of stability on horseback and that, therefore, gives mounted warriors (among others) a significant edge. The airplane was invented right here in America, yet the U.S. military was reluctant to develop aircraft as weapons. When the United States entered World War I in 1917, the European Allies had no use for the few already obsolescent aircraft America had to offer.

The point is this: *Most people, most of the time, are happy with things as they are.* This doesn't mean things couldn't be better, but if a person is happy with things as they are—however they are—he will see no advantage to investing in change. A genius inventor may conceive of a better way of doing things. But what good does that do her if most people are happy with the way things are? (Remember Edison's failed vote tabulator.)

In fact, it can be argued that some of the most innovative companies have succeeded precisely by avoiding market research. In the 1980s, Sony Corporation became legendary (or notorious) for seldom conducting market research. Its management held that market research could not identify needs people didn't realize they have. The fabulously successful Walkman, for instance, in all its varieties and variations, was not the product of market research, and it is certainly true that consumers perceive Sony as an innovator and manufacturer of high-quality products.

On the other hand, Sony continued to champion the Beta-format VCR long after the VHS format had eclipsed it and consumers ceased to want it. Sony and a handful of enthusiasts persistently touted the technical superiority of Beta over VHS, but consumers bought VHS in droves, movie companies stopped releasing Beta-format tapes, and Sony belatedly had to cave in to the marketplace. It licensed VHS technology and started producing the VHS machines. Who can calculate the revenue Sony lost by closing its eyes to the needs and desires of the marketplace for so long?

Prototype

Here's an example of the limits of market research in a world where most people are happy with the way things are. Gerald Schoenfeld, a new product idea-generation consultant in New York, related in *Fortune* (February 7, 1983, page 61) that Church & Dwight Company, makers of Arm & Hammer baking soda, plodded through questionnaires from 5,000 consumers in an effort to discover what their "refrigerator needs" were. Five thousand consumers really couldn't think of any. Fortunately for Church & Dwight, new product development didn't stop there. They put aside the questionnaires, continued with their in-house idea sessions, and came up with the concept of baking soda as a refrigerator air freshener. The product wasn't new; however, an entirely new use for it had been identified. But identified by whom? Not the consumers. And how *should* they know? They're not baking-soda experts. The experts were at Church & Dwight, and at least one of them understood that baking soda could absorb the moisture-laden odors of a closed refrigerator. In effect, the company had been asking the wrong people—5,000 amateurs, instead of a small group of their own in-house professionals.

A Tool Is Not a Magic Wand

Well, this is just *great*! Management experts say that most new product failures are due to inadequate market research, but the market can't be depended on to know what it wants—or, left to its own devices, can take up to 700 years to want something. What are you supposed to do now?

My advice is that you should do what you are paid to do, which is to think. If you are depending on market research for magic—crank in information at one end, get new product answers at the other—you're earning your salary under false pretenses. You're not thinking. You're waiting for magic.

Market research is not a magic wand. It is a tool, and like any other tool, it can be used skillfully or clumsily.

Don't Pick Up the Hammer Unless You Really Need It

The hammer is a useful tool, provided that you really need to hammer something. If you don't, then you'd better leave the hammer alone. The danger is, if all you've got is a hammer (as the saying goes), the whole world starts to look like a collection of nails.

Know when *not* to use your "hammer." If you are dealing with a product concept that is so unusual or such a breakthrough that the prospective consumer cannot easily see the benefit or even relate to it in his current situation, market research will tell you little or, worse, may kill a visionary idea. Market research is of limited use if the concept depends on an extensive infrastructure of supporting elements, such as cable TV or a digital transmission network for the Internet. And then there are concepts that are so sweeping that they will change the way people do things. The personal computer was such a product. Market research will tell you little about these.

Prototype

The personal computer was not born of market research for the simple reason that, in the 1970s, there *was* no market for a personal computer. It was a concept in the minds of a few electronic hobbyists, including one Ed Roberts, a civilian laser technician working for the Air Force in Albuquerque, New Mexico. In 1974, he developed the PE-8, which *Popular Electronics* rechristened the Altair 8080 when it ran a construction project story about this $397 computer hobby kit, which had few practical applications, but which was nevertheless fascinating—to a small number of computer enthusiasts. (Like the PC market, the phrase "computer nerd" did not yet exist in 1974.)

Other manufacturers made some computers, most notably Apple, beginning in 1977, but it wasn't until August 12, 1981, that IBM introduced the IBM PC. The marketing folks at Big Blue predicted that the world population included about 100,000 people—total—who would buy the product, which, like Ed Roberts, they saw as primarily a hobbyist's instrument. No one was more shocked than IBM when, in the first few months following its release, demand for the PC far outstripped supply.

If, however, the proposed new product (like most "new" products) is an innovation rather than an invention, if it is clearly linked to something your prospective customer base is already familiar with, then market research may well yield very useful information. Market research is the tool of choice when you think you already have the answer or, at least, have narrowed down a range of possible answers. If you *believe* that the product you propose clearly addresses a consumer need or desire, or it solves a current problem consumers are aware of, or it solves a problem with current (especially competitive) products, or it fills a gap that current (especially competitive) products have left unfilled, then use market research to test, confirm, disprove, and suggest ways to modify your beliefs.

Don't Pay Too Much for Your Whistle

One of old Ben Franklin's many homely anecdotes is about himself as a little boy who spends all the money in his pocket on a shiny pennywhistle, which soon breaks. From this incident he learns a valuable lesson: Don't pay too much for your whistle.

And, indeed, you shouldn't. Balance the cost of the market research—in dollars as well as in added development time and consequent delay to market—against the cost of the risk of new product misfires. Some new products are not worth testing. That doesn't mean they're not worth creating. It means that the revenue they are likely to generate does not justify the expense of a market research campaign. Book publishers, for example, are often criticized for largely neglecting market research. The fact is, most books that are profitable generate nothing greater than a modest profit, which would be eaten up by money spent on market research.

Buzzword
Consumers are buyers and users of economic goods or goods of certain class, whereas *customers* are people who have bought products specifically from you. *Prospects* are potential customers.

You are paid to assess risks and use your judgment. New product decisions that are critical, difficult to change, impossible to retreat from, or that involve substantial investment (a high risk-to-reward ratio) are good candidates for market research.

Five Golden Rules of Market Research

Here's a half tablet (only *five* Commandments) for using the market research tool:

1. *Develop a set of business norms as an index against which to analyze market research findings.* It's a mistake to regard market research data as *absolute* data. It is information that's meaningful only as it *relates* to your past successes and failures (that is, your business "norms").

2. *Test and offer alternatives.* Don't develop a single product, price, position, etc., and then test this unit in isolation. Formulate a set of alternatives—different product features, price points, positionings, colors, styles, distribution venues, and so on—and include them all in your research project. Use the results to help refine and develop an optimal solution.

3. *Make sure you will be able to do something with the research.* If you invest X amount—no, let's be realistic—if you invest XXXX amount on market research that provokes praise and compliments and remarks like "Isn't that interesting," then you've failed. Research should yield praise, but it should also produce action—whether that action is a *go* to develop a product, a *go* to modify a concept, or a *no-go* that kills a proposed product before it costs a bundle. Before starting or authorizing or proposing any market research project, make certain of the following:

> ➤ Define possible outcomes ahead of time

> ➤ Define a range of realistic decisions and feasible actions

4. *Make the most of research to stimulate creativity.* Whatever else market research does or fails to do, it buys you something that is valuable to any business: the opportunity to talk (directly or indirectly) to consumers, customers, and prospects. Exploit this valuable contact as a chance to develop new opportunities. Involve all the key people on the new product development team in the market research, including in the creation of questionnaires and in the analysis of the results. Review results collectively in order to generate new ideas.

5. *Use it. Don't believe it.* Market research is a model. It is not real life. *Use* the information your research yields as input into the following stages of a new product development process:

> ➤ Idea generation

> ➤ Screening

> ➤ Design and development

> ➤ Product evaluation

> ➤ Marketing

Use market research techniques to feed and modify your own ideas rather than to transform the data into ironclad articles of passive belief.

Skinning the Cat

There's more than one way to do it. In the balance of this chapter, we'll take an overview of the development process and outline how market research can be used at each stage. In the next chapter, we'll look more closely at research techniques and which techniques are appropriate during the preliminary investigation of new product concepts and (if the concept survives the preliminary stage) during the more detailed investigations that follow. Then, in Chapter 11, we will open up the "stage gate" system of product development.

Idea Generation

If you're looking for ideas, you can simply ask your current customers or even wait for them to say something to you. Or you can use more sophisticated research techniques in order to answer at least four key questions:

1. What segments of need exist in the market?

2. What gaps exist in the competitive fulfillment of these needs?

3. What bothers customers/consumers?

4. What benefits do customers/consumers desire?

How Do I Get the Answers?

Several research techniques can be used. In focus groups, a trained moderator leads small groups of consumers from the target market in a discussion of problems, needs, product concepts, competitive brands, and new ideas. The focus group can be assembled from your current customers. You can read more about focus groups in Chapter 10, "Groundbreaking Research."

If a broader sample is required, quantitative analysis of responses to customer/consumer questionnaires can be carried out in order to identify product attributes and perceptions of product benefits, and to identify groups whose needs are not being satisfied. Specifically, quantitative research should answer such questions as:

➤ What are the products in the market and how do consumers react to them?

➤ How are the products used?

➤ Who uses them?

➤ When and under what circumstances are they used?

➤ Which products compete with or substitute for one another?

➤ What product attributes lead consumers to use the products?

➤ What product attributes lead consumers to use the products *in the way that they do*?

Waking Sleeping Dogs

Much of your business life is spent avoiding problems. In market research, however, you eagerly seek out problems. Problems are very strong motivators of consumer purchases. People will buy something they believe will solve a problem that afflicts them.

Problem detection studies are quantitative surveys designed to define problems in a category, and then rank them based on *intensity* (How bothersome is the problem?), *frequency* (How often does the problem occur?), *duration* (How long does the problem last?), and *preemptibility* (What is the extent to which currently available products/services handle the problem?).

Watch It!

To discover needs and ferret out problems, you can conduct surveys and ask questions. You can also arrange actually to *watch* a process, whether that process is machining a precision part, mowing the lawn, or opening a bank account. By studying the process, you can identify problems, gaps, and needs. This is an extension of the time and motion studies that pioneering "efficiency experts" such as the husband-and-wife team of Frank and Lillian Gilbreth carried out in the early 1900s—except that, instead of looking for ways to arrange work processes so that they're more efficient, you're looking for ideas about new products that will appeal to consumers by making tasks or processes easier, more efficient, more pleasant, more profitable, and so on.

Prototype

Frank Gilbreth (1868–1924), a New York City–based contracting engineer, and his wife Lillian (1878–1972), a psychologist and teacher, creatively applied the social sciences to industrial management. Their use of motion-picture photography to study the human movement involved in manufacturing processes, including human interaction with machines, revolutionized concepts of efficiency. Perhaps the Gilbreths' most spectacular "time-motion studies" (a phrase they coined) were of surgical operations. In an era before sophisticated life-support systems, speed was of the essence in surgery, and the Gilbreths' work probably saved many lives.

Task observation should be combined with questions:

➤ Ask the potential consumer to list all the tasks or steps involved in a project.

➤ Ask him to rate the steps from pleasant to unpleasant.

➤ Ask why he finds a given step pleasant or unpleasant.

➤ Ask *if*, *why*, and *how* he would like the step, task, or process changed.

Concept Screening

You may use customer or consumer research to generate ideas, or you may use it to *screen concepts*. This involves introducing product concepts to groups of customers or consumers and getting their responses. The two major questions you're trying to answer are:

➤ Is there a market for the proposed product?

➤ How large is the potential market?

Beyond this, you are also looking for answers to such questions as:

➤ What are the important concept attributes and product benefits?

➤ What is the best positioning for the product?

➤ Is the market segmented?

➤ How is the market segmented?

➤ What are the characteristics of the target market segments—in terms of demographics, psychographics, and product class usage, for consumer products; and in terms of end user needs, for industrial products?

Focus groups are useful for concept screening. The concepts being screened are described verbally and/or visually. If three-dimensional models and mock-ups are available, so much the better. Quantitative surveys are also appropriate, such as shopping mall intercepts, field survey office interviews, and mail surveys. These also can employ descriptions, drawings, renderings, and samples.

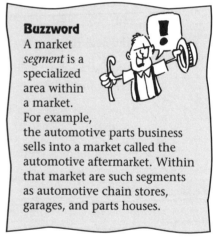

Buzzword
A market *segment* is a specialized area within a market. For example, the automotive parts business sells into a market called the automotive aftermarket. Within that market are such segments as automotive chain stores, garages, and parts houses.

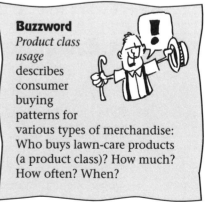

Buzzword
Product class usage describes consumer buying patterns for various types of merchandise: Who buys lawn-care products (a product class)? How much? How often? When?

The manner in which the concept is presented is critically important and will be discussed in detail in the next chapter. You will see that the trick is to present the concept in normal, everyday language that is closer to the style of advertising than to the prose of a formal essay—yet that studiously *avoids* the creative twists and slogans normally used to hard sell a product. Remember, your objective in concept screening is to get customer/consumer response, *not* to *advertise* or *sell* the concept.

Product Design and Development

Market research for this phase should answer such questions as:

➤ Which design features are important and should be included in the product?

➤ Which features are not important?

➤ Which features are undesirable and should be deliberately excluded?

➤ How should the product be packaged and presented?

➤ How will the product be used?

➤ What kind of durability and reliability expectations do customers/consumers have for the product?

➤ How will the product be maintained? (What are service and support expectations/needs?)

➤ How much will consumers be willing to pay?

➤ How likely are consumers to buy the product?

Group discussions can be used to ascertain some of this data but, usually, a larger database is desirable, amassed from responses to mailed questionnaires. In addition, customer/consumer response to actual prototypes, working models, or mock-ups may be tested in the laboratory or in the field.

Product Evaluation

To borrow a phrase from the slogan of a popular tire manufacturer, this is where the rubber meets the road. At this stage, your firm has invested in a "final" design, usually in the form of prototypes or even pilot manufacturing runs. Questions to answer include:

➤ Does the final design meet target consumer expectations?

➤ If it is an industrial product, does it meet the needs of the end user?

➤ Are enough consumers—or, for industrial products, end users—willing to pay the price necessary to generate an adequate return?

➤ How many can be sold?

➤ How long will it take to sell that many?

➤ For consumable products, what will trial and repeat-purchase rates be?

➤ Is the product packaging right? (Does it generate a high perceived value?)

Research at this stage typically involves large sample tests, whether in-house or in the field. For commercial and industrial products, a panel of expert evaluators and/or personal interviews with end users can be used.

Jump Start
By the time you reach the *product evaluation* phase, you should have identified your target consumers. It is these individuals—and not general *consumers*—that you should be working with at this point.

The Marketing Plan for the Launch Phase

Common sense suggests that the marketing plan is the final phase of the new product development to test. But common sense doesn't always put beans on the table. Because speed has become increasingly critical in new product development, it's better to put aside linear assembly-line thinking and look at this stage of the evaluation in terms of parallel processing. You can test marketing concepts quite early in the development stage—even as part of concept screening and certainly parallel with product design.

The four important questions to ask are:

➤ What is the best positioning for the product? That is, how do we communicate the most important benefit(s) to the "best potential customers"—the most important target market segment(s)?

➤ What is the optimum price?

➤ What is the optimum distribution channel?

➤ What are the optimum promotion techniques and advertising strategies?

For industrial goods with high-tech contents, ask:

➤ What is the optimum way to educate our sales force?

➤ What is the best way to educate end users?

Buzzword
Consumable goods are purchased, used up, and must be purchased repeatedly. Toothpaste is a consumable. *Durable* goods last longer. An electric toothbrush is durable and will not be purchased again—at least for quite a while. (But is a regular old-fashioned toothbrush—your dentist says replace it every three months—durable or consumable?)

Jump Start
Evaluation of the market plan can begin early in the development phase, but may also be employed later, as a means of "course correction," using a live test market.

Focus groups are useful during early stages of testing, as are mail- and telephone-survey questionnaires. Traditionally, certain industries (especially the consumer packaged-goods industry) have employed testing in a live test market as a "final check" of the marketing plan. This is expensive and involves a test period of anywhere from six months to a year. But if millions and millions of dollars are involved in an effort to carve out a big chunk of market share, live tests can be invaluable.

So Many Choices, So Little Time

No matter what research techniques you use at whichever stage of product development, each has advantages and disadvantages.

Focus groups are relatively inexpensive and are probably quite valuable for generating ideas and getting individual responses to concepts. However, critics charge that the small size of these groups makes them statistically unreliable. While this drawback has little bearing on idea generation, it can be disastrous for final decision making.

Concept tests permit testing before expensive prototypes are developed and, therefore, allow product modifications at lower cost. They also reduce the risk of premature disclosure of new products to competitors, and they certainly help define market characteristics and needs. However, concept tests tend to be imprecise. Consider these questions:

➤ Are you measuring product idea, ad copy, or product position?

➤ Will the test accurately predict market share? (Not if the finished product fails to deliver adequately on the promises of the concept description!)

➤ Will today's prediction hold true tomorrow? (Not necessarily. A lot of time can go by between the concept test and the introduction of the product.)

Quantitative surveys have numbers on their side. The laws of statistics are well understood and reliable. The problem is that many quantitative techniques permit little, if any, *direct exposure* to the product—although in the case of package goods, it is feasible (if costly) to send out large quantities of samples.

Just what techniques you choose depends on just what kind of information you're trying to obtain. The following figure summarizes a range of techniques and categorizes their effectiveness in measuring certain market characteristics and meeting project needs. Note that the vertical axis—the techniques—progresses from cheapest to most expensive method, with the cheapest listed at the top.

	Consumer acceptance	Trade acceptance	Competitive effects	Cannibalization	Promotional effects	Price effects	Estimate demand	Realism	Control	Quick results	Low costs
Focus groups	•								••	••	••
Employee panels	•								••	••	••
Central location testing	•					•			••	••	••
In-home consumer testing	••					••	•	•	••	•	•
Controlled distribution tests	••		•	•	•	••	••	•	••	•	•
Test markets	••	••	••	••	••	••	••	••	•		

A range of market-research techniques in order of increasing cost. Source: Edwin E. Bobrow and Dennis W. Shafer, Pioneering New Products: A Market Survival Guide *(Dow Jones-Irwin, 1987).*

The Least You Need to Know

➤ Market research can be useful, but it does not guarantee success.

➤ Blindly pursued, market research can stifle creativity and cause you to miss viable new product opportunities.

➤ Weigh the potential benefits of market research against the cost (in direct dollars as well as time consumed) for each new product you develop.

➤ Remember: Certain products (such as the personal computer) *create* new markets and, therefore, defy research into existing markets.

➤ Market research may be best for product modification, line extensions, and so on, rather than new-to-the-world products.

Chapter 10

Groundbreaking Research

In This Chapter

➤ Reducing risk by making a preliminary investigation

➤ Doing it quickly and on the cheap

➤ Your research resources

➤ Focus groups

➤ Preliminary technical assessment

I've said it before, and I'll say it again: Market research can be costly—not only in actual dollars spent, but in time consumed. And who can really tote up the cost of time? While you're *testing* the market, your competitors may be *profiting* from the market. On the other hand (and there's always another hand), flying by the seat of your pants can result in losing your shirt. As usual, you're on the horns of a dilemma: risk time and money on market testing, or accelerate development and just hope for the best.

The most effective way of negotiating the horns of any dilemma is to steer clear of those horns. The fact is that you don't *have* to start off by plunging into elaborate market testing. Instead, dip a toe with preliminary research.

Preliminary Investigation

Here's where you're at with this stage: You've generated a bunch of seemingly good ideas. Now you've got to start screening those ideas in order to determine which of them is worth more of your time and money. The initial screening process—in effect, the *pre-preliminary stage*—is the start of the "stage gate system," which we will discuss fully in Chapter 15. Right now, however, we're talking about market research, so let's just assume that you've gotten an idea generated *and* you've gotten it past the initial screen. Your next step is a preliminary investigation.

The Quick and Dirty Spirit of Stage 1

The purpose of the preliminary investigation—"Stage 1" of market research—is to spend a small amount of money to gather enough information to find out whether or not the new product idea in question is worth taking to Stage 2—*detailed* investigation.

Jump Start
Burn this into your memory banks: Spend a *little* money at Stage 1. There is no need to risk substantial funds at this point.

You expect fancy things from a full-dress market study: a *measurement* of market potential, an *anatomy* of the consumers, and a *forecast* of potential sales. From a preliminary market assessment, you can't expect a finished Rembrandt oil portrait of your new product prospects, but, rather, a quick-and-dirty sketch of them: an *assessment* of market attractiveness and potential; a *gauge* of probable product acceptance; a *guesstimate* of the competitive situation.

How Much Is Enough?

How much is a "little money"? What should your Stage 1 budget be? Ultimately, only you can answer this. But the point is, you *must* answer it. And not just in dollars. Set a deadline for a report on the preliminary investigation. Within an explicitly limited budget and by a clearly set date, determine as much as you can about:

➤ Market size

➤ Market growth

➤ Market segments

➤ Consumer interest

➤ Competition

You Have Resources

Do what common sense tells you to do when you don't have much time or money. Use what you've already got. Look around you. Look *in*-house before you walk out that door. Talk with your sales force. Talk with your customer service staff and with your tech support people. Then take nothing more than a half step out of house to talk with your distributors and dealers. Depending on the size and nature of your business, it may be a very simple matter to speak directly with customers: Float the idea by a few of them.

Now move on to easy-access secondary sources. These include:

> **Jump Start**
> Try asking your customer service staff about what customers want—and *don't* want. Customer service staff are under-used assets in most businesses. Too often, they are regarded as nonrevenue-generating "support" personnel rather than what they *really* are: a continuous finger on the pulse of your customers.

➤ *Trade journals.* They offer reports, articles, and new product news.

➤ *Publications from trade associations.* From these you can learn a lot about what most concerns industry leaders.

➤ *Government studies.* The government is a great gatherer of information. Make use of it.

➤ *Articles in the popular press.* Monitor the general press to get ideas about what's hot and what's not.

➤ *Trend and product discussions on daytime TV talk shows.* Like popular press articles, these can clue you in to current trends.

➤ *The Internet.* Search the World Wide Web (WWW) using keywords relevant to your new product concept; maybe you'll find something worth noting.

➤ *The Industry "buzz."* Pick up the industry "buzz;" listen to what others in your industry talk about. What are the hot-button items and issues? How do they relate to the new product concept you are considering?

Finally, get a bit more aggressive. Contact potential customers. Start with your own customer database. At this stage, you probably don't even have to go beyond these individuals—unless the new product you are contemplating is so different from the kind of product(s) you currently deal in that it targets an

> **Jump Start**
> Consider hiring an unpaid intern or a work-study student to comb through research sources.

entirely new set of consumers. You don't need a fancy mailing and a specially prepared questionnaire for this work. Just get on the phones.

Depending on your budget and deadline, you may also want to invest in a focus group at this stage. I'll discuss this later in the chapter, but, as long as you've got your fingers hovering above the telephone touchpad, try dialing some *free* (or relatively inexpensive) outside sources. These may include informal discussion with industry experts, the editor of a trade journal, and anybody else you know whose opinion you have reason to believe is worth listening to.

Jump Start
Your best *potential* customers are your *current* customers.

Is any of this preliminary work "scientific"? Of course not, but it's not supposed to be. Right now, you have neither the time nor the money for science.

Finding Your Hidden Data Assets

Let's explore in a bit more detail some of the information assets you probably have.

➤ *Your own sales force and service reps.* Sit down and talk to them. Interview them. Present the concept under consideration, and ask them to tell you how it is likely to be received.

➤ *The Internet.* The Internet can be a valuable source of information related to potential new products. Recent developments in Internet search engines (software to facilitate keyword searches) make it possible to search fairly quickly and painlessly. You may or may not find on the Internet detailed information relating to your new product idea, but chances are that you'll pick up something of the "buzz" on the concept. Ever changing, the Internet can provide a feel for what's hot and what's not.

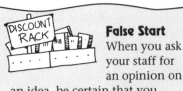

False Start
When you ask your staff for an opinion on an idea, be certain that you make it clear that you aren't asking for approval of *your* idea. It's hard to tell the boss—or even a colleague—that he's wrong. Beware of presenting the idea as something you've hatched or have a lot of ego invested in. You'll get "false positives."

➤ *The government.* Use your government. Goodness knows, they use you. Governments—especially the feds—collect a lot of information, including statistics that might tell you something about the market for a new product you have in mind. Who ya gonna call? You might start with the "blue pages" found in the "business" volume of most White Pages telephone directories. The "blue pages" list phone numbers of federal, state, and local government agencies. The federal government annually publishes the *United States Government Manual* (available from the U.S. Government Printing

Office—or at the public library) to guide you through the bureaucracy. Or check out federal government information on the Internet. The quickest way to get to the data you need is by starting out with Fedworld on the World Wide Web at **http:/ www.fedworld.gov/** or, via Telnet, at **fedworld.gov.** Many federal agencies maintain their own sites on the Web, but Fedworld is a good, central place to start.

➤ *Ads.* Read ads. Finding out what your competitors are doing does not require costly (and illegal) industrial espionage. Examine your competitors' ads and get ahold of their trade literature—not for the purpose of coming up with a "me too" product, but in order to gauge how competitors are positioning their products, what features they promote, what customers they're trying to snag. Look for gaps—features that are missing from competing products, problems that go unaddressed, customers and market segments that remain unserved.

➤ *Trade associations.* Talk to any trade associations relevant to your industry or to the new product you're considering. These folks are in the business of promoting their industry and are often eager to help. Ask them about sources of market data.

➤ *Your library.* Check out your library. If you don't have a company library, go to the public library. You'll need to search the indexes of trade journals and popular magazines for keywords relating to your new product idea. Many trade journals publish quarterly or annual indexes to their articles. These will make your search easier. You'll also find in the public library a remarkable publication called *Reader's Guide to Periodical Literature.* This is a frequently updated subject index of articles in an impressively wide range of magazines and journals. Want to find out something about widgets? Look it up in the *Reader's Guide.* In many libraries nowadays, you'll find computer terminals to make your search easier. Type in a keyword, and a list of relevant articles and publications will be spat out at you.

> **Buzzword**
> A *keyword* is a single word or short phrase, highly relevant to the subject you're researching, that you type during a computer database search. A good keyword is the kind of term you would look up in a book index in order to find your topic.

➤ *Consultants.* Consultants don't *have* to cost an arm and a leg—at least, not at Stage 1. You might be able to purchase multiclient, standardized, one-size-fits-all consultant-published reports that provide a good snapshot of a particular industry, market, or even market segment. For a few dollars, you may well find information on customer habits, preferences, peeves, competition, market trends, government regulation, and the like.

➤ *Industry experts.* Go out and rent an industry expert. Hire a consultant for a *strictly limited* period. Don't pay for an expensive report. Just sit down and ask questions.

➤ *Your broker.* Talk to your broker. Is your business day ever punctuated by some stockbroker cold-calling you about investing in one mutual fund or another? Now's your chance to turn the tables. Talk to a broker about the prospects for a given industry. Financial houses are also good sources for annual reports and 10K reports (documents that publicly held companies must submit to the stock exchange).

➤ *Your customers.* Take a few key customers to lunch—separately, of course. Discuss the concept in informal detail. Make it clear that you value the customer's *candid* opinion.

Consumer vs. Business-to-Business Products

Let's catch our collective breath for a moment and take note of an important distinction between two broad types of products: consumer products and business-to-business products. Which kind of product you're developing will determine where you should direct your preliminary research.

Consumer products are purchased and used by the population at large, sometimes through direct distribution (for example, mail-order), sometimes through authorized dealers, but, most characteristically, through retailers. Because you're usually dealing with a large and diverse set of consumers, it can be very difficult to predict what will and what will not appeal to them. All of the techniques we have just examined can be useful in making a preliminary market assessment.

Business-to-business products are non-consumer products, which are usually sold to product producers or manufacturers, resellers (retail as well as wholesale), government, institutional, and professional customers. A look at the characteristics of business-to-business markets tells us a good deal about those markets and, by contrast, about consumer markets as well:

➤ An individual "consumer" usually does not make the purchase decision. A business entity does. Often, more than one business entity is involved—as, for example, a retailer and a wholesaler.

➤ Although you may be dealing with more than one purchasing entity, purchase criteria are often more clearly defined than is the case with products sold to consumers. Determining what a business purchaser wants in a product *may* be a more straightforward task than guessing at what an individual consumer wants (especially when the consumer is not always sure himself).

➤ What I've just said notwithstanding, business-to-business purchasing situations often involve multiple buying influences and several individuals: dreaded committees and people with conflicting needs, wants, and desires.

➤ Consumers are not necessarily out of the picture when it comes to the reception of business-to-business products. They generally play an indirect role. A business may be the original purchaser, but the ultimate user may well be an individual consumer.

These differences and distinctions should be kept in mind when you're conducting market research. It's important also to realize that the final selling situation is usually more personal in business-to-business markets than in consumer markets. The customer base is smaller, and one's success characteristically depends on creating close relationships with customers/clients. This has the benefit of giving you a better shot at reaching the right people to ask your market research questions.

The Truth about Focus Groups

In Stage 1 market research for business-to-business products, you may have the luxury of being able to go directly to the horse's mouth. Your customer base may be quite small and well focused. Preliminary research might consist of little more than presenting a concept to a customer and asking:

➤ Would you buy it?

➤ If not, what can I do to it to *make* you want to buy it?

➤ Is it hopeless, and should I just forget about it?

In the case of consumer products, however, it is often difficult to locate the right horses, let alone find their mouths. That's where focus groups come in. At its most basic, a focus group is a gathering of a small number of "real people" (usually eight to ten or thereabouts) who are consumers likely to find your product(s) of interest.

Jump Start
Focus groups are an opportunity to experience the market firsthand. They are among the most widely used forms of marketing research. Focus groups are also commonly called group interviews, group discussions, group depth interviews, and qualitative research. All of these terms are synonymous.

Starting a Focus Group

Many firms start a focus group by calling in an expert, an individual or consulting firm with expertise in recruiting focus-group members and in leading focus-group sessions. However, there's no law against recruiting and leading your own group yourself, especially at Stage 1, where you want to save money. Here's an outline of the steps:

1. Find eight to ten people who satisfy criteria you believe important to marketing your product. For example, you'll probably want people of a certain age or ages; male, female, or perhaps people of both genders; people who exemplify a certain lifestyle, use a certain class of product, or have expressed interest in a new product similar to yours.

2. Get them into an informal and comfortable setting—for example, a private room with cushy chairs, or even an outdoor setting where people do not feel pressured.

3. Interview them. For example, ask them questions about their purchasing habits. Make sure you record the interview—preferably with a video camera.

A session usually lasts an hour—two at most. Continuing much longer than two hours is fatiguing and becomes counterproductive.

Even at Stage 1, it's usually best to set up more than one session per product or issue. Three is a good number. Depending on the type of product concept you're evaluating, it may be best to strive for variety in the various characteristics of the participants in each group. For example: One group may be young. Another older. And a third mixed. You may also want to spread the groups out over different geographical areas.

Finding Focus Folk

Even if you entrust to a professional the job of conducting a focus group, you need to work out the criteria for recruiting your participants. Once you have clearly established these criteria, you need to find your people. The most obvious place to begin is with your current customers. If you have a customer database, use it to make the necessary phone calls. If you have a file of questionnaires returned by customers (for example, as part of the "user registration" packet included with your products), use these.

Jump Start
Focus groups can be used to evaluate business-to-business product concepts as well as consumer products. You might invite a group of your best customers to chat about a concept. The opportunity to contribute to the development of products that may ultimately be good for a customer's bottom line is often sufficient incentive to participate.

Beyond your own customers—and without hiring a professional recruiter—you might gather your groups from:

➤ Responses to mailed invitations. You may purchase a mailing list tailored to certain criteria you specify.

➤ Shopping mall intercepts. You invite shoppers to participate.

➤ Ads in journals or magazines that reach readers who are likely to be your target consumer.

It helps to offer a modest incentive to participate in the focus group session—a "gift pack" of inexpensive items, discount offers on your products, even cash. However, be certain that the incentive is not misinterpreted as a "bribe" to elicit falsely positive responses.

Take Me to Your Leader

Focus groups operate on a principle similar to group therapy: People tend to speak more freely in a *group* than they do one-on-one to an *individual* with whom they are not well acquainted. But the focus group is not a stream-of-consciousness free-for-all. It requires the moderating presence of a skilled leader to provide direction, albeit without contaminating results by skewing opinion. For this reason, leaders—moderators—are usually trained professionals hired to conduct the focus group.

➤ The moderator should be given a *discussion guide*—a list of the issues to be covered.

➤ The moderator should lead the group from a *general* discussion of the product category, to a progressively more *specific* discussion of the product concept under investigation, and then, even more specifically, to a discussion of specific characteristics, benefits, and problems associated with the proposed new product.

➤ The moderator should encourage participants to be wishful, even unrealistic. This is a way of getting at what people *really* want and need in a product. It requires that the moderator maintain an absolutely non-judgmental attitude and, if necessary, gently "correct" any inhibiting remarks from participants.

➤ The moderator should get *everyone* involved in the discussion, even to the extent of calling on reluctant participants.

➤ The moderator should focus participants on their feelings rather than on abstract ideas. If designing a new product were simply a matter of having people list their requirements for a given product and then taking these requirements to your design department, there would be very little risk (or challenge) in new product development. The fact is, however, that emotions—not rational concepts—are the most powerful motivators of buying decisions. Often, the consumer himself is unaware of his feelings. Bringing the feelings to the surface can provide valuable information. ("How do you *feel* about cleaning windows?")

➤ The moderator should keep score. He might use flip-chart pages to jot down ideas as they come, then tear off the sheets as they are filled, and tape them to the walls. This is a sign of progress that encourages the group to keep producing. It also demonstrates that the moderator honors and respects each idea.

➤ The moderator should do what he can to foster feelings of security, freedom, enjoyment, and community.

➤ Consider dual moderators when the product under consideration involves a need for specialized knowledge or is highly technical. One moderator keeps the group moving, while the other, the technical expert, follows up on technical issues as necessary.

Idea Generation

Let's understand what focus groups are and what they are not. They are:

➤ Descriptive

➤ Subjective

➤ Exploratory

➤ Approximate

They are not:

➤ Diagnostic

➤ Objective

➤ Definitive

➤ Precise

These latter qualities are the goals of quantitative research—that is, research based on large (statistically significant) numbers of respondents to questionnaires. But, because focus groups are what they are—descriptive, subjective, exploratory, and approximate—they can be useful even before you reach Stage 1. Focus groups can be used to generate ideas. The moderator may present a topic or a problem, then ask the group for ideas about solving it. Even more effective is the use of the focus group to generate new ideas about *existing* products, including modifications and alternative uses.

False Start
Do not think that focus groups are a prudent shortcut to making cost-intensive design, marketing, and manufacturing decisions.

Concept Screening

Focus groups are most widely used in concept screening: presenting a new product concept and eliciting responses to it.

The first challenge is to present the new product concept in a way that communicates the idea clearly to the focus group participants.

The product concept is often presented in a straightforwardly written product description, which includes such items as:

➤ Benefits

➤ Features

➤ Size

➤ Packaging

➤ Price

A conceptual line drawing or a realistic rendering of the product may accompany the written description.

The language of the concept description should be informal and clear. It should be free of technical or marketing jargon on the one hand, but it should not be punched up with ad-style copy on the other. You don't want to *sell* the concept; you want to get feedback about it. If you are presenting more than one concept, it's very important that all the concepts be presented in the same style. If you present Concept A in flat prose backed up with a line drawing, and then present Concept B in ad-style copy accompanied by a beautifully rendered painting, most participants will vote for Concept B. And you will have learned absolutely nothing of value. They are reacting to the presentation, not the product.

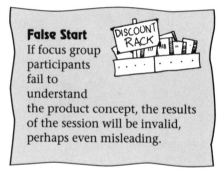

False Start
If focus group participants fail to understand the product concept, the results of the session will be invalid, perhaps even misleading.

Tech Assessment at Stage 1

It's one thing to make a stab at determining whether customers will or will not buy a product and quite another to judge whether or not the product can be created—and created cost effectively—in the first place. This is the purpose of the preliminary technical assessment, which is the second phase of Stage 1 research. In the case of manufactured products, this assessment involves the participation of key R&D, engineering, and manufacturing engineering staff. In the case of proposed new services, it requires the input of the staff that will actually design and perform the proposed service.

The preliminary technical assessment aims at three objectives:

. 1. To sketch out rough technical and performance criteria

2. To evaluate—in a preliminary way—feasibility

3. To flag technical risks and pitfalls

You'll probably want to stay in-house for this preliminary stage, discussing the three objectives with appropriate staff, who may, however, need to research the literature relating to the product in question. In addition:

➤ Perform a preliminary patent search. Patents are discussed at greater length in Chapter 19, "The Fine Print."

➤ Check out competitors' literature, and pay close attention to physical and performance specs.

At the end of this preliminary stage, you should have some answers for the following questions:

➤ What are the proposed requirements/specs?

➤ Can these requirements/specs be achieved technically?

➤ Can they be achieved feasibly?

➤ Can *we* manufacture it?

➤ At what approximate cost can *we* manufacture it?

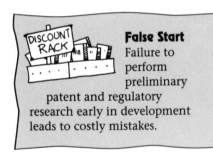

False Start

Failure to perform preliminary patent and regulatory research early in development leads to costly mistakes.

➤ What is the patent situation for this type of product generally and for this product in particular?

➤ What is the regulatory situation? Will government rules or local ordinances impact on your new product?

➤ What are the technical pitfalls—and can they be overcome feasibly?

And Then There's the Money

Finally, someone must take the responsibility of reviewing the Stage 1 data for a back-of-the-envelope "sanity check." This is a ballpark estimate of payback:

➤ What's the magnitude of the investment required?

➤ How much revenue is the product likely to generate on an annual basis?

➤ How long will it take before we break even?

Accountants hate this phase of Stage 1 because it is largely based on fiction. Far from being carved in stone, the relevant projections are written in air. But you should be able to pause, crack your knuckles, scratch your head, and determine, say, if a million-dollar idea is going to end up costing your company 100 million dollars to develop. (If it looks like it will, my advice is not to develop the product.)

The Least You Need to Know

➤ The object of preliminary research is to spend as little money and time as possible to determine whether a given new-product concept is worth taking to the next step.

➤ Focus groups function mainly to stimulate your own creative and evaluative processes; they do not provide statistically significant data. Be careful how you use the results of focus group studies.

➤ The technical assessment is critical. What good is positive market research if you can't feasibly build the product?

Chapter 11

Needs and Wants

In This Chapter

➤ Building the three-legged business case

➤ Finding out what customers want

➤ Identifying gaps in the market

➤ Designing a needs and wants study

I ended the last chapter with a profound article of advice: If a "million-dollar idea" looks like it will cost $100 million to build, don't bother building it. Same is true if your preliminary research suggests that nobody on earth will buy the proposed new product or if your R&D and manufacturing people tell you that it is just too hard to make.

But what if the concept gets a green light in Stage 1? *Now* what do you do?

This chapter will help you take the next step toward a more detailed and definitive investigation of the prospects for a new product. The transition to Stage 2 (detailed marketing research) is something called the "User Needs and Wants Study."

Building the Business Case

The case for developing a new product rests on a three-legged stool:

Leg 1: A *definition* of the product. What is it? For whom is it intended?

Leg 2: A *justification* for the product. Why should it come into being? Why should *we* produce it?

False Start
Beware—he who sits on a bad three-legged stool risks cracking his coccyx.

Leg 3: A *plan* for creating, marketing, and selling the product. How will we do it? And who among us will do what parts of it?

All three legs are necessary, and none may be allowed to wobble; that is, all the key people who will be involved in developing the new product must agree on the content of each of the legs.

What and for Whom?

In Stage 1, you produced a rough sketch of a product definition. Now you need to move into a three-dimensional definition, which spells out the following:

➤ Who is the target for this product? Who will *buy* it? Who will *use* it? (These aren't always the same!)

➤ What are the product's benefits?

➤ What are the product's features?

➤ What are the design/manufacturing requirements?

Prototype

The elements of a product definition are tightly interrelated. Let's look at a definition of Brand X Roll-On Deodorant. The benefits of any product are all the positive gains a user will derive from the product. These quite emphatically include emotional gains. A benefit of Brand X is the pleasing masking of offensive body odors. That's basic to the definition of any deodorant. What begins to set Brand X apart from other deodorants, however, is the definition of its emotional benefit: It "takes the worry out of being close." That benefit—taking the worry out of being close—bears sharply upon the target consumer for Brand X: youngish people who are interested in "being close." And that benefit will also influence some important product features: The deodorant fragrance of Brand X must be subtle. (Who wants to "be close" to someone who *smells* like deodorant?) The effect of the deodorant must be long-lasting. (Who wants to worry about smelling bad when you're trying to "get close"?) Finally, all three of these elements—benefits, target consumer, features—bear directly on design and manufacturing requirements.

By the conclusion of Stage 2, you should have a clear and concise product definition that is complete in all three dimensions. This is critically important, because a great deal of what is done in developing the product depends on the definition:

1. Marketing and sales efforts depend on a definition of the target consumer.

2. Positioning strategy depends on a definition of product benefits.

3. Deliverable benefits depend on a definition of product features, which should be prioritized into such categories as "must have," "would like to have," and "must avoid."

Now: Why?

By the end of the detailed stage of new product development, you should have an unequivocal answer to *why* your company should invest in the project. Dimensions to be considered include, of course, the financial aspects—risk versus reward—but financials in and of themselves are projections. In essence, they are fictions—hopes, really. The new-product justification should also be based on such non-directly financial issues as:

➤ *Competitive advantage.* Does developing this new product position your firm for a significant edge over the competition? (This is usually a longer-term advantage, which may not be readily quantifiable, but is very real nonetheless.) For example, the automatic garage-door opener you create should be easier to install than what the competition offers and perhaps include a special "hotline" phone number for instant answers to installation questions.

➤ *Exploitation of synergies.* Does the new project product take special advantage of certain company strengths? For example, a manufacturer of special "healthy" dog food may decide to exploit the synergy of its penetration into this segment of the dog-related market by also creating a line of "healthy" dog chew toys.

➤ *Market attractiveness.* Developing a certain new product may be justified because it opens up to a firm a particularly attractive market. For example, it was a very good idea for Brother, long known as a manufacturer of electric typewriters, to move into developing a line of laser printers. The typewriter market is hardly attractive in the age of the PC, whereas the market for laser printers continues to grow. In particular, there is increased demand for *inexpensive* product in this market.

Jump Start
The project plan should be clear, not rigid. This early in the development process, it must be flexible enough to adapt to changing circumstances.

And...How and by Whom?

By the end of Stage 2, you should have a fairly detailed plan of action that takes the new product from development to launch. At minimum, the plan should include a time line aimed at a set launch date, with a specification of the resources (the people, equipment, and cash) required at each stage.

What Does the User Need and Want?

Well, look. I can save you a lot more work by just telling you up-front what it is that your customers need and want. Get ready. Here it comes. The envelope, please…

Buzzword

Value is not synonymous with "good price" or "bargain." It is the perceived ratio between product features/benefits/quality and product price.

Your customer wants a superior product that delivers unique benefits and excellent value.

Simple, huh?

Value is a function of the benefits, features, and quality that are built into a product versus the price of the product. The more benefits, features, and quality a product can deliver at a low (or reasonable) price, the more value the product has.

"*…the more value a product has.*" Actually, that perfectly reasonable-sounding phrase is misleading. A product does not so much *have* value as the consumer *perceives* value in the product. It would be quite convenient if you could simply pour value into a product as you pour a quart of oil into your automobile. But value is not an absolute quantity. It is relative. It is a perception.

Hearing the Voice of the Customer

The fact is, *you* don't know value. Only the customer knows it. (At least, he knows it sometimes and about some things. It is actually more a perception, a feeling, a sense.) And it is your job, in market research, to find out what the customer defines as value in a particular product or class of product. That is the purpose of a needs and wants study—to assess how the customer defines *value,* which requires also determining how the customer defines:

➤ Benefits

➤ Desirable features

➤ A reasonable price

For the study of such customer perceptions, focus groups are a good place to start, but, depending on the financial risks versus rewards involved in the product you're developing, Stage 2 may require more definitive information than focus groups can provide. Depending on the product and market, you may need *quantitative* (statistically significant sampling) as well as *qualitative* (small focus group results) data to make an informed decision. Often, focus groups and quantitative data can be supplemented by face-to-face interviews with individual customers. This step refines the data further. (But the research dollars pile up, and the clock keeps ticking!)

What Is Value?

There really is little point in rigorously trying to separate the study of value from the study of benefits, but questions you need to ask that relate most directly to value include:

➤ What do you look for in product X?

➤ What criteria go into making your purchase decision?

➤ Relating to the first two questions: What are your "must haves" for product X? Your "would like to haves"? Your "unimportants"? Your "do *not* wants"?

➤ How important is durability to you? (And how much are you willing to pay for it?)

➤ What does "durability" mean to you in product X?

➤ How important is performance to you? (And how much are you willing to pay for it?)

➤ What does "performance" mean to you in product X? (Note: You can ask similar questions about other value-related attributes.)

➤ What trade-offs are you willing to make to save money? What features or level of performance are you willing to live without to save money?

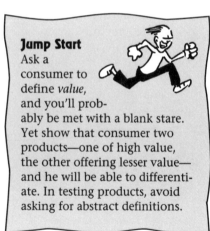

Jump Start
Ask a consumer to define *value*, and you'll probably be met with a blank stare. Yet show that consumer two products—one of high value, the other offering lesser value—and he will be able to differentiate. In testing products, avoid asking for abstract definitions.

What Are Benefits?

Questions designed to assess what product benefits customers consider important are really questions about feelings—about feelings associated with a product or a task. Benefits are positive effects a user derives from a product. Typically, these effects are strongly related to feelings. (The function of a sports car is to get you from point A to point B. For a single man of 45, the product *benefits* of a sports car are—well, you know the rest.) If you were creating a new personal deodorant, for example, you might ask a group of consumers:

➤ How do you feel about using a deodorant?

➤ How do you feel about spraying on a deodorant?

➤ How do you feel about rolling on a deodorant?

➤ How do you feel about applying a stick-type deodorant?

➤ Complete this sentence: When I use a deodorant I feel…

➤ Complete this sentence: When I use a deodorant I would like to feel…

And so on. It helps to provide a list of "feeling" words for the respondent to choose from. This saves the respondent brain work, forestalls his resorting to misleading and vague cliches, and also makes responses easier to measure by introducing a degree of standardization. We'll say more about interview questions later in this chapter (see "Designing the Needs and Wants Study") and in Chapter 13.

Glorious Problems

I've already pointed out one unique feature of new product development. Whereas in many business activities folks devote their workday to *avoiding* problems, in new product development, you *seek* problems. A problem calls for a *solution*—i.e., a new product. Ask consumers:

➤ What problem(s) do you have with task X?

➤ How do you currently solve these problem(s)?

Jump Start
I've repeatedly cautioned against the me-too approach to new product development. But there is nothing wrong with looking at how competitors solve—and fail to solve—problems, and there is nothing wrong with borrowing aspects of their best work and improving on their worst. Actually, that's called *progress*.

You will also want to get more specific by asking questions such as:

➤ What product(s) do you currently use to solve problem(s) with task X?

➤ Why did you choose Brand X to solve problem X?

Then you may begin assessing the competition in terms of problems:

➤ What problems do you have with currently available task X products?

By identifying problems, you pinpoint gaps in the market. As nature abhors a vacuum, so the marketplace "wants" its gaps filled. This is where profit lives.

The User Study: What to Expect

What can a user needs and wants study tell you? Let's look at an example.

A company that makes a variety of plastic bag products wants to enter the crowded but attractive trash bag market. A concept has emerged at Stage 1 involving a bag that must offer at least *one* distinctive feature and related benefit to set it apart from the competition. But what will that feature/benefit be?

A user needs and wants study is commissioned. It reveals:

➤ Users dislike wire-tie garbage bags. The ties get lost.

➤ Users don't like tying up bags that have integral plastic ties, which are too short or easily come untied.

➤ Users feel bad about garbage and use words like "gross" and "disgusting" to describe it.

➤ Users fear that bags will break.

➤ Users hate wrestling with clingy plastic bags when they dispense them from the roll and try to get them open.

➤ Users have trouble getting the bags to fit properly around the rim of the garbage basket.

➤ Users *really hate* when the bag comes off the rim and garbage ends up outside of the bag—and they end up having to hose out the inside of the garbage basket. The study suggests that users want:

➤ A bag that's very easy to close—without extra parts to misplace.

➤ A bag that really *gets rid* of the garbage.

➤ An "anxiety-free" bag that won't break.

➤ A bag that dispenses easily.

➤ A bag that is easy to open.

➤ A bag that fits the garbage basket with ease and absolute security.

It's clear that no competitive product currently addresses all of these needs. Because there are *problems* with competitive products, market *gaps* exist.

Here are some ideas for features and benefits to incorporate into the new product:

➤ A bag with a variation on the "zip-lock" feature currently used in certain food-storage bags.

➤ A absolutely opaque bag. Can't see the garbage.

➤ A bag that seals so tightly, it forms an "odor barrier."

➤ A bag that features boldly printed humorous cartoons—to make the user feel better about taking out the garbage.

➤ Brightly colored bags—also to make the user feel better about taking out the garbage.

➤ A super-strong bag that takes the worry out of hauling the trash.

➤ A bag made out of special plastic that changes color if it stretches too much— thereby warning the user that the bag is packed too full and may break. Call it a "smart bag."

➤ A lightly powdered bag that will not cling and is therefore easy to open when it is dispensed. The powder smells good, too.

➤ A bag that incorporates a flexible stiffened rim that makes it easy to mount inside the garbage basket and that prevents it from collapsing once it is inside.

Designing the Needs and Wants Study

Shake your head and splash some cold water on your face. You need to remember where you are. This is Stage 2: *detailed* market research. You've already developed some new product concepts, and you've subjected them to Stage 1 screening. The user needs and wants study is *not* a fishing expedition. You design it with certain new product ideas already in mind. It may even be that you have a somewhat developed new product concept prepared and you're testing the "fit" of your concept with the market, trying to learn how you can shape and modify that fit so that it will smoothly lead to a profitable product. This doesn't mean that you should design the study expressly to confirm your preconceptions. There is no point in that. But you do need to design the study specifi- cally to gather the data you need to develop your particular product.

Information Objectives

Our hot-wired, Internet-bound, infobahn-paved age is suffocating under multiple blanket layers of "information." Too much data is like shopping mall music. It dwells meaning- lessly in the background. It's there, but we don't really hear it.

Make sure that the information you gather is meaningful. How do you define *meaningful information*? It is information that actually informs your decisions. Here are three meth- ods for filtering out the useless stuff and collecting the nuggets:

➤ Draw up a list of the key decisions you need to make.

➤ Draw up a *written* list of the information you believe you need to make those decisions. These are your information objectives.

➤ Create your questions based on the information objectives you have defined.

Three Information Commandments

Even if your needs and wants study is little more than a series of interviews with consumers, prepare a formal questionnaire. This will help to ensure that you obey the three commandments of a useful needs and wants study:

    I. Thou Shalt Be Thorough. A well thought-out, *written* questionnaire will help ensure that you cover all the bases.

    II. Thou Shalt Be Consistent. You want each respondent to be questioned in the same way. Compare apples to apples.

    III. Thou Shalt Write It All Down. What good are the responses if they aren't recorded—neatly, clearly, and unambiguously?

Cover Your Preposterior

You've sketched out a questionnaire. Heck—you've even *typed* it! Now you rush out the door to the nearest respondent. The Great User Needs and Wants Study is about to commence. Right?

Not yet.

Before taking your questionnaire on the road, perform a preposterior analysis. This means imagining that you've already done the study and that all of your questions have been answered. Now, armed with these answers, can you go ahead and make the decisions you need to make?

If you don't *imagine* that you can, you'd better make the necessary revisions to your questions before you commit to the actual test.

The Right Handful

There was a time when almost no one in the state of Iowa would vote for a Democrat. Folks out there had a saying: *Iowa will vote Democrat when hell goes Methodist.* If you were doing a needs and wants study prior to developing commemorative coffee mugs featuring portraits of favorite presidents, you probably wouldn't want to restrict your pool of respondents to Iowans.

Make certain that you have a representative sample of potential customers—not just people who happen to be available. This is also true when you're dealing with business-to-business products. Don't interview just one person from each client firm. Find out who makes purchasing decisions and who actually uses the product. Then interview several of the key people you identify.

Customers Don't Know What They Need

Oh, yeah. I forgot to mention one last thing. Customers don't necessarily know what they need.

Oops.

Consumers are very influenced by what the last supplier they spoke to told them. They are influenced by what advertising tells them they need. They often don't think through their needs. They believe they need Solution A to Problem A, when, actually, the real problem is Problem B. They jump to conclusions without analyzing the situation. They want instant gratification, even when a long-term solution is better.

The essential fallibility of consumers is the Achilles heel not only of needs and wants studies, but of marketing research generally. If consumers reliably knew what they needed, *everyone* would be an inventor. (But the world would probably be rather dull.)

False Start
Do not assume your customers know what they want or need. This is especially true in the case of truly innovative high-tech products. Five years ago, who knew they needed or wanted a 56Kbps modem?

To get around the problem of the consumer's limited self-knowledge, do not settle for *asking* questions about wants and needs. Supplement your questions (and the answers you receive) with an investigation of how the proposed product will actually fit into the consumer's environment and/or the system in which he works—the context in which the product will be used. Get to know the consumer in his "natural" setting. Weigh what he *says* he wants and needs against what he actually *uses* and *does*.

The Least You Need to Know

➤ The business case requires defining the product, justifying the creation of the product, and planning how to make and market the product.

➤ The user needs and wants study is the first major step in the *detailed* phase of new product market research.

➤ Assessing user wants and needs should not be a fishing expedition; the study should be designed to obtain specific information relevant to a set of new product concepts you want to test.

Chapter 12

Resting Your Case

In This Chapter

- ➤ Analyzing the competition
- ➤ Assessing technical feasibility
- ➤ Concept screening
- ➤ Interpreting concept tests
- ➤ Overview of market and financial analysis

After completing a user needs-and-wants study—and assuming that users appear to need and want what you propose to offer—you're ready to complete the business case for developing the new product. The major dimensions involved in this phase of Stage 2 market research include a detailed analysis of the competition, a detailed assessment of technical feasibility, and steps to assure that the product can be executed in a financially feasible manner. Finally, the "finished" product concept is tested—with consumers—yet again.

The Competition

Remember from the last chapter what it is that your customer wants? (Hint: *Your customer wants a superior product that delivers unique benefits and excellent value.*)

Look at the word *superior*. Men and women "of a certain age" were schooled at a time when English grammar was tediously drummed into unreceptive heads. I happen to remember the bit about absolute, comparative, and superlative degree: "good," for example, represents the absolute degree; "better," the comparative degree; and "best" the superlative degree. The word "superior" is a representative of the comparative degree, and that implies the existence of other things—in this case, other products—to compare it to.

That's right: You have competition. And if your object is to make your product "superior" to competing products, you'd better know as much as you can about those products.

What, Me Worry?

It's no secret that Americans partake of many different cultures and values, but most of us seem to share at least one cultural value in common: for better or worse, we tend to "mind our own business." In our personal lives, that can be a fine thing. But, in business, it can be fatal. When an ostrich buries its head in the sand, what part of its anatomy is most exposed?

Exactly.

Unless you're in a field without competitors—and that is indeed rare, or a situation that is short-lived—you need to regard competing products as indexes against which you measure your own. Why? Because, inevitably, the consumers will make just such comparisons.

By studying the competition, you can also learn about how the competitor competes, how he plays the game, what leads to success, and what ends up in failure. Finally, there is, quite simply, the *game.* I know that your livelihood and the success of your business are serious matters. But, like it or not, you are also, every working day, playing a game. Your opponents are the competition. Skilled players of any high-level game soon learn the value of "psyching" their opponents, of getting into their heads, of figuring out and predicting their strategy. This is certainly true in the new product game. It's a mistake to think that Company A creates a product and so does Company B, then they put the competing merchandise on the market and sit back while the two items duke it out between themselves.

False Start
If you think you have the perfect product and there is no need to worry, think again. You need to understand how competitors approach the market and how they address technical problems.

Few companies can afford to be so passive. Instead, they *play the game*. Company A brings out a product. Company B *responds*—perhaps by slashing the prices of its existing competitive products precisely at the time of A's launch. By studying your competition, you may be able to anticipate how competitors will respond to the introduction of your new product.

What to Find Out

Begin by determining just who your competitors are. Take an inventory of the actual products that will directly compete with yours. Then do the following:

➤ Make a list of each competing product's features, benefits, price, *value*.

➤ List each competing product's special strengths and weaknesses.

➤ What problems do the competing products solve, and what problems do they fail to solve?

➤ What problems do the competing products *create*?

➤ What's the profile of each competitor? Does the competitor have a strong sales force? Good distribution? Is it known for high-quality customer service and tech support? What are the weaknesses of each competitor?

➤ What kind of advertising does the competition use?

➤ What customers—market, market segment—are the competition targeting?

➤ How does the competition get business? Attractive price? Skilled sales force? Great product? Heavy-duty promotional effort?

➤ How well is the competition doing? Struggling? Maintaining? Excelling? Growing? Shrinking? Dying?

➤ What are the competitors' costs like? What are they paying for raw materials? For labor? What kind of volume do they produce and move? (It may not be possible to answer all of these questions, since data in these areas is usually confidential, and the price of industrial espionage can be criminal prosecution.)

Information: Perfectly Legal, Supremely Ethical

You can't scope out your competitors the way you test the consumer market. Understandably, your competition will probably not be willing to sit down for a heart-to-heart, nor will the rival CEO fill out a questionnaire for you. Even if you ask nicely.

Nevertheless, there's plenty of information out there. I've mentioned some of it in the previous chapter:

➤ Get the competitors' advertising, promotional, and descriptive literature. You can even write to competitors to request this material. If it makes you feel more comfortable, have your spouse or child write, and use your home address. Or ask a staff member to do the same. (But such subterfuge should not really be necessary.)

False Start

Beware of "reverse engineering"—essentially taking a product apart (in the case of computer software, decompiling it) to see what makes it tick for the purposes of copying the process. In many instances, reverse engineering is illegal, and the very fact that you have done it can cause potentially ruinous legal problems—even if the product you finally create is not a direct result of reverse engineering.

False Start

Don't confine yourself to the obvious trade shows in your field. Take an excursion or two to shows in fields that are peripherally related to yours. What competitors are exhibiting at these?

➤ Buy your competitors' products. Look them over. *Use* them. Try to *enjoy* them. What features are good? What features are great? What features could use improvement? What features are lacking?

➤ If a product is too expensive to buy—say you are in the business of manufacturing factory-size printing presses—you might ask a friendly customer to let you have a look at his new installation of Brand X equipment.

➤ Have a conversation with some of your own key suppliers. They might be willing to talk about matters relating to the competitor's production capacity: volume of raw materials ordered, installed equipment base, and so on.

➤ Acquire as much financial information as you can relating to the competitor. This is easy, if the competing firm is publicly traded. Just obtain an annual report. Ask your stockbroker's analytical department to make an appraisal of the competitor. Through your investment house, obtain the firm's obligatory 10K report. But if the company is privately held, it may be virtually impossible to get thorough financials.

➤ Attend every trade show possible. These are showcases for new products. And don't just look at the *products*. Take note of the traffic patterns. What exhibitors attract the most visitors? Why? What's hot? Why?

Don't forget two other easy-access sources of information about the competition:

➤ *Your customers*. Your needs-and-wants study should include thorough questions about your competitors, their products, their prices, their sales force, their distribution, their customer service and support, and so on.

➤ *Your own sales and service staff.* That's right. These are the people in the trenches, who not only see competing products in action, but often hear a lot of customer talk concerning them.

Finally: you *can* hire consultants who specialize in "competitive intelligence." These are not spies, but people who, for a fee, will perform the kind of legwork I've just outlined.

> **False Start**
> When hiring a competitive intelligence consultant, be certain that your contract spells out what the consultant will and will not do. At minimum, the consultant must agree to engage in no illegal activity.

Tech Stuff

In an earlier chapter, I mentioned the danger of letting technology lead new product development: the *if you build it, they will buy it* syndrome. Conversely, before huge sums of money are committed to product development, you need to make certain that the wish list resulting from the user needs-and-wants study can be realized technically. And the question is not just whether the new product can be built, but whether it can be built in an economically feasible, viable way.

The issue your R&D, production, and other creative and technical staff must address is what range of technical solutions can be arrived at in order to produce a product that meets the requirements of the marketplace. Once a range of technical options is established, the technical staff should proceed to formulate a statement of just what it will take to create the technical solution:

> **Jump Start**
> Practical lab work during market research is nothing more than a confidence check—an effort to determine, with a high degree of assurance, that the product under discussion *can* be created. Usually, you will have neither the time nor budget at this stage to build a full-scale prototype.

➤ A new invention or set of inventions?

➤ Substantial innovation upon established technology?

➤ Application of established technology in an innovative way?

With this assessment in place, the next question to answer is whether or not your firm has the expertise and equipment in-house to create the product. If not, can these things be obtained in an economically feasible manner?

The next step is risk assessment from a technical point of view. How many at-home do-it-yourself projects have you started, only to leave unfinished (and tucked away in a dark corner of closet or garage) because, somewhere along the way, you ran into a problem you just couldn't get around? Well, it's a lot harder to take a half-developed product and find a dark corner of your firm to hide it in—especially if several hundred thousand dollars has already been spent on it.

➤ Make an effort to inventory all of the technical risks and roadblocks. Can they be overcome? How?

➤ Inventory the patent, regulatory, and safety liability issues the product may involve. Can these be dealt with? How?

Finally comes the black magic: figuring out the cost per unit to create the product. At this stage, all you can hope to determine is a ballpark figure based on several volume-of-production scenarios. Be sure to bring in production people to review your technical solution and provide cost estimates.

Screen That Concept

We've looked at ways of investigating, analyzing, and reporting what customers need and want. I've just concluded a brief survey of steps necessary to translate those needs and wants into a technically viable product. The word "translate" is the key. Think of market research as a way of translating one "language"—the words of customers—into another "language": technically feasible concepts for a new product. These may be different languages, but both are expressions of wants and needs. Now, before proceeding to Stage 3—development of the actual product—it's a good idea to ensure that nothing has been lost in the translation. That's where the concept test comes in.

Time to Stop Prospecting and Start Testing

Another test? But haven't we already tested the concept?

No, not really. In preliminary market research and in the user needs-and-wants study during the detailed phase of market research, you may have *proposed* a number of product concepts. But they were broad concepts—ideas, really. You weren't so much testing their validity, as you were prospecting for more ideas. You were looking for direction, for clues. From this set of hints, you formulated some technically feasible product solutions. *These* are the full-fledged product concepts.

With the concepts in hand, it's time to go to potential customers and *test* them. You show consumers what you have—it may be a full description, drawings, 3-D renderings, a mock-up, spec sheet, a ballpark price—and you ask: *Is this what you had in mind? Would you buy this?*

Putting Together a Concept Test

In some respects, the concept test is a replay of the user needs-and-wants study. You can make use of focus groups, which will give you qualitative feedback on the concept. However, at this stage, you *should* be nervous about relying on statistically insignificant numbers as a basis for making sweeping decisions about your new product. Supplement the qualitative focus group data with quantitative input from a survey of a larger number of potential customers.

In presenting concepts and ideas during the Stage 1 study, you attempted to pack the essence of a new product into fifty or a hundred words. For the concept test that concludes Stage 2, you should present a more fully developed concept. Get as close to the finished product as you can *at this point.* Keep the following in mind:

> **False Start**
> The way a focus group votes on a concept can be misleading. Eight or ten people do not a statistically significant sample make.

➤ You'll probably want to supplement written descriptions with renderings and other visuals. Although you most likely won't have a prototype at this stage, perhaps you have a crude working model or at least a mock-up. Use it. (Some companies—3M is an example—do introduce prototypes early on.)

➤ In presenting concepts for packaged goods, you'll need to have—what else?—*the package*.

➤ If you have oodles to spend, you might produce a brief video dramatizing the product in use.

However you go about making the presentation, the idea is to ensure that the respondents understand the concept fully and at significant depth.

If you're confident that the respondents understand the concept, then you can measure response with some hope that the results will be meaningful. At the most basic, you're looking for the respondents' *interest* in the product. Is it high, low, or in between? From this foundation, you develop more refined measurements:

> **Jump Start**
> The purpose of a concept test is to gauge customer reaction in order to assess market acceptance—i.e., expected revenue.

➤ What does the customer like?

➤ Why?

➤ To what *degree* does the customer like a feature, benefit, or the product as a whole?

➤ What does the customer dislike?

➤ Why?

➤ To what *degree* does the customer dislike a feature, benefit, or the product as a whole?

➤ In the customer's view, how does the new product stack up against competing products?

➤ What would the customer be willing to pay for the product?

Chapter 14, "Making Sense of It All," will show you some ways to construct an effective questionnaire to get at some of these answers. For the moment, however, you should know about the need to ask both closed- and open-ended questions. Closed-ended questions are either multiple-choice, yes/no, or call for rating along a scale (for example, 1–5). Open-ended questions allow the respondent to answer in his or her own words. Closed-ended questions are easily quantified and standardized, but they may inhibit expression and, therefore, skew results. Open-ended questions, while they are more challenging to compare and contrast between one respondent and another, may provoke more thought and unexpected ideas.

Making Heads and Tails Out of It

A concept test is not like a thermometer or a barometer. Its measurements are not guaranteed to be accurate. In fact, even carefully designed concept tests, in which the concept is presented with crystal clarity, the questions asked are comprehensive, and the sampling of potential customers is truly representative, have built-in defects:

➤ Almost invariably, concept tests overstate market acceptance. That is, no matter how you plead with a group to "be candid," there's a natural tendency toward a positive bias. People want to be polite, they want to please, and they want to make you feel good. These are unconscious motives, and, endearing as they are, they can really mess up a concept test.

Prototype

A group of individuals were told they were going to be tested on their productivity. The researchers were experimenting with different strengths of light in a factory environment. The researchers found that productivity would increase every time they tried to raise *or dim* the lights. This did not make sense, until they realized that it was because the individuals knew they were being tested. This type of response became known as the Hawthorn effect. The *Hawthorn effect* describes the tendency of people under observation to respond more positively than people who are not being observed.

➤ It's easier to respond positively when you don't actually have to dig into your wallet and commit to a purchase. (For this reason, some concept tests introduce an element of role play by giving the respondent a limited quantity of play money to "spend." It is believed that this introduces greater realism—and conservatism—into the test.)

Here's another problem. Let's say that 50 percent of your test group expresses an "intention to buy" product X. Let's say that you wisely take this with a grain of salt—because of the naturally inflating factors just mentioned—and cut the figure in half. *Ah*, you say, *I can expect at least one quarter of the market to buy product X.*

No way.

The concept test has a 100 percent captive audience, who are deliberately exposed to the message of the product. But there is no such way to "capture" the entire market once you're in the real world. A sizable number of potential buyers will *never hear your message.* They won't see your advertising. They won't receive your catalog. They won't shop at the right store or look in the right department. They just won't get it.

To make a realistic calculation of your likely market share, then, you not only have to allow for test inflation, but also factor in your ability (and inability) to communicate your product to the market.

With all of its possible complications, interpreting the concept test seems deceptively simple. The top box score—that is, the percentage of respondents who tell you they would "definitely buy" the product—is usually a good indicator of how the product will fare in the marketplace. Except for one problem. There is no cut-and-dried formula for translating this number into a predicted market share. A high number suggests ultimate success. But just how much success? And will that degree of success be enough?

False Start
Is it possible for a test to *understate* product acceptance? Yes—especially if the category of the product is very new and very unfamiliar to consumers. You can't blindly rely on tests.

Here is as close as you can get to a rule of thumb: For frequently repurchased consumer goods (the largest category of which are packaged goods), a top box score of 40 percent or better is considered strong. Now, what does "strong" mean? Roughly, it means that about 30 percent of *target* consumers will *try* the product. A score of 30 to 39 percent on the concept test suggests that fewer than 30 percent of target consumers will try the product. A "definitely would buy" response of under 30 percent suggests that fewer than 20 percent

Jump Start
Concept tests are most reliable for new products in familiar product categories.

of target consumers will try the product. (Source: Edwin E. Bobrow and Dennis W. Shafer, *Pioneering New Products: A Market Survival Guide* [Dow Jones-Irwin, 1987].)

On Target?

I've mentioned the phrase "target consumer." If you were once a Boy Scout or Girl Scout or attended a summer camp, you probably spent some time on an archery range. Maybe you hit the bull's-eye. Maybe you didn't. But at least you knew where the *target* was.

Buzzword

A *target consumer* is a buyer who has (through test results or purchasing history) shown himself *likely* to buy products in a given category.

It's not always that easy when you're developing a new product.

If you're committed to doing market research, you're not done yet. In addition to a user needs-and-wants study, a competitive analysis, and a concept test, you'll need to do an analysis of the market—not so much to help you hit the bull's-eye, but to find the target in the first place.

Chapter 17 is devoted to sizing up the market. For now, just be aware that you'll have to determine something about:

➤ Market size

➤ Market growth

➤ Market trends

➤ Market segments (what they are, their size, their growth, their trends)

➤ How buyers behave (who they are, when they buy, why they buy, how they buy)

Prototype

Think you haven't been targeted as a consumer? Have you ever been handed coupons along with your receipt when you leave the supermarket? Bet you didn't know that the selection of coupons was based on what you bought.

For instance, when you purchase some cheese danishes, you might receive a coupon for a competitor's doughnuts. This is targeting you, the breakfast snack purchaser, for another potential breakfast snack.

You have to admit, your chances for buying the doughnuts with a coupon are greater than if they gave you a coupon for rump roast.

And Then There's the Money...

But you're *still* not done. Read Chapter 16 to learn the ins and outs of the financial analysis.

Once you have a picture of user needs and wants, the competition, a prediction of product acceptance (concept test results), and an estimate of the dimensions of the market, you can make a meaningful stab at predicting

➤ Payback period: How long before we get our money back?

➤ Return on investment (ROI): What will you get for what you've put in?

These make up the bottom line, and the bottom line is, for better or worse, the final score.

The Least You Need to Know

➤ Market research prior to developing concepts is aimed at prospecting for ideas, whereas the object of research after developing concepts is to test those concepts.

➤ Don't deceive yourself into thinking that concept test results directly predict your probable percentage of the market.

➤ Establish technical feasibility simultaneously, with your market research.

➤ A thorough business case requires study of the competition, technical feasibility, consumer response to the product concept, study of the market, and, finally, a financial analysis.

Chapter 13

Marketing Research Nuts (and Bolts)

In This Chapter

➤ Using market-research consultants

➤ In-person consumer surveys

➤ Telephone surveys

➤ Mail surveys

➤ Planning and executing market-research projects

You now have a picture of the range of testing tools and techniques that are used to analyze markets and market conditions at various stages of new product development. Let's face it: This book cannot make you an expert in market research. But you can learn enough to make informed decisions about using market research that is conducted by outside consultants you may hire. You can also learn enough to construct some tests on your own. This chapter explores a variety of specific methods and techniques for conducting the research discussed in chapters 10, 11, and 12.

You Need Help

If you've read the last three chapters and feel somewhat inadequate to the task of market research, take heart. You're not alone. In fact, market research, like so many functions of management, has become a specialty unto itself and, therefore, beyond the in-house resources of many companies, including some of the largest firms. Fortunately, the market research field is replete with suppliers who can design and execute market testing at almost any level.

The plenitude of market research consultants is the good news. The fact that these suppliers come in all degrees of ability and competence is the not-so-good news. Choose your outside helpers wisely. Consider the following questions when you evaluate market research firms:

1. What techniques does the supplier propose?

2. Why does he propose them?

3. Does the supplier have experience with the technique(s) he will use?

4. How much experience?

5. What is the quality of that experience?

6. Can the supplier conduct both qualitative and quantitative research? (Even if the consultant recommends one type of research only, does he have expertise in both areas? You don't want his recommendation to be made solely on the basis of what he *can* and *cannot* do.)

7. Is the methodology proposed tied to the overall goal(s) of the research?

8. How detailed and how well thought-out is the analytical plan that has been proposed?

9. Are cost and time-frame requirements realistic?

10. Has the supplier outlined hypothetical outcomes?

Jump Start

Hiring a consultant need not be a grim necessity or an admission of incompetence. Bringing in someone from the outside not only can help you to get a necessary job done, it can also add a fresh imaginative voice and point of view to your organization.

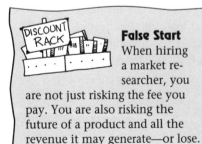

False Start

When hiring a market researcher, you are not just risking the fee you pay. You are also risking the future of a product and all the revenue it may generate—or lose.

This last point is crucial. You aren't hiring a fishing buddy. The consultant should be able to tell you where he expects to arrive at the end of the study. This doesn't mean that he should start out by giving you the results, but, rather, that he should be able to predict a range of probable results and tell you what *kind* of information will be obtained.

Finally, *do* check the supplier's references.

Choose Your Method

In essence, most marketing research is a process of interviewing consumers. The interview may be conducted in person, on the telephone, or in the mail. If one method were always best, I wouldn't have to discuss the other two. But each method has its place, depending on two factors:

➤ Suitability to the objectives of your study

➤ Feasibility from the point of view of budget and time frame

I'll review the positives and negatives of each method.

In Person

The personal interview is among the most useful of research methods and is the method of choice when you have something to show or give the respondent, as in product, advertising, and package tests, and is very important in testing complex—especially industrial—products. The personal interview is also called for when conducting complex attitude and opinion studies.

It would be great if you could personally interview consumers every time you do market research. No other method offers so much:

➤ *Freedom:* You are free to pursue whatever line of questioning seems most productive. You can get at details of attitude and opinion. You can probe and clarify answers to open-ended questions, obtaining both detail and precision in responses.

➤ *Opportunity to exhibit products or concepts:* Face to face, you can easily show respondents mock-ups, models, drawings, test packages, and so on.

➤ *Opportunity to observe:* A good interviewer can observe such things as the respondent's body language, facial expressions, and other gestures, which often speak more truly and fully than

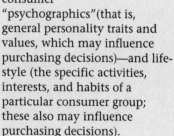

Jump Start
Consider two additional questionnaire forums: product inserts and surveys on your company's World Wide Web site. It is a good idea to motivate customers to fill out and return inserts by offering some incentive, such as a free sample of another product, an extension on the warranty, and so on. Without a good incentive, expect fewer than 20 percent of purchasers to reply. Web surveys work only with highly motivated consumers and are therefore more suited to hobby and enthusiast products as well as professional products rather than general consumer goods. Inform site visitors that their comments will help you to create the products *they* need.

Buzzword
Attitude and opinion studies measure consumer "psychographics"(that is, general personality traits and values, which may influence purchasing decisions)—and lifestyle (the specific activities, interests, and habits of a particular consumer group; these also may influence purchasing decisions).

143

words. The interviewer can also observe how a respondent uses a sample product or opens a package that is being tested.

➤ *Swiftness of completion:* Properly executed, personal interview studies can be conducted quickly—certainly faster than mail research and sometimes faster than telephone studies.

Despite the advantages, personal interviewing can be cumbersome and is certainly the most expensive type of research to conduct.

Door-to-Door No More

Once the dominant method for the personal interview, door-to-door interviewing is virtually extinct today. Two other methods have supplanted it:

➤ The *intercept interview* characteristically takes place in a shopping mall, supermarket, or in whatever retail setting is most appropriate to the product concept being tested. The interviewer approaches potential respondents and asks for a moment of their time. Often, a free sample or other small gift is offered.

False Start
Door-to-door interviewing is almost a thing of the past. Fewer people (especially with many women now in the workplace) are at home during the day, and evening interviews are inconvenient. Fewer people these days are comfortable welcoming strangers into their homes, and, for that matter, the safety of the interviewer is also a consideration.

➤ In *central location studies*, respondents are recruited by mail or telephone and are asked to meet at a central location at a certain time. The telephone or mail recruiting process is used as a screen in order to select respondents who meet certain criteria (age, income, interests, etc.). Central location interviews are useful when the complexity of the issues involved necessitates a lengthy and detailed interview—forty-five minutes to an hour. Payment or other compensation is almost always required, and it is wise to consider that the proportion of qualified respondents will be low.

By Phone

The telephone is widely used in marketing studies and is especially well suited to:

➤ Collecting facts and opinions from a broad sample of people

➤ Tracking studies

➤ Contacting respondents from specific lists (for example, people who redeem coupons or register certain products)

➤ Callback interviews (with people who have been previously contacted in person)

Telephone interviewing offers many advantages:

➤ There is no easier way to reach a large, geographically dispersed, or geographically targeted sample.

➤ If at first you don't reach the respondent, try, try again. Just call back.

➤ You can hire a relatively large number of telephone interviewers at a relatively low cost.

➤ It's fairly easy to monitor the performance of your interviewers for quality.

Buzzword
Tracking is the ongoing consumer testing that is conducted after a product is introduced into the marketplace. Basically, it asks the question former New York mayor Ed Koch was famous for: "How'm I doin'?" If necessary, course corrections (product, packaging, advertising modifications, etc.) are made.

➤ Because the interviewer rather than the respondent retains control of the questionnaire, the questioning process can be flexible and more probing while avoiding dead ends that waste time.

➤ Telephone interviewing is a speedy process.

➤ It's easy to pretest a telephone questionnaire and make modifications as you go along. You don't have to wait for results to come in by mail.

For all of its advantages, telephone interviewing certainly has its limitations:

➤ You can't talk too long. Ten minutes on the telephone with a stranger is a substantial amount of time. Interviews much longer than this will be perceived as an imposition. (However, for highly motivated consumers—including industrial and professional buyers—longer interviews are quite acceptable.)

➤ You can't control background distractions: needy children, an incontinent dog, a "call waiting" interruption.

➤ You can't show the respondent a mock-up, sample, or drawing. (So far, video phones have not found wide market acceptance, but you can use phone and fax in conjunction.)

➤ You can't ask very complex questions, except in the case of professional or industrial customers.

False Start
Be careful not to give a bad representation of your product. A lot of people resent unsolicited telephone interviews. They tend to come at unwanted times, such as during dinner, the most likely time for a target customer to be home.

➤ You can't administer lengthy scales. ("Rate on a scale of 1 to 10..." and the like.) These become too complex as well as tedious. Industrial and professional customers will tolerate greater complexity than general consumers.

➤ You may encounter hostility. The best thing that can happen in this case is that the respondent will tell you up front that he's not interested in participating—or perhaps he'll just hang up on you. Less desirable are respondents who don't really want to participate and therefore become restless and irritable about halfway through the session.

Boiler Rooms

That's what a cynical public calls them. Telemarketing and marketing research professionals prefer the term "interviewing centers." These are places where dozens or scores of telephone interviewers gather to make their assigned calls. The chief advantage of an interviewing center, as opposed to having researchers make their calls from home, is the ability to supervise interviewers.

The interviewing center may also be equipped with computers for CATI: *Computer-Assisted Telephone Interviewing*. A computer monitor is located at each calling station. The screen displays questions for the interviewer to ask, and the interviewer types the responses directly into a computer system, thereby eliminating the need for a paper questionnaire and additional keyboarding costs.

In the Mail

Surveys—concept questionnaires—sent through the mail seem like a great idea. After all, they offer significant advantages:

➤ Compared to other research methods, they don't cost much.

➤ Mail-borne research tends to offer economy of scale. The more questionnaires you send out, the lower the cost per questionnaire.

➤ As with telephone research, mail research reaches people over a broad and dispersed geographical area.

➤ A mailed questionnaire eliminates interviewer bias by eliminating the interviewer. (But this also allows no possibility for probing for detail or clarification.)

➤ Mailed material can include product photographs, charts, graphs, and other visual material. This is a distinct advantage over telephone interviewing.

So much for the good news. Mail research is also replete with problems and disadvantages. The two most important are *low rate of return* and *nonreturner/returner bias:*

➤ *Low rate of return.* Go to your mailbox, and what do you get? Bills and "junk mail." Well, guess what? The questionnaire you labored at so lovingly (and spent good money on) is, so far as most people are concerned, junk mail. It will be trash-canned 90 to 95 percent of the time.

➤ *Nonreturner/returner bias.* Who are the 5 or 10 percent of respondents who actually return a mailed questionnaire? The relative smallness of their number should tell you that they are probably *not* typical of the total sample. Usually, returners are "extremists," who either love the product category or the new product concept or they hate it.

In addition to these two major problems, you are also faced with:

➤ An inability to control just who fills out (or even actually receives) the questionnaire. The questionnaire may well reach an unintended party.

➤ Mailed questionnaires are, of course, self-administered. No interviewer is present. Therefore, questions must be fairly simple. Most—if not all—must be closed-ended. No probing is possible.

➤ Mail surveys take time. Bulk-rate mail is none too fast, and it may take days or weeks before respondents get around to filling out the questionnaire.

False Start
Mail studies tend to skew toward older people because it is this group who typically has the time to fill out and return a questionnaire. No problem—if you want to reach mainly retirees. More often, however, it is the younger consumers that researchers are most interested in reaching.

False Start
A bevy of complex questions will frustrate the respondent, who is therefore likely to crumple up the questionnaire and toss it away.

Don't Give Up on It (Maybe)

Despite its disadvantages, there are situations in which mail research can be quite useful. The cardinal rule here is that *mail studies work best with respondents known to have a special interest in a product category.* For example, few consumers have a "special interest" in laundry detergent, so a mailed questionnaire concerning a new product concept for a laundry detergent is not likely to produce a high volume of responses, let alone a high volume of reliable responses. However, it is possible to identify purchasers of certain types of special-interest products—let's say high-end audio equipment—and target a large group of these consumers to receive mailed questionnaires.

Professional, medical, industrial, and certain other business-to-business markets also provide fertile fields for questionnaires. If you ask questions concerning professional/ business products that will increase profits, make a job easier, or improve performance, you stand a good chance of engaging a respondent's self-interest; therefore, you can expect a reasonably good response rate.

In addition to targeting potential respondents most likely to be interested in a given product category, you can take other steps to make the questionnaire appealing:

Jump Start Hobbyists are good candidate groups for receiving questionnaires targeted to their interests.

➤ Send a good-looking package.

➤ Avoid "Occupant" or "Resident" addresses; personalize the address.

➤ Use first-class postage rather than bulk rate. This can be a significant added expense, but the fact is that bulk rate postage screams *Junk mail! Toss me!*

➤ Enclose a cover letter with the questionnaire that makes clear how much you value the respondent's opinion and how his answers will help you serve *him* better, more efficiently, more cost effectively. Personalize the letter by addressing it to the respondent by name.

➤ Make the questionnaire itself attractive and as simple as possible.

➤ Keep the questionnaire short—no more than four pages (a *single* folded sheet, printed on both sides).

➤ Provide a special incentive: discounts, coupons, a gift, even cash.

Jump Start Consider including a trial-size sample along with a coupon, if possible. If the potential customer likes the product, he can purchase it with the coupon and the knowledge that he already approves of the product.

The Steps

A research project is, first and foremost, a *project*. Like any other project your firm undertakes, it consumes time, effort, and cash. Better make the most of this investment by carefully planning the project.

Recognize that the project needs to be managed—led by a dependable, able, and well-organized individual accountable for completing the project satisfactorily and on time. The project manager will oversee a process of:

➤ Planning

➤ Preparation

➤ Field work

➤ Tabulating

➤ Reporting

The first step in the *planning* phase is to define the purpose and objectives of the research project. Remember, research at this stage is not a fishing expedition. You need to know what information you're after and why you want it.

After you've defined your purpose and objectives, you need to design the research project. What kind of study will serve your purpose and attain your objectives? What respondents do you need to reach? How will you reach them?

Once you've defined your purpose and objectives and designed the project, write this up in the form of a project proposal. Share the proposal with every key person involved in the development of the new product in question.

After the proposal is approved and agreed upon, *schedule* in-person interviews (if the study calls for them). The calendars of other people create deadlines you must accommodate. At this time, too, compose the questionnaire. If you're using interviewers in this research, prepare instructions for them at this point.

The next step is to mail or ship any necessary materials. This may include interview kits sent to various sites selected for interviews. It may include questionnaires sent to telephone interviewers. Or it may include questionnaires to be mailed directly to respondents. Once all necessary materials are in place, the interviews (if any) are conducted.

As results are received, go through a check-in process:

➤ Count the number of interviews or questionnaires received.

➤ Review questionnaires for internal inconsistencies in order to prevent tabulating false results later. For example, if a respondent answers one question by saying that he loves Brand X, then, three questions later, responds that he has never used Brand X, discount the response to the first question.

To enable statistical tabulation, responses must be coded. We'll discuss this in the next chapter, along with how to create a data-processing plan, how to generate reports, analyze results, and make your report.

The Price

The direct cost of a research project can be boiled down to a very simple formula:

cost = labor hours required × $ rate per hour + expenses

Labor includes paying interviewers and data-entry personnel, as well as paying for administration and project management: the people who design, direct, and oversee the study. *Expenses* may include some of the following:

➤ Printing

➤ Telephone charges

➤ Postage

➤ Mainframe computer time

➤ Travel

➤ Rental of locations and equipment

➤ Incentives for respondents

➤ Cost of samples, mock-ups, etc.

Jump Start
Always allow for contingencies. A good rule of thumb is to build in a 10 percent contingency allowance over and above whatever figure you budget.

The Least You Need to Know

➤ Even if you intend to turn over your market research to consultants, you should be familiar with the available options and processes, and their advantages and limitations.

➤ There is no single tried-and-true way of conducting consumer surveys.

➤ Questionnaires are best used with well-defined, highly motivated consumers—for example, industrial and professional customers—rather than the general public.

➤ Choose your methods based on the kind of product concept being tested, the cost of the research, and the amount of time you can invest.

Chapter 14

Making Sense of It All

STOP THE INSANITY!

In This Chapter

➤ Writing good research questions and building effective questionnaires

➤ Preparing data for analysis

➤ Analyzing data

➤ Presenting the data in a report

This is a chapter about interpreting the results of your research. But the first interpreting that gets done is not by you. In the beginning, the people who respond to your questionnaire or to your interviewer reading to them from *his* questionnaire must understand the questions. And not just *understand* the questions, but understand them as you intend them to be understood. Before you can make sense of it all, your respondents must make sense of what you present to them. This chapter begins, then, with a discussion about creating an effective questionnaire. After *that* matter is settled, we move on to methods of interpreting research data.

What Is the Question?

The heart of the interview or the questionnaire is, understandably enough, the question. How would you answer the following?

If a cheap electric home-office stapler were available,
would you purchase one? Yes ❑ No ❑ Maybe ❑

If a cost-effective electric home-office stapler were available,
would you purchase one? Yes ❑ No ❑ Maybe ❑

If an electric home-office stapler were available for under $10,
would you purchase one? Yes ❑ No ❑ Maybe ❑

If a high-quality electric home-office stapler were available for under $10,
would you purchase one? Yes ❑ No ❑ Maybe ❑

Unless you are either dead set against ever owning an electric stapler for your home office or are uncontrollably lusting after one, my guess is that you might answer each of these questions differently.

Jump Start
Many times questionnaires ask you the same question worded in a couple of different ways to see what *words* motivate you. Words that might have caused you to answer positively toward the purchasing of a product can be used later in product advertising material.

How you ask your questions *will* influence the responses you receive. You need to ask questions in such a way that:

1. You attain the objectives of your research project.

2. You motivate respondents to give honest, accurate answers.

This is not always easy. In fact, a detailed treatise on developing questionnaires is well beyond the scope of this book. However, we can establish guidelines for

➤ Creating clear questions that invite good answers

➤ Combining good questions into an effective questionnaire

Asking the Questions

Most questionnaires call for three types of questions:

1. *Qualifiers:* These questions determine whether the respondent is qualified to partici-pate in the study. If you're testing a new brand of cat litter, better begin with "Do you own a cat?"

2. *The "real" questions:* These are the questions directly related to the concept or product category being studied.

3. *Demographics:* Questions here concern age, gender, income, and so on.

Questions for #1 and #3 are always closed-ended, whereas #2 questions often combine closed-ended and open-ended questions. Closed-ended questions are variations on the multiple-choice questions familiar from school:

➤ They may call for a yes/no response.

➤ They may call for choosing a response from a list of responses.

➤ They may call for an answer that rates something on a defined scale.

➤ They may call for sorting items according to preference or importance.

Open-ended questions fall into two categories:

➤ Basic or primary questions.

➤ Follow-up questions, calling for more detail or clarification.

Buzzword
Closed-ended questions limit the respondent to a stated choice of answers. *Open-ended questions* both invite and require the respondent to answer in his own words.

A Smorgasbord of Closed-Ended Questions

The quickest way to get an idea of how to construct effective questions is to look at some examples.

1. *Yes/no* questions.

> Do you own a computer with a CD-ROM drive?

This, of course, is the simplest, most straightforward kind of question to ask. Just make certain that a yes/no response really is the only response possible.

2. *Multiple choice* questions.

> Which of the following brands of widget have you purchased during the past six months?
>
> ❏ Brand A
>
> ❏ Brand B
>
> ❏ Brand C

The multiple-choice question is the format of choice whenever the range of possible responses can be

Jump Start
Closed-ended questions can be followed by open-ended questions that ask for a "why" explanation of the respondent's answer.

153

determined in advance. The format is easy to tabulate and evaluate—certainly easier than open-ended questions—and it introduces an apples-to-apples consistency among responses. Of course, you must be certain that the question you're asking really is closed-ended and that you have included all of the possible relevant responses.

Prototype

Questions are sometimes set up on even scales, 1 to 6. For example: Rate the value of this product from 1 to 6.

Poor Value 1 2 3 4 5 6 High Value

Ostensibly, 6 would be the best rating. But you are testing the ratio between price and perceived value. You don't want to charge too much for the product, but you don't want to give it away, either. So, while the respondent may believe that 6 is the most desirable rating, you see the winning product—the one with the best price-to-value ratio—as a 4. Structuring a question in this way effectively removes the middle-of-the road option, which tells you nothing, except that the respondent is unsure of what he feels.

3. *Scaling* questions.

How would you rate the flavor of the corn chip?

❏ Excellent   ❏ Poor

❏ Very good   ❏ Very poor

❏ Good   ❏ Terrible

❏ Fair

Questions calling for good-to-bad ratings are easily assigned numerical values for tabulation. In fact, you can construct the question that way from the start:

Please rate the flavor of the corn chip from 1 to 5, with 1 being *very poor* and 5 being *excellent.*

The two preceding questions are examples of "unipolar" scales—they go from good to bad or from bad to good. Many products are more effectively rated using "bipolar" scales, in which the "best" (most favorable) response is in the middle:

Which of the following statements best describes the "heft" of the golf club?

❏ Much too heavy   ❏ Somewhat too light

❏ Somewhat too heavy   ❏ Much too light

❏ Just right

Bipolar scales are usually useful for evaluating response to products and particular product attributes, and they are easy to quantify for tabulation.

Another type of rating question calls for indicating how much or how little the respondent likes something:

How do you feel about the design of the widget?

❏ I like it very much   ❏ I dislike it mildly

❏ I like it moderately   ❏ I dislike it moderately

❏ I like it mildly   ❏ I dislike it very much

❏ I neither like nor dislike it

You should construct this question symmetrically, providing as many "like" as "dislike" responses, with a neutral response in the middle.

The like-dislike rating illustrated above (often called a "hedonic" question, from the Greek word for pleasure) does not necessarily tell you much about the respondent's intent to actually purchase the product. For that, use a buying-intent scale question:

How likely would you be to buy this product?

❏ Definitely would buy   ❏ Probably would not buy

❏ Probably would buy   ❏ Definitely would not buy

❏ Might or might not buy

Finally, there are rating questions that ask for the respondent to fix his opinion along a scale of agreement and disagreement. This kind of question is best used to gauge the accuracy of your assumptions about target consumers:

For each statement, indicate whether you

❏ Strongly agree   ❏ Slightly disagree

❏ Moderately agree   ❏ Moderately disagree

❏ Slightly agree   ❏ Strongly disagree

❏ Neither agree nor disagree

155

Statements might include, for example:

Telephone answering machines are generally difficult to use.

VCRs are difficult to program.

Automatic dishwashers make too much noise.

4. *Sorting according to preference or importance* questions.

These kinds of questions can be as simple as the following:

Which of the two widget designs do you prefer: number 1 or number 2? Or do you like them equally?

Note that you should provide an alternative to a simple either/or response.

In many cases, you want the respondent to rank more than two items:

Please rank the following colors in order of preference, with 1 being most appealing and 5 being least appealing.

❏ Blue

❏ Red

❏ Green

❏ Yellow

❏ White

Note that the range of responses is listed in neutral alphabetical order.

You can also use ranking questions to gauge what issues or product features consumers regard as most important. For example:

Please rank the following features from most important to least important, with 1 being most important and 10 being least important.

False Start
Ranking questions quickly become tedious. Ask them sparingly.

Another type of rating question asks the respondent to express his feeling or opinion along a sliding scale you define:

Fill in the box that best represents your feelings about programming a VCR:

Very difficult ❏ ❏ ❏ ❏ ❏ ❏ Very easy

Some Open-Ended Questions

Open-ended questions have a number of disadvantages. They can be difficult to code, tabulate, and analyze, and they ask for some creative thought on the part of the respondent, which the respondent may not be willing to give. However, they are an excellent means of collecting information when the range of possible responses is very broad. Because open-ended questions provide a minimal amount of prompting and impose the fewest limitations, they may evoke the most authentic possible response from the respondent.

Probing questions are very simple in form. Following a round of closed-ended questions, you ask—either in person or on a questionnaire—something like:

> What else didn't you like about the widget?

Clarifying questions are more specific than probing questions. They relate directly to answers already given. The respondent has rated the VCR as too difficult to program. A good clarifying question would be:

> In what ways was it difficult to program?

Useful phrases to include in open-ended questions are:

> What exactly did you mean when you said…
>
> Can you explain that…
>
> In what ways is…
>
> What did you like about…
>
> What made you think about that?

Jump Start
Open-ended questions are most effective as probing or clarifying follow-ups to closed-ended questions.

False Start
Probing questions should not be leading questions. "Didn't you like the sure-grip handle?" is a leading question. If the respondent had nothing to say about the sure-grip handle, that in itself tells you something about the relative importance of the product feature.

Building the Questionnaire

Now that you have the basic vocabulary of question writing under your belt, it's time to create the questionnaire. Begin by reviewing the objectives of your study. This process should help you generate a list of the information you need to obtain. Once you have this list, you can write the questions required to obtain the information. You should also consider the method of data collection you will use: mail, Internet Web site, phone, or personal interview. This will affect the number, type, and complexity of the questions.

After you draft the questionnaire, get a colleague to look it over. Ask for frank critical input, then make any necessary revisions. It is advisable to pretest the questionnaire on a small group in order to be certain that the questions are clear and that you're getting all the information you need.

There are no hard-and-fast rules for building the questionnaire, but there are some common-sense rules of thumb:

False Start

Ask questions that are too hard, and you'll get false data. Respondents tend to make up answers rather than risk looking dumb.

Jump Start

What is a "significant sample" of completed questionnaires? Ideally, 25 percent. With very large surveys, 10 percent may be more feasible to work with.

1. Begin with the general and work toward the specific. Don't begin by hitting the respondent with a bunch of complicated product attributes. Instead, start by asking for some general likes and dislikes.

2. Make the questions easy. It is legitimate to ask respondents to make purchasing decisions, but not marketing decisions. That's *your* job.

3. Be careful about digging too deeply for answers concerning quantity and volume. Do *you* remember how many times you ate Brand X cereal during the last twelve months?

4. Break up complex questions into several simpler ones.

5. Don't let respondents overlook the obvious. When you ask why a respondent likes Brand X floor wax, he or she may *think* that you want some esoteric answer ("Because it produces an especially hard shine that is perfectly transparent"), even if the answer the respondent *really* has in mind is simple ("It's cheaper than the others"). In closed-ended multiple-choice questions, be certain to include the obvious.

The Next Step: Coding

Now that you've got a stack of completed questionnaires, what do you do with them? You need to translate the results into a form that can be tabulated and expressed in a statistically meaningful way. The first step in this process is *coding*.

Coding reduces complex verbiage into a set of simpler categories and numerical labels relating to those categories. Quite frankly, this part of the analysis is not much fun. You—or whoever the researcher is—must analyze a significant sample of the questionnaires to determine the *kinds* of responses that have been given to the questions. The kinds of responses are then logically grouped into categories, which are labeled with numbers that correspond to columns on an evaluation sheet. For example, in a test concerning house paint, you may find that respondents most frequently comment on brilliance of color, ease of application, durability, drying time, and so on. Each of these qualities (and, presumably, many others) will become a category assigned to a column—for example, "Brilliance" or "Ease of Application."

Next, all of the comments (attributes) relating to each category are placed in the appropriate column and assigned a code. For example:

Jump Start Obviously, it's easier to code closed-ended questions than open-ended ones. With predominantly closed-ended multiple-choice questionnaires, category columns and attribute codes can be determined in advance.

Brilliance	Code
Loved brightness of color	1
Loved vividness of color	2
Liked brightness of color	3
Liked vividness of color	4
Disliked too bright color	5
Hated garish color	6
Thought color not bright enough	7
Thought color not vivid enough	8
Disliked dull color	9
Hated flat color	10

Now...A Data Processing Plan

Next, it is necessary to develop a data-processing plan that achieves three objectives:

1. Provide informative data.

2. Perform cross-tabulation to show what differences exist among demographic or attitudinal groups within the whole sample studied. Cross-tabs are the sub-group categories relevant to the information you're trying to obtain. Typically, cross-tabs include:

Buzzword

A *cross-tab*—sometimes called a banner or break—is a significant sub-group within a sample. Typical cross-tabs are defined by demographic characteristics (age, sex, etc.), geographical location (city, region, neighborhood), and frequency of usage (those who regularly use a given product, those who do not regularly use it, etc.).

➤ Demographic categories: sex, age, income, education, size of the household, number of children, and so on

➤ Geographic categories: city, region, etc.

➤ Usage categories: respondents who regularly use a conditioning shampoo, respondents who rarely use a conditioning shampoo, respondents who never use a conditioning shampoo, and so on

➤ Purchase intent: will definitely purchase, will probably purchase, might purchase, will probably not purchase, and so on

3. Choose among the types of analysis tools available to interpret results in order to answer the key overall issues of the study.

A Statistics Toolkit

Statistical analysis is a complex subject well beyond the scope of this book. But it's important to understand the *range* of analytical options available for arriving at the information you said you needed when you wrote up your research proposal. (Remember *that*?)

For each question that is being analyzed, you need to know the *base*—that is, the number of respondents. The total number of respondents for a given question is 100 percent. From this base, you can meaningfully calculate the percentage of each response to the question.

It is, of course, important to know that 45 percent of the 340 people who responded to a question about intent to buy answered that they "would definitely buy" the product being tested. But most studies analyze the data beyond expressing simple percentages.

Simple cross-tabulation is an example of basic multivariate analysis. Other, more complex multivariate techniques you should be aware of include:

➤ *Regression analysis:* This technique is used for prediction. It takes a dependent variable (also called a criterion variable), which is a variable you are trying to predict (for example, the number of toothpaste tubes that will be purchased by a typical household in a year) and a set of independent variables (also called predictor variables), which explain or predict differences in the dependent variables (for example, the number of children in the household), and it develops an equation relating them.

➤ *Factor analysis:* These techniques analyze interrelationships among variables in order to reduce them to a smaller set of underlying variables called *factors.* The idea is to reduce a welter of data to a relatively few manageable attributes that become key factors to consider in developing a new product.

➤ *Cluster analysis:* These techniques attempt to identify groups (of people or of products) that are similar in some significant way(s). Cluster analysis is obviously quite useful in identifying target markets because it identifies groups that have similar needs, similar interests, similar buying patterns, and so on.

➤ *MAPPing, or Multidimensional Scaling:* The acronym MAPP stands for Mathematical Analysis of Perception and Preference. And the acronym is apt, because this technique represents consumers' product perceptions and preferences as points within a defined space. That is, the technique creates a "map" of perception and preference, which indicates the most important product attributes (as perceived by consumers) and also suggests gaps in the market, which are opportunities for new products.

➤ *Conjoint Analysis:* This is a technique for separating and measuring respondents' judgments about complex alternatives—usually product characteristics or attributes—into distinct components. The technique assigns "utility values" to each of the characteristics of each product or product concept under study. In this way, the characteristics of Product A can be compared quantitatively to those of Product B. The utility values can be added up, and the product or product concept with the greatest total is the one most likely to appeal to consumers.

Buzzword
The definition of *multivariate analysis* is simple: any analysis that studies several variables together. In practice, however, multivariate procedures can be quite complex.

Making Yourself Heard

Research is useless until it is reported. You have to make yourself heard, and to do this you need to find a way to communicate effectively. The following guidelines are useful whether you are preparing a research report or evaluating the work of an in-house or outside researcher:

➤ The report should look attractive, clear, and interesting. Above all, it should appear well organized.

➤ The report should have a clear, descriptive title that identifies the subject being investigated.

161

➤ All other things being equal, an effectively organized report has three parts:

1. The *digest:* This is an "executive summary" of the report's findings. It states within three or four pages why the study was done, how it was done, and what was learned from it.

2. *Presentation of detailed findings:* This is the nitty-gritty—the detailed presentation of findings. The user of this part of the study will be the product manager or whoever is most directly responsible for new product development.

3. *Tabulations:* These are the numbers—*all* the numbers, raw and cooked. They are useful as documentation and for other researchers, but are not usually read by executives or product managers. (In practice, this section is often bound separately from the rest of the report.)

➤ The report should interpret and explain all findings—not just put numbers and words together. Telling your reader that "64 percent of respondents prefer product A" is less useful than declaring "Most consumers prefer product A."

Jump Start
A market research report should draw conclusions. It should not simply present results.

➤ The report should be written for product managers or other staff most directly responsible for new product development. It should not be directed at other researchers.

➤ The report should strongly and unmistakably relate to the stated purpose of the research project. This does not mean that peripheral findings should be discarded, but, rather, that they should be clearly subordinated to the essential issues. Consider placing peripheral material in an appendix.

The Least You Need to Know

➤ Effective research questions are clear, concise, and complete. They evoke the information needed without "leading" the respondents and thereby contaminating the data.

➤ Determine which analytical techniques are best for studying your data in order to obtain the information you need to make new product development decisions. Avoid getting lost in peripheral data and analysis—interesting though it may be.

➤ Devote great care to formulating cross-tabs. Errors here will lead to false assumptions.

➤ Show the results of research in a clear, concise report that is effectively organized and intended for an audience of *managers*, not researchers.

Part 4
Is It Worth It?

Suppose that you conclude that the world will look favorably on your new product. Does that ensure a profitable experience?

Not necessarily.

The next step is to translate the product concept and your picture of what the market wants and needs into a product that is technologically and economically feasible and eminently marketable. The four chapters that follow take you through an orderly system of checks and balances ("stage gates") that contribute to successful product development, lead you into a comprehensive business evaluation of the new product, suggest strategies for identifying the best markets for it, then conclude with a discussion of the available options for distributing the new product.

Chapter 15

Opening the Gates

In This Chapter

➤ Understanding the stages and gates

➤ Building your gates

➤ Stage-gate pitfalls

➤ Process overview

It's time to put together the new-product development processes and procedures we've covered so far. We'd better stop and do this now, before we get lost.

We move from idea generation, to preliminary (Stage 1) investigation, to the detailed (Stage 2) study, and then on to Stage 3, the actual development of the product. Beyond this comes further testing and the product launch. What's it all about? And how do you know when—or if—to move from one stage to another?

You pass through the gates. This chapter will show you how.

The Not-So-Gentle World of Go/Kill

As you may have gathered from the preceding fourteen chapters, new product development can be highly exciting each step of the way, but each of those steps costs time, effort, and cash. And each step delays the launch of the new product—a cost that is difficult to calculate, but one that may mean the difference between the success and failure of the product.

At each step of the new product process you need to make two judgments:

1. When to terminate the present step

2. When—and if—to go on to the next step

That's where the stage-gate system comes in.

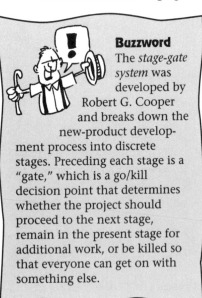

Buzzword
The *stage-gate system* was developed by Robert G. Cooper and breaks down the new-product development process into discrete stages. Preceding each stage is a "gate," which is a go/kill decision point that determines whether the project should proceed to the next stage, remain in the present stage for additional work, or be killed so that everyone can get on with something else.

Buzzword
Scoping is the quick, low-cost preliminary research that is carried out in Stage 1 and that constitutes the initial development screen.

Stages

We have already examined two of the major stages of new product development:

Stage 1. *Preliminary investigation:* This is where the project is quickly investigated and "scoped."

Stage 2. *Detailed study:* This is where the business case for the project is built.

In this book, chapters 8 through 11 relate mainly to Stage 1, while chapters 12 through 14 cover Stage 2. Much of the rest of this book relates to the remaining stages:

Stage 3. *Development:* This is the actual process of designing and developing the new product, as well as the launch marketing plan and preliminary production plans.

Stage 4. *Validation and testing:* Once a prototype or test run of the product exists, it's tried out in the lab and test-marketed. The extent of the test marketing depends on the product type and market conditions. Responses are analyzed, and adjustments made.

Stage 5. *The launch:* The product is commercialized and swings into full production, marketing, distribution, and sales.

Having mapped all the stages out, it's important to realize that each stage is multifunctional, with parallel activities going on simultaneously and people from various departments working hard at each stage. The five stages mentioned here are not all mandatory—nor are they the only five that will work. Maybe four stages will do for you. Or maybe you'll need to break the stages down further into six, seven, or more stages. For example, you may want to think of the idea-generation process as one of the stages—though, usually, it's thought of as a preliminary stage, free from the inhibition of gates. The important thing is to formulate some orderly, staged system in order to organize the process of development, control costs, allocate resources, accelerate where necessary, and/or apply the brakes when necessary. Gates and stages are *one* way to do this.

Gates

Arguably, gates are more important than the stages they "guard." Gates tell you whether to continue with the project or scrap it. They also act as quality-control checkpoints, signaling what aspects of a project need further thought before the whole thing moves on from one stage to another. Out West, a sturdy set of gates keeps the rancher's hoofed assets from disappearing. The gates *you* need serve an analogous purpose, even if your assets aren't four-footed.

The rancher makes his gates of wood, iron, and barbed wire. Yours are built of "deliverables," which are lists of criteria that are predefined for each stage. These deliverables include mandatory criteria (minimum requirements the project *must* meet at Stage X in order to progress to Stage Y) and desirable criteria (requirements that *should* be met, that are desirable, but not mandatory). The "output" of the rancher's gate is either to keep cattle in or, at will, let them out, perhaps for more fattening. The "output" of the new product development gate may be:

➤ *A go/kill/recycle decision.* The gate embodies criteria designed to measure whether or not the project is worth doing and is right for the company. It may be passed along to the next stage, killed, or sent back (recycled) for further work.

➤ *Quality evaluation.* Have the "deliverables" reached the gate in good shape?

➤ *The path to follow.* Which way should the project go at this point—forward or back?

Buzzword
Deliverables are criteria for progress at each stage of development. Usually, planners draw up a list of mandatory deliverables and desirable deliverables.

Swinging the Gates

The gates swing—open or shut—on three go/kill (must-meet criteria) questions and any number of less dire (should-meet criteria) "prioritization" questions. The go/kill questions are:

1. *Is the project real?* At this point in the process, is it feasible? Can we get it done? Does it fit within the strategic plan of the firm? Is it consistent with company policies? Is there anything on the horizon that will squash it (government regulations, an emerging competitive technology, and so on)?

2. *Is the project worth doing?* Here is where all the market research comes in. Use the research data to answer whether or not the market is big enough, the payback period brief enough, the profit margins fat enough.

3. *Is the project a winner?* You can't afford to put in all this time and effort merely to create a feasible project that will make back costs or eke out some slim profit. With limited resources (and we *all* have limited resources), develop only those projects that are clear winners in terms of market share, profit, and potential to open up new markets and market segments.

False Start
Beware the difference between *benefits* and *features*. This is especially important at this stage because benefits are the true motivators of purchase—especially in a new product.

For these three key gate questions, you will need to establish absolute minimum criteria. For prioritization questions (the "should meet" factors) criteria may be looser and will likely include considerations of degree—for example, the degree to which the proposed product:

➤ Offers unique benefits

➤ Offers value

➤ Solves a problem either unaddressed by current products or created by them

➤ Exploits a large and growing market

➤ Combines short- and long-term potential

➤ Offers high profit margins

➤ Is relatively free from competition or has no dominant competitor

➤ Fits exceptionally well with the firm (good synergy with *current* R&D, production, the sales force, the customer base, etc.)

Gate building can be part of the strategic planning outlined back in Chapter 6. The criteria that go into each gate are usually the result of management consensus based on the input of key personnel from all departments. Usually, a review of past projects comes into play, including an analysis of past successes and failures.

Gate construction can be a way of formalizing the creative processes discussed in the first ten chapters of this book; that is, a project can be developed first as a set of "deliverables" or criteria for each stage of a projected development path. Working this way can sharpen focus and speed the development process by avoiding time-wasting detours. In effect, the gate-building process can be used to telescope the formulation of questions and answers, so that the process of establishing what-we-want is carried out in parallel with the process of how-we'll-get-what-we-want.

What Not to Build

The potential *parallel* quality of gate building can greatly accelerate new product development.

If it works right.

I and *f*—two little letters even giants stumble over. Let's look at the downside:

➤ Gates and stages can lead to serial processing, which is much slower than parallel processing.

➤ Gates can be inhibiting if the *kill* half of the *go/kill* decision is overemphasized.

➤ Gates can lead to rigid systems, which not only inhibit creativity generally, but in particular inhibit breakthrough thinking.

➤ Gates can promote more paperwork and bureaucracy. (The very things a properly managed gate system is designed to avoid!)

➤ Gates and stages can lead to serial processing, which is much slower than parallel processing.

Gatekeepers

The existence of gates implies a need for gatekeepers. These are the people who actually make the go/kill and other judgments that must occur at each gate. While certain core members of a new-product evaluation group remain constant, the gatekeepers may vary somewhat from gate to gate, depending on their areas of expertise and authority. Typically, the gatekeepers at the earliest stages of development, where expenditures are low and allocation of resources is limited, are the less senior members of the management team. They evaluate ideas preliminarily, essentially screening them with a fairly coarse

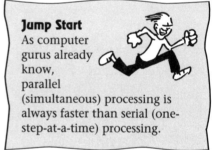

False Start
As the philosopher George Santayana said, those who do not learn the lessons of history are doomed to repeat the errors of the past. However, merely attempting to replicate past successes is never a firm foundation for building new products. Don't abandon the past, but remember that the operative word in new product development is *new*.

Jump Start
As computer gurus already know, parallel (simultaneous) processing is always faster than serial (one-step-at-a-time) processing.

sieve. However, as the project progresses closer to a commitment to production, more of the gatekeepers are senior personnel empowered to make high-level financial decisions. Gatekeepers should possess the following qualifications:

➤ To the extent that development resources are required from different departments, the gatekeepers should be representative of the departments involved.

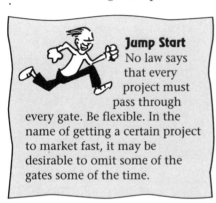

Jump Start
No law says that every project must pass through every gate. Be flexible. In the name of getting a certain project to market fast, it may be desirable to omit some of the gates some of the time.

➤ Whatever other attributes gatekeepers may have, they need to be empowered to approve the resources required for movement to the next stage.

➤ Gatekeepers must be sufficiently disciplined to avoid the seat-of-your-pants approach by applying consistently established gate criteria. The gatekeeper cannot rely on a gut feeling, but must have a thorough familiarity with the company's strategic plan and with all other factors relevant to deciding whether or not to open the gate.

Product Development as a Stage-Gate Process

Let's imagine we're on a hill and can look in two directions: back, to where we've been, and ahead, to where we will go. Here's an overview of the stage-gate process.

The *idea* triggers the process. Without an idea, the gates rust on their hinges. Gates have no business at this stage, which is devoted to pure creativity—the "fuzzy front end" that makes cost accountants nervous, but that is so essential to striking a creative spark.

Gate 1 to Stage 1

Brainstorming and other idea-generation strategies typically avoid judgmental thinking, which inhibits creativity. At some point, though, certain ideas stand in bold relief as being possibly worth developing. The first gate is the initial screening of these "standout" ideas:

➤ Gate 1 should be relatively easy to pass through, excluding only those new product ideas that very obviously are incompatible with company strategy and resources, that seem essentially unfeasible, that run contrary to company policy, and so on.

➤ Financial criteria should not be a part of the first gate. Information is too sketchy to make financial decisions at this point.

If the idea passes through Gate 1, it goes to Stage 1, the preliminary investigation. This stage is often called *scoping*, and it is to product development what a very rough sketch is to an artist contemplating the investment of a great deal of time and effort in a large-scale oil painting. Keep these two things in mind:

➤ The essence of the preliminary investigation is speed and low cost.

➤ The Stage 1 sketch includes a preliminary assessment of the market and a preliminary assessment of technical feasibility.

Stage 1 is usually a sharing of the idea with people beyond the original brainstorming or other creative group. If this shared experience results in excitement—and the preliminary market and technical studies don't turn up a major roadblock—the project has a good shot at passing through Gate 2.

False Start
Unfortunately, some managers will be all too rigidly focused on financial criteria for a new product. You need to make them understand what you are trying to assess at this stage and when you will have accurate financial information.

Gate 2 to Stage 2

The second gate replays the first gate, but applies the criteria more rigorously, using the information obtained in Stage 1. The second gate might also include more "should meet" criteria than were present in the first gate, and it is likely that a rapid, back-of-the-envelope financial estimate will also figure in this gate.

Jump Start
Gate 2 needs to be a sturdy one. It passes the project on to a stage in which substantial money and time must now be committed.

Gate 2 opens onto Stage 2, a more intensive version of the preliminary study stage. The most time- and cash-consuming aspect of this stage is acquiring the data needed to make a decision—especially if you rely on extensive research and concept testing.

Gate 3 to Stage 3

Gate 3 is the point at which the business case built in Stage 2 is evaluated. This is a critical gate because it marks the transition from data-gathering, research, and testing to development. If Stage 2 was more costly than Stage 1, Stage 3 usually represents far more substantial spending, which has corporate-wide impact. The requirements for Gate 3 include the following:

➤ First, Gate 3 should review the procedures of Stage 2, ensuring that they were executed in a high-quality and reliable manner.

➤ Next, the same mandatory criteria applied in Gates 2 and 3 need to be applied now, but in light of the detailed information generated by Stage 2 research. In addition, careful consideration should be given to any "should meet" criteria turned up by analysis of Stage 2 data.

➤ Whereas financials play little if any role in Gate 1 and only a ballpark role in Gate 2, they are a critical aspect of Gate 3. Accurate financial analysis is important here.

Assuming the project gets a green light, it goes on to the third stage, development proper.

While many may view this as the heart of the new product process, little of substance can be said about this stage in a general book on developing new products because this is the most specifically technical phase of the process. Either you know how to put together a widget or you don't. However, this stage does have a number of characteristic features common to many industries, products, and services:

➤ The objective—the "deliverable"—of this stage is a prototype of the product or service. Usually, the prototype has been tested in-house.

Buzzword
Milestones are checkpoints in the development of a product. They are places to pause for review and control, but they are not go/kill points.

➤ This stage is usually complex, containing within itself any number of additional gates, which might be more accurately described as *milestones*, since, unless something truly unanticipated occurs here, they are not go/kill points, but checkpoints that provide opportunities for review and control.

➤ Testing—both technical and user-oriented—may occur at this stage in order to make modifications to the evolving prototype.

➤ While technical folk are front and center in this stage, marketing does not bow out. Marketers continue to work with the technical people in shaping the prototype.

Jump Start
The government provides the means for protecting innovation, thereby taking some of the risk out of new product development. Trademark and patent information will be covered in more depth in Chapter 19, "The Fine Print."

➤ The production staff also gets into the act, ensuring that the evolving prototype remains feasible for manufacture.

➤ During this stage, post-development consumer testing plans may be created, along with production plans. This may involve the planning of new production facilities and quality-assurance methods.

➤ At this point, all regulatory, trademark, and patent issues should be nailed down.

Gate 4 to Stage 4

Gate 4 consists of a quality dimension, a financial dimension, and a plan-review dimension. The characteristics of Gate 4 follow:

➤ The development process is reviewed to ensure quality of execution. Of course, the prototyped product must harmonize with the mandatory criteria (as they were last defined at Gate 3), but now the "should-meet" criteria become critical as well.

➤ At each stage, financial data becomes more significant and complete because more development costs move from the *projected* to the *actual* column of the ledger; therefore, Gate 4 has a strong financial component.

➤ Now is the time to review plans for post-development testing, which is also called *validation*. A validation plan may be approved at this gate.

Stage 4 activities are addressed primarily in Chapter 22, although many of the evaluative methods discussed in chapters 12, 13, and 14 may be employed here as well. Validation processes may include some or all of the following:

➤ Further in-house testing to tweak aspects of product performance.

➤ Field trials to verify "real world" performance.

➤ Trial production of limited quantities of the product. This stage may be tied to field trials.

➤ Test marketing. Actual production products—not prototypes and not trial products—may be marketed initially in geographically limited areas to gauge consumer response and acceptance, to make adjustments to the launch plan, to get a more accurate fix on revenue and market share, and to set final quantities for production.

➤ All financials are reexamined and refined at the end of this stage as more projected figures become actual.

Buzzword
Field trials, also called *user trials*, are sometimes referred to as *beta testing*. The *beta version* of a product is more fully developed and perfected than a prototype (or "alpha version"), but is still subject to user input for modification. The beta version may also be the product of the trial production phase.

Buzzword
Pilot production is another word for the trial production of a product. Production is limited and, therefore, may be more or less feasibly tweaked as necessary.

Gate 5 to Stage 5

The last gate opens on to full production and the product launch. Or not.

This gate ensures the quality, and it reviews the results of the testing and validation procedures of Stage 4. A kill decision is still possible here, but, usually, the less dire output

False Start
Don't suffocate your newborn product in too many layers of review and testing. Depending on the type and scope of the product, not every review and testing step may be necessary, desirable, or even survivable.

of this gate—short of a full *go*—is a recommendation for further modification of some aspect of the product, the marketing plan, or the pricing. Gate 5 also offers a final opportunity to review production, operations, and marketing plans.

The final stage—full production—is not really final. The performance of the product—in both a technical sense and in the marketplace—is monitored and periodically reviewed with an eye toward making any mid-course corrections that may be required. Radical corrections may result in the development of—guess what?—another *new product!*

What's Wrong with This Picture?

Take a look at the various headings in this chapter. Pretty orderly, huh? Maybe you're thinking: *Why couldn't he have presented the whole book this way?* Step-by-step, paint by numbers, some assembly required.

Unfortunately, new product development is rarely as orderly as this chapter suggests, and that's why I haven't patterned the whole book after it. As long as you don't let it get too rigid, too inflexible, the stage-gate approach is a rational, workable way of *balancing* creative forces against the discipline of available resources and the marketplace.

Now, I shouldn't have begun the preceding paragraph with the word *unfortunately.* Because there's nothing at all unfortunate about the wilder, less logical aspects of creativity. For you—and for consumers!—part of the fun, the allure, of new products is surprise: the *wow factor.* If you fail to *balance* the wild against such taming considerations as available resources, technical feasibility, and potential market, you may indeed have fun—but not for long. (The money will run out and Daddy will indeed take the T-bird away.) However, if you let the so-called realities of cash, technical traditions, and "tried-and-true" markets weigh down creativity, you'll have no fun at all—*and* (sooner or later) you'll probably go out of business anyway.

The Least You Need to Know

➤ The stage-gate system is a rational plan for balancing creative energy against resources, technical feasibility, and the realities of the marketplace.

➤ If you find the stage-gate concept useful, feel free to adapt and modify it to fit your product and company.

➤ Applied too rigidly, the stage-gate system will discourage, perhaps destroy, creativity. Beware.

The Business Evaluation

A business evaluation—how a proposed new product will fit with what your company does, how it promises to fare in the marketplace, how much it will cost (in time, effort, and direct funding) to create, produce, and market—should be a part of every stage of thinking about a project. However, the final business evaluation or business review (often called a BE) is an intensive effort that comes after the product is evaluated in terms of technical and production feasibility, after the market is researched, and after the basic business case is built. The final BE includes detailed sales forecasts, pricing analysis, expense and investment projections, and a final check against corporate strategy and company goals. In the context of the stage-gate system discussed in the preceding chapter, the BE may be part of Stage 4 or even Stage 5, since it should function as the basis for a final go/kill decision prior to full production and market introduction.

As Certain as Death and Taxes

The most stable posture a human being can assume is prone. In this position, you certainly will never fall down. You may get stepped on, of course. You may be rolled over, trampled, and crushed. But you won't fall down.

In contrast to the prone position is motion—walking or running—which involves considerable risk of falling down, since it is a process of alternate balance and loss of balance. Is the risk of falling down worth it?

Only if—

➤ You want to avoid being squashed

➤ You really want to get somewhere

Benjamin Franklin told his countrymen that the only things certain in human existence were death and taxes. He might have added one more certainty: *There is no reward without risk.*

We've discussed a good many complex methods and procedures for creating and evaluating new product concepts and the new products themselves. Really, they are all aimed at a single objective: obtaining the maximum reward for the least risk.

Jump Start
To gain something of perceived value, you must risk something of perceived value: money, time, effort—resources. Remember the old saying: *It takes money to make money.*

In developing a new product, you are much like a consumer pondering the purchase of a new product. The prospective purchaser (if he's savvy) wants the most product for the least money—not *more* product for *more* money, nor less product for *less* money. That is, the wise consumer wants neither an expensive nor a cheap product, but one that offers maximum *value*. This is what you're looking for when you ponder investing in the creation of a new product: value—not necessarily the product that will cost the least to develop, nor the super-product with a super cost to boot, but the product that will deliver the greatest reward for the amount of risk you are willing (or able) to invest in it.

The Decision: Boiling It Down

You need a framework for analyzing risks and rewards, for seeing them clearly and without emotion or recourse to gambler's hunches and inscrutable gut feelings. The simplest and most widely adopted framework for boiling down the risk-reward equation was developed and popularized by the Forum Corporation in product planning seminars as early as the 1970s. We saw a version of it in the last chapter. It calls for asking and answering three questions about each proposed new product:

1. Is it real?

2. Can we win with it?

3. Is it worth it?

Is It Real?

Early in this book, I mentioned—repeatedly—Thomas Alva Edison, who learned, with the very first invention he tried to market, that just because you can invent something, it doesn't necessarily mean that anyone will want it. For that matter, thinking up a concept does not necessarily mean that the actual product can be manufactured feasibly, reliably, and cost-effectively.

None of this means that the concept is unreal. It exists. You thought it up. But:

Is the market real?

Is the product real?

These are questions that should be asked (and answered as best as can be) at every stage of the new product's development. In the final BE, the answers should be nailed down as definitively as possible. Here's what it takes to get good answers:

➤ Determining if the *market* is real requires assessing the degree of user need and want for the proposed product.

➤ It also requires assessing whether customers *can* buy the product, even if they do want it. You need to assess the structure of the market, its size, and its potential. You need to know what your target customers can afford to spend.

➤ Then, apart from need/want and ability to buy, there is the question of whether or not consumers *will* buy. What are their purchase priorities? And how does the proposed product address these? What *value* does the product clearly and compellingly present to the consumer?

➤ Determining if the *product* is real requires assessing its feasibility. *Can* the product be

Jump Start
There are probably a lot of people who would like an automobile with all the best features of a Mercedes, Lexus, BMW, and Infiniti combined. But how many of these automotive wish makers could actually afford to purchase such a car? A question like this is an important part of assessing market realities.

designed and developed? Can it then be put into production at a reasonable cost and within a workable time frame?

➤ After you determine what is and is not feasible, are you left with a product that satisfies the market? Does it offer the right design and performance features at the right cost? Can you produce it in the right quantities?

Can We Win with It?

This question focuses on your company in relation to the competition, and answering it involves focusing both on the proposed *product* and on your *company*. The question has three parts:

➤ First, can the proposed product be competitive? This requires a hard look at the proposed design and performance features—their quality, utility, color, style—and, most of all, their uniqueness. What does *your* product offer that others do not? What problems does it solve that others fail to address or that other products create?

➤ The product (if it is a consumer product) must also be competitive in terms of promotion. Can it be packaged and advertised competitively?

➤ Will the product come at the right time?

Prototype

Knowing when the right time is for a product is a hard one. Sony marketed a minidisc recorder-player when everyone was buying CD players. Even though the minidisc holds more data (so it can deliver more music, video, or whatever at a potentially greater degree of fidelity), and even though it is recordable (whereas a standard CD is read-only or play-only), the minidisc failed when it is was first introduced. With CDs gaining wider and wider acceptance, the timing was wrong. As of this writing, Sony was just reintroducing the minidisc into the market. Maybe the time is now right.

Then there is the company to consider. Can *it* compete? Consider the following:

➤ Can your company compete in terms of engineering and production? Do you have the expertise, the experience, the capabilities, the plant facilities, the plant locations, the proprietary processes and patents? Do you have the creativity?

➤ Can your company compete in terms of sales and distribution? Is your dealer network up to the new-product task? How are relations with your present customers? (Remember, *present* customers are always your best *potential* customers.) Is your marketing department in gear?

➤ You also have to assess management: Is it prepared for the challenges of the new product?

Is It Worth It?

The final question the BE must nail down is, quite simply, whether or not the product under consideration is *worth* doing. The overriding consideration here is, of course, profitability. But there are other factors to take into account as well, most notably whether or not the new product will position the company advantageously for long-term development. Consider the following:

➤ First, can the company afford the product? This is usually a matter chiefly of calculating cash flow and impact on cash flow.

➤ Will the return on the investment be adequate? This needs to be considered not only in terms of absolute, per-unit profits, but also in comparison to other investments. Is this the best place to put the company's money at this time?

➤ Is the risk acceptable? Heed Murphy's Law—what *can* go wrong *will* go wrong—and anticipate all the bad that can befall you. If you-know-what happens, will you survive, and will it be worth it?

There are other factors to consider in evaluating whether or not a project is worth proceeding with. These include:

➤ The impact of the new product on long-term goals: Does it open new areas for the company? New markets?

➤ Impact on external relations: Will the new product improve relations with current customers? With the dealer or retail network?

➤ Impact on image: Will the new product enhance the company's image?

Jump Start
Company image should not be a matter of corporate egotism, but should enhance long-term profitability and attract talented employees. Image is valuable, and it is mostly created by the products you produce.

The Laws of Venture Capital

It's important to ask and answer the three questions—Is it real? Can we win with it? Is it worth it?—in as much detail as possible. But getting at that detail can be difficult. There is no doubt about it, answering the questions requires both data and judgment.

Buzzword
Venture capital is money made available for innovative enterprises, especially where the reward and the risk are high.

If you are asked to participate in decisions about new products, *judgment* is precisely what you're being paid a salary for. That's a fact, and I suppose I could just get up now and leave you with that.

But I'm not out the door yet. Adequate data is essential to clarifying your judgment, and nothing can substitute for that. You might also find helpful the following formula, which has been adapted from the work of A. David Silver, a well-known venture capitalist. He proposes three "laws" of venture capital:

1. Accept no more than two risks per investment.

2. $V = P \times S \times E$, where V = valuation, P = size of the problem, S = the elegance of the solution, and E = quality (excellence) of the entrepreneurial team.

3. Invest in big P companies, because the public market will accord them unreasonably high Vs, irrespective of S and E.

These "laws" are interesting because they can be readily adapted to a business review of a new product:

Law #1 can be taken as is, with the proviso that the limit be on two substantial or major risks (minor risks abound in any new product).

Law #2 is also valuable, but "P" needs to be translated specifically as the problem the new product will solve, and "E" must account for the quality of the company as a whole: the people and organization that propose to create and market the new product.

Law #3 is likewise helpful, if we translate it slightly: Invest in products that solve big "P" (problems), because the market will accord them unreasonably high Vs, irrespective of S and E.

I would add a fourth law to Silver's three, whether you're contemplating an investment in a new business or in a new product:

Invest in businesses or products where there is an opportunity to capture a dominant market share. The market share may mean capturing a unique niche or an entire market.

Before I leave Mr. Silver, it is well worth looking at his five-way breakdown of the risks he sees start-up companies having to face. The same risks apply to new products:

1. The development risk: Can we develop the product?

2. The manufacturing risk: If we can develop it, can we produce it?

3. The marketing risk: If we can make it, can we sell it?

4. The management risk: If we can sell it, can we sell it at a profit?

5. The growth risk: If we can manage new product development, can we grow the company?

The Dimensions of a Business Evaluation

I've outlined the questions that a final business evaluation must ask and answer before a launch can be reasonably justified. The answers to these questions should be addressed in at least five dimensions:

➤ Market share

➤ Market attractiveness

➤ Product evaluation

➤ Cost forecast

➤ Sales forecast

Market Size

This subject will be explored in detail in Chapter 17. The size of the market for the product under consideration is obviously important and should be estimated as accurately as possible. Beware of mistaking an entire market for what is really a market segment or niche. Know what consumers you're targeting.

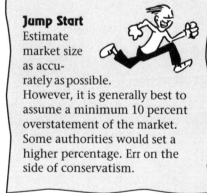

Jump Start
Estimate market size as accurately as possible. However, it is generally best to assume a minimum 10 percent overstatement of the market. Some authorities would set a higher percentage. Err on the side of conservatism.

Market Attractiveness

Market size is important, but it's rarely an eternal figure. Relying exclusively on market size in making your business evaluation is like using a snapshot to judge how well Fred Astaire dances. It's a static picture of a point in time. What you really need is a movie. And that's where an assessment of market attractiveness comes in, since it is a dynamic measure of the market for a given product.

The subject of market attractiveness will be examined further in Chapter 17, but here are the overall factors to consider in estimating market attractiveness for a final business evaluation:

➤ *Growth rate.* Size is valid for a moment in time. But what will future moments bring? It's bad enough to miss an opportunity because the market looked too small at Moment A and you failed to anticipate growth when Moment G rolled around, but it can be downright disastrous to plunge ahead with a new product and gear up production for the market as it appears at Moment A, having failed to anticipate how it would shrivel by Moment G.

➤ *Stage of the market's life cycle.* Is the market in a growth stage, a shrinking stage, or at a plateau?

➤ *Diversity of the market.* A more diverse market gives you the opportunity to precisely target various segments of the market.

➤ *Cyclical demand.* Is the market cyclical or seasonal?

Buzzword
Demand for a product is said to be *cyclical* when it rises and falls in recognizable, predictable patterns not necessarily tied to seasons.

Jump Start
Rarely do major new product concepts meet or beat the cost target that is set early in the development process. You can reduce the variance between the forecast and the actual cost by thoroughly and frequently reestimating throughout the development process.

These are the principal size-related components of market attractiveness. Beyond these, the BE should address such factors as the "captivity" of customers, the concentration of customers, competition, industry profitability, social and political factors, and technological factors. All of these will be discussed in the next chapter.

Product Evaluation

The business evaluation should present a finalized version of the feasibility assessment described in Chapter 12. In addition, the final BE should give details on specs, features, and benefits, with a justification (usually based on some form of testing) for all of these product dimensions. The BE must clearly state the product objectives and how these can be met.

Cost Forecast

The most meaningful figure the final business evaluation aims at in calculating the cost of developing and manufacturing a product is the unit cost. It's meaningful because it is cost relative to the volume of units produced during a given period. Chapter 17 includes guidelines for forecasting costs.

Sales Forecast

This dimension is explored in chapters 17 and 18, where you'll find three techniques to make estimating easier:

➤ *The top-down approach.* This is the most comprehensive approach, and it attempts to arrive at the "total company demand" for the product. This figure represents the *total industry volume* that would be *bought* by a *defined customer group* in a *defined geographical area* in a *defined time period* in a *defined market environment* under a *defined marketing program* that results in a *defined market share*. It's a rigorous method that depends on having a great deal of information.

➤ *The bottom-up approach.* This is the most common and conceptually simplest approach—although it can require a lot of legwork. It is a grass-roots forecast based on a detailed actual count of prospective customers who meet a certain set of defined criteria.

➤ *The cross-sectional analysis.* This approach collects sales data on existing products that provide customer benefits similar (or analogous) to those of the proposed product, but in totally unrelated categories. For example, let's say that you were proposing a new kind of portable weed trimmer. You might include in your final business evaluation sales forecast data on such existing products as chain saws and portable water pumps, which (as you see it) share certain key attributes with your proposed product and, therefore, are predictive of potential sales. (All are home maintenance products used outdoors, used fairly infrequently, have no adequate technological substitutes, retail for under $200, require little service, are highly durable, and work fast.)

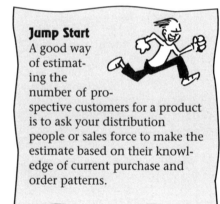

Jump Start
A good way of estimating the number of prospective customers for a product is to ask your distribution people or sales force to make the estimate based on their knowledge of current purchase and order patterns.

GIGO

The analytical tools that are used to make predictions and estimates throughout the new-product development process and that come together in this pre-launch final business evaluation are both complex and seductive. Their very complexity *makes* them seductive: Something this fancy has *got* to be right!

This is the kind of thinking you frequently heard expressed back in the days when computers were not commonplace objects on every desktop, but big clusters of consoles in air-conditioned "clean rooms" manned (and they were *always* men) by guys with short-sleeve white shirts and plastic pocket protectors. Whatever analysis "The Computer" spat out must be right. After all, it had lights, spoke in tongues only specialists could understand, and required air conditioning to do its work!

But when the figures turned out to be all wrong and the forecast way off, those short-sleeved guys would reply to any complaint with a muttered acronym: GIGO. It stands for *Garbage In, Garbage Out.*

Sophisticated analytical tools are only as good as the intelligence and hard work that go into gathering the raw data. A forecast is only as good as the data on which it is based. And, usually, smarts and legwork aren't enough. A liberal dose of imagination and common sense are also essential when forecasting the market for a proposed product.

The Least You Need to Know

> ➤ The final business review is a full presentation of the rewards and risks of developing the proposed new product.

> ➤ The BE addresses the product, the company, and the market.

> ➤ Make sure you can answer these three questions: Is the product real? Can you win with the product? Is the product worth the effort of developing?

To Market, To Market...

Throughout much of this book, I've been talking about markets and estimating market size and market demand and market potential. I've reviewed a variety of tools and measures for gauging the number of potential buyers for a new product. By the time you've reached the "Is it worth it?" stage of your evaluation, major expenditures hang in the balance, and it suddenly becomes important to be able to make more than a back-of-the-envelope estimate of market potential. This chapter provides a closer look at some of the tools and techniques you need to complete your final business evaluation prior to launch.

How Big Is It?

Earlier in this book, I suggested methods for making preliminary estimates of market size. You'll find these discussed in chapters 9 through 13. If, as is often the case, you have a working familiarity with the intended market for your product, you can plunge right in with a top-down, bottom-up, or cross-sectional market size estimate. You might also consider using some combination of these methods. However, if you're innovating in a market that is new to your company, you might want to begin your size estimate by defining the boundaries of the size of your target market. You can do this by consulting U.S. Department of Commerce statistics on annual factory sales of the business category within which the new product would compete. Usually, you need to determine the SIC code for your target industry, then look up the statistics by the appropriate code.

Buzzword
SIC code—Standard Industrial Classification code—is a system that breaks business activity into a defined and number-coded set of industrial segments organized by major divisions, industry groups, subgroups, and, finally, specific industries.

Another approach to zeroing in on unfamiliar markets is to estimate the number of ultimate potential customers and an annual penetration or usage rate.

If a business is related to certain types of consumers, Census Bureau data can be used to begin to gauge the size of the market. Private consumer polling organizations, such as A.C. Nielson Company, can furnish segment statistics on households and consumers, allowing you to focus on very specific demographic groups. Penetration rates can then be estimated by historical growth of categories of products similar to yours. For consumable products or for services, annual usage can be projected based on the frequency of use of similar or analogous items. Good data can often be found in the relevant trade publications.

Buzzword
Penetration is the degree to which a product is sold or recognized in a particular market.

Use the Internet to access the entire *SIC Index:*

www.wave.net/upg/immigration/sic_index.html

Or try:

edgar.stern.nyu.edu/sic.html

Prototype

A company was considering developing an automotive accessory product for older consumers living in urban areas. The product would offer benefits related to safety and protection, but it would not be *essential* for the operation of an automobile. A check of *Merchandising Week,* a retailing trade journal, indicated current annual sales of safety items as follows: smoke detectors, $153 million; CB radios, $283 million; auto radar detection, $68 million; and home security systems, $94 million. A further check of what might be considered nonessential consumer equipment products showed the following volumes: circular saws, $59 million; toaster ovens, $58 million; floor polishers, $23 million; and trash compactors, $72 million.

Commerce Department and Census Bureau data indicated that the total number of persons 40 years or older living in urban areas and owning automobiles was 7.4 million. If half of these people owned the product and replaced it every 10 years (at $79 each), a mature market would be $29 million annually (100 percent target market ownership would equal a $58 million annual market). A quick evaluation based on this information would indicate that the ultimate market size was probably somewhere between $10 million and $50 million and would grow at a rate proportionate to automobile sales and the 40 and older population segment.

What About Non-Consumer Markets?

If you're planning to develop a new product or service in a non-consumer (business-to-business, professional) market with which you are unfamiliar, you can use a size-estimating approach similar to what is used with consumer products:

1. Define the primary target market in demographic terms—age, income, place of residence, occupation, and so on, if you're developing a consumer product; SIC codes, volumes of business, number of employees, geographic location, if you're developing a non-consumer (industrial, professional, business-to-business) product.

2. Estimate the percentage of the target market likely to eventually own or use the product or service.

3. Estimate a product life, if it is a durable product, or the annual usage rate per user, if it is a consumable or a service.

4. Estimate a market share factor based on the uniqueness of the product and the degree of competition in the market.

5. Check your estimates against the annual market size of similar or analogous product categories, services, or industries.

Prototype

A company intends to establish a network of diagnostic radiology centers in 25 leading markets. A rough approximation of the market potential is estimated by multiplying the number of radiologists times their average annual gross income. A telephone call to the American Society of Radiologists indicates that there are 18,000 radiologists at an average annual income of $100,000, or a $1.8 billion annual market. A check of census data reveals that the 25 target cities represent 60 percent of the population, or $1.1 billion. Based on the uniqueness of product features and benefits, the company thinks its concept could capture at least a 10 percent market share, resulting in about $100 million in annual revenues.

(Note that this is only a start. For the final business evaluation, this company would want the support of up-to-date research on demographic usage of radiology and segments of providers—such as university hospitals—with their own equipment. Direct personal interviews with radiologists would also be part of the BE estimate.)

Top-Down

In the previous chapter, I mentioned three methods for refining market size estimates into volume estimates. The most comprehensive method is the top-down approach, which segments the "total potential"—the gross market size estimate—to arrive at "company market demand." At its most thorough, the top-down method determines company market demand for a *product* as

> The *total industry volume* that would be bought by a defined *customer group* in a defined *geographic area* in a defined *time period* in a defined *market environment* under a defined *marketing program*, resulting in a defined *market share*.

Here's how top-down forecasting might work if approached geographically. Demand for a new pharmaceutical could be projected as:

Buzzword
Buying power is disposable income factored by retail sales factored by population.

The *national market* for the product category (×) the *percentage of total national buying power* in target markets (×) the *percentage of retail sales* accounted for by target distribution channels or stores (drug stores only—no grocery, convenience, or department stores) (×) company estimated share of store volume (taking into account existing brands) (=) *demand* for a new pharmaceutical.

An alternative to the geographical approach is the category spending approach, in which (for example) demand for a new "light" beer could be estimated as:

Total *population* (×) personal *discretionary income* per capita (×) *average percentage* of discretionary income spent on *food* (×) *average percentage* of amount spent on food that is spent on *beverages* (×) *average percentage* of amount spent on beverages that is spent on *alcoholic beverages* (×) *average percentage* of amount spent on alcoholic beverages that is spent on *beer* (×) *expected percentage* of amount spent on beer that will be spent on *light beer* (=) *demand* for a new light beer.

Jump Start

If detailed category sales data is currently available, demand forecasts may be generated by segmenting the category volume by specific product attributes; for example, market demand for high-end hi-fi VCRs might be a function of total unit volume of all VCRs times percentage greater than $400 retail price times percentage of homeowners owning audio stereo systems greater than $600 retail.

Yet another approach to the top-down method is demographic segmentation. For example, demand for a new cross-country ski product might be estimated as:

Total *population of* persons of legal drinking age (×) *percentage* in the *snow belt* (×) *percentage* over *16* years old (×) *percentage* with *household income greater than $35,000* (×) *percentage* active in *outdoor sports* (×) *market share estimate* (=) *demand* for the product.

Bottom-Up

Bottom-up forecasting is highly important because, sooner or later, a prospective customer has to purchase the product. Forecasting from the bottom up is a grass-roots estimate of who will actually buy the product. It is an effective balance to the numbers yielded by top-down methods. The bottom-up approach also helps generate a sales plan and, because sales personnel are usually used to gather information, it gets the sales force involved in the new product and committed to it early on. Bottom-up forecasting is conceptually quite simple, although it can take a good deal of legwork. For example:

➤ An industrial machine company directly asks 1,500 manufacturers about their buying interest in a new piece of machinery.

➤ A lathe manufacturer asks its distributors to project sales of a new model by customer within an SIC code.

➤ A garden tool manufacturer asks its key retail customers how many units of a new line they would stock and what kind of turnover rate they expect.

Cross-Section

Cross-sectional analysis substitutes detective work for legwork. In this method, sales data is collected for products that provide customer benefits similar to what the new product is to provide, but in totally unrelated categories. I've given an example of this method in Chapter 16, in the section titled "Sales Forecast." The hard work is deciding which current products will provide an accurately predictive analogy to the new product, and, of course, one must also be able to obtain the data on the analogous products. Yet even if such data is not available, you can still use the cross-sectional technique by preparing panel group research. A number of firms—including National Family Opinion Poll, Datagauge by Market Facts, and others—can prepare a usage questionnaire targeted on your proposed product as well as analogous products and send them to the consumer panel members they maintain.

Jump Start
About new product sales forecasting: In general, do it, but don't believe it.

Can You Trust It?

How reliable are forecasts based on the techniques just discussed? The best answer is that they are better than no forecast at all. The more history you can draw on, using actual sales of analogous products, the better. But this cannot be relied upon alone. Cross-sectional analysis should be balanced by top-down or bottom-up estimates—or both. Then you ought to heft in a very substantial grain of salt. The big danger is that forecasting errors tend to compound with each layer of assumptions you lay on, as each layer introduces its own +/– percentage of variance.

Is the Market Attractive Enough?

Market size is important, but it isn't the only factor that figures in assessing the attractiveness of a market. Remember, size is a snapshot, but the *real* market is a *moving* target.

Growth

The growth rate of a category can be estimated on the basis of

➤ Industry projections

➤ Growth of similar categories

➤ Historical data for similar or analogous products

You can venture beyond these simple methods by using a "chained relationship" thought process. This is a challenging procedure that attempts to link various market facts and consumer demographics into a profile of the target market for the new product. Based on this profile, growth can be more accurately predicted.

Prototype

A few years ago, a company wanted to bring out a new line of easily assembled case furniture with European styling. To estimate market size, the following chained relationships were considered:

1. 35-to-44-year-olds make up the fastest-growing population segment, having increased 38 percent from 1983 to 1993.

2. This age group is the greatest purchasing segment of household furnishings.

3. The build-it-yourself industry has grown generally by 10 percent during the preceding ten years.

4. Houses were continuing to get smaller, because of cost and affordability factors.

5. The "European look" had been a steady trend in contemporary home furnishings during the preceding five years.

The chained relationships suggested that the market potential for the company's line should grow at 8 to 10 percent, largely on the analogy with the build-it-yourself industry and the sharp growth in the target population segment.

Looking at Other Market Factors

Growth is not the only determinant of a market's attractiveness. Consider the following:

➤ The market's diversity provides opportunities to segment the market, which means that such elements as packaging, optional features, advertising, and so on can be more precisely targeted in order to capture more of each segment. On the other hand, a highly diverse market may pose an excessive number of challenges to capturing buyers with a single product.

➤ Growth is not always one-dimensional, up or down; a market may be cyclical, with periods of growth followed by periods of shrinking.

➤ Some markets are seasonal. It's important for the developer of a new product to understand the impact of season on the market for the proposed product.

➤ Some products lend themselves to functional substitution, while others do not. For example, the market for electric toothbrushes will be limited as long as most people feel they can *substitute* the plain old "hand-operated" toothbrush. However, gas-powered non-riding mowers are less subject to functional substitution: electric mowers tend to be less powerful; the range of corded electric mowers is limited by the cord; the battery of a cordless electric mower soon runs down and must be recharged; non-power mowers are impractical for larger lawns; riding mowers are practical only for very large lawns. Conclusion: There are no viable substitutes.

➤ Some products tend to command a captive customer base. For example, customers who own a brand of personal computer that requires proprietary accessories are captive to new accessory products for that type of computer—unless they wish to make an investment in an entirely different system.

What Does It Sell For?

Pricing is typically a subject of hot debate prior to a new product launch. The dilemma couldn't be simpler or scarier: If you price the product too low, you lose money. If you price it too high, the sales just aren't made.

There are two principal strategies for pricing:

➤ *Penetration pricing* puts an aggressive, must-buy price tag on the new product. This should generate maximum initial sales, which will lower per-unit costs by allowing high-volume production to meet increased demand. Penetration pricing is a good way to capture a large share of the market and thereby either outdistance or pre-empt competition. However, the danger here is that you may never realize a workable margin per unit. Worse, pricing too low is not an easy mistake to correct. While you can always reduce a high price, consumers are not receptive to increasing an initial price.

Buzzword
Skimming is a pricing strategy that sets the initial price of a new product high in order to establish high perceived value for the product. Later, the price may be reduced to promote wider sales.

➤ *Skimming* sets the initial price high. Only the most motivated buyers—the "purchase leaders"—will buy, so sales may be modest. Over time, however, the price can be reduced, thereby motivating more purchases. Why skim? Selling at a high initial price establishes the perception of high value among consumers. Subsequent price reductions make the product seem like a bargain.

Which strategy is better? The answer depends on the nature of your new product. If the new product is unique and clearly superior to the competition's, a significant number of consumers will be willing to pay a premium for it, and a skimming strategy may succeed. If the product is not unique and faces strong competition, penetration is usually a better way to go.

In the next section, I'll talk about calculating the *cost* of the product—and, of course, cost is important in setting the price. In fact, traditionally, a company projected how much it would cost to produce the product, added an acceptable profit margin, and,

Jump Start
A variation on penetration pricing is the special introductory price. The product is introduced at a low price up to a stated deadline, after which a higher price is put in place.

voilà, came up with the product's retail price. But there's a better way to set a new product price. "Value-based pricing" is a strategy that uses the value *consumers* place on the product as the primary guide to pricing. Remarkably enough, this figure has little direct relationship to manufacturing cost. If consumers perceive the new product as something they need and that provides benefits no other product provides (or provides as well), they will value the product highly. If, however, you find that consumers do not value the product highly enough to allow you to meet costs and make a profit, you cannot simply revert to the cost-plus-margin strategy. Either you have to redesign the product and/or reconfigure the promotion, or you take consumer valuation as a final kill signal and go on to develop something else.

Obtaining the data on which to base your value price should be an objective of whatever market research you do. Once you have enough data to set this figure, factor in an estimate of sales volume based on a range of price points. *Then* factor in manufacturing and other costs, based on a corresponding range of production volume. The object is to balance the value price, the market size at a given price point, and the unit manufacturing cost at a corresponding production volume in order to net the highest level of profit.

Calculating Costs

The cost of creating and manufacturing a new product includes overhead costs as well as direct costs. *Overhead* includes the cost of facilities and equipment you already own insofar as they become dedicated to developing and manufacturing the new product. This includes, for example, the amount of hours your salaried in-house R&D, marketing, and production staff devote to the new product. Direct costs include outside consultants, testing, and the actual materials that go into the manufacture of the product.

Estimating the cost of materials for the final business evaluation can be tricky. The most efficient way to proceed is to develop a preliminary bill of material (a PBOM), which is an informed forecast of just what parts will be needed for the new product. Creating a PBOM should begin as early as possible in the product-development process and should be repeatedly refined and carried into the final business evaluation. The PBOM typically involves four steps:

1. An overview of the product's assembly structure is laid out. This shows the basic assemblies and subassemblies.

2. Once the necessary assemblies and subassemblies are determined, each is broken down into its component parts—as far as this can be determined at each evaluation stage.

3. The PBOM should be updated continuously, right through to the final BE.

4. The PBOM at the stage of the final BE—just prior to a production go/kill decision—should be made very accurately and in great detail.

With each iteration of the PBOM, parts costs should be loaded into the document. Components of cost include:

➤ Purchase of parts

➤ Cost of raw materials

➤ Direct labor costs

➤ Time required for various processes (machining, heat treating, etc.)

As the PBOM develops so that parts required become finalized and specific, costs associated with each part should be nailed down precisely.

Sizing Up the Competition

In developing the new product, you ignore competition at your peril—especially during the early stages of concept development. A consideration of competition should figure relatively late in the game, too, and should be a part of the final BE. (Review chapters 8 and 12 for research methods you can use to size up your competition.) In the final business evaluation, you should be able to make an intelligent forecast of the market share the new product will capture relative to the market share held by your competitors.

Considering the Climate

Often overlooked in the final business review are social and political factors that may impinge—negatively or positively—on consumer reception of the new product. Be certain that you have considered:

➤ Relevant social attitudes and trends

➤ Government regulatory factors

Prototype

Failure to understand regulatory factors can be disastrous. For example, you'd think that government regulations would have little or no impact on creating, say, a new peripheral product for a personal computer. After all, it's non-polluting and non-hazardous. On the contrary. In the U.S., the peripheral manufacturer must obtain FCC (Federal Communications Commission) certification of its product in order to ensure that the electrical signals it produces will not interfere with assigned and protected radio, TV, and other communications frequencies. Obtaining the certification adds cost—and time!—to the development process.

The Tech Scene

Technical feasibility must be established early in the development process. Relevant technical factors should be stated in finalized—albeit digested—form in the final BE, with special attention paid to:

➤ Patent issues—which will be considered in Chapter 19.

➤ Technology position—especially the proprietary advantages the new product will create. Will the new product offer a technology that no other manufacturer offers and that, therefore, will capture consumers?

The Final Fit

The final business evaluation may conclude by making the case that the new product *fits* the company. Any good tailor knows that a suit should fit the body overall, but a *great* tailor knows just where the fit counts most. For the final BE, pay special attention to these critical areas:

➤ *Fit with current markets*. Product extensions are usually easier to justify than new products that grope for entirely new markets.

➤ *Fit with distribution*. Demonstrate either how your current distribution network can handle the new product or what needs to be done to that network to enable it to handle the new product.

➤ *Fit with company image and identity in the market*. It's easier to justify a new product that is strongly related to the company's identity and image. If Ford Motor Company starts trying to sell wristwatches, stunned consumers may well ask what business Ford has making such products.

➤ *Fit with technological expertise.* Ford is good at making cars, knows nothing about wristwatches, and probably will never develop and manufacture them. The final BE should demonstrate how the new product is suited to the company's established expertise.

➤ *Fit with production capability.* Either show how the company is currently well positioned to produce the product, or prove that retooling will be worth the effort and expense.

➤ *Fit with materials availability.* Will the raw materials required for production be readily—and dependably—available? Do we know how to get them?

➤ *Fit with vertical integration.* Show how the product leverages company strengths. For example, you are an IC (integrated circuit)—"chip"—maker. The new product you propose is a personal computer. The vertical integration here is obvious, since you already have the capacity to produce the "heart" of the computer, whereas most PC manufacturers have to rely on outside suppliers for their chips.

Jump Start

Sometimes products that radically depart from an established corporate image can reinvigorate that image and attract special attention. When it introduced its PC in the early 1980s, IBM saturated TV and print media with ads featuring—of all things—Charlie Chaplin's famous "Little Tramp." The antithesis of Big Blue's monolithic corporate image, the Little Tramp successfully launched a radical new product.

The Least You Need to Know

➤ Market estimates usually overstate market size. Avoid this by using more than one estimating method.

➤ An estimate of market *size* is a snapshot, whereas an estimate of market *growth* is a motion picture. Don't neglect to factor in other aspects of market attractiveness as well.

➤ Set price strategically by deciding whether *skimming* or *penetration pricing* is more appropriate to the product. Don't let product cost alone determine price.

Chapter 18

Distribution, Distribution, Distribution

> ## In This Chapter
>
> ➤ Finding the right distribution channel
>
> ➤ Distribution as innovation
>
> ➤ Your first "customer"—the distributor
>
> ➤ Analyzing available distribution channels

Remember Ralph Waldo Emerson's misguided advice to would-be inventors? *Build a better mousetrap, and the world will beat a path to your door.*

Great philosopher. Lousy marketer.

Emerson's advice works no better for the inventor than it does for those who are responsible for launching a new product. The fact is, customers don't beat a path to *your* door. If you have created a killer product, they will beat a path to the door of some distributor: a retailer, a value-added reseller, a warehouse operator, a wholesaler, a direct marketer—someone.

Before you can reach the customer—the end user—you have to get to and into the distribution channel. And *that* can make or break your new product.

Who Ya Gonna Sell It To?

You have more customers than you think. Sure, there are the thousands, tens of thousands, maybe millions of folks "out there" who may be willing to separate themselves from their cash for your benefit. But the first customers you must excite about your new product are those who operate the distribution channel. This has always been true, but, today, in many industries, distributors are more powerful than ever. The chain "superstore"—whether it deals in general merchandise (Wal-Mart, etc.), home improvement goods (Home Depot, etc.), toys (Toys "R" Us, etc.), computers and software (CompUSA, etc.), or consumer electronics (Circuit City, etc.)—has come to dominate one retail category after another. In the realm of packaged goods, the great supermarket chains are now so powerful that they can demand—and get—"slotting fees" from manufacturers in return for granting them shelf space. (You pay *me* to carry *your* product. What a deal.)

Jump Start
To reach your customers, you must first sell into the appropriate distribution channel.

Now, here's the trick: You have to match up the distribution channel with what you know about your target customer. Let's say you've developed a line of high-end radio-controlled model airplanes, with price tags ranging anywhere from $300 to over $1,000. You look at the superstores—Toys "R" Us paramount among them—and you think: *Wow! If I could only get distribution like this!*

But there's a problem. The superstores do stock some radio-controlled model airplanes, but the top price is $175. Now, you could go to the buyer responsible for the department that handles radio-controlled models and try to convince him that now is a great time for the superstores to start carrying $300-and-up models. Unfortunately, this tactic won't work.

And it shouldn't. It's not that the buyer is being rigid or obstinate, but that he understands who his customers are: mass-market toy shoppers. High-end radio-controlled model airplanes appeal to more sophisticated, more motivated, more focused consumers: hard-core enthusiasts (generally men, whose obsession imperils their marriages). These folks don't go to *any* toy store—let alone a superstore—to buy their models. The appropriate distribution channel for the high-end remote-controlled model is through hobby shops and, perhaps, direct-mail catalogs that are targeted specifically at hobbyists. Of course, no hobby shop has the reach or commands the traffic of a superstore. But you don't need a gazillion shoppers who have no interest in your product. What you need is a far, far smaller number who *are* motivated to buy what you're selling.

Innovating through Distribution

Marketing is like life. For just about every rule there is an exception. Sometimes it's a *good* idea to venture outside of what seems like the "appropriate" or "traditional" distribution channel. In fact, doing so can sometimes be a product innovation in itself. Earlier in the book, I cited the example of L'eggs, which took pantyhose out of the department store hosiery department and put them in the supermarket. At first thought, this may seem even more far-fetched than trying to market a $500 radio-controlled model airplane in a mass-market toy store. But there is method to the L'eggs madness. Sure, a supermarket *looks* like a very different place from a hosiery department, but:

➤ Women are the most frequent shoppers in department stores as well as supermarkets.

➤ Pantyhose are not very durable. Indeed, they wear out so quickly that they are just about as "consumable" as food. And no one would argue about food belonging in a supermarket.

➤ The price point of pantyhose is compatible with grocery price points.

➤ Packaged like food—eggs—the product is made very cleverly to fit into the super-market environment.

➤ Considering the packaging and the product, the name is perfect—and it suits the supermarket context.

The point is this: If you have a good reason to push the envelope and innovate in the area of distribution, build your case and take your shot.

And How Ya Gonna Reach 'Em?

Let's look at the options for formulating a channel strategy. Each distribution channel has advantages and disadvantages for new products.

Department Stores

Distributing through department store chains gets you national exposure with cost-effective centralized buying. Advertising is usually extensive and well developed, and you may have cooperative advertising possibilities. In addition, the chains offer extensive customer credit, are conveniently located, and often command considerable customer loyalty.

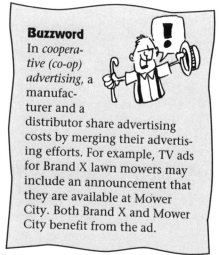

Buzzword

In *cooperative (co-op) advertising*, a manufacturer and a distributor share advertising costs by merging their advertising efforts. For example, TV ads for Brand X lawn mowers may include an announcement that they are available at Mower City. Both Brand X and Mower City benefit from the ad.

Merchandise is typically displayed to maximum advantage. There are also drawbacks, however.

Chains tend to be slow and cautious to add or change merchandise lines. ("Slow" and "cautious" are two words a product innovator never wants to hear.) Moreover, they tend to subject products to extensive testing—which may actually help you tweak a product and its promotion, but which also makes the adoption process slow and possibly painful. With computerized inventory procedures, new products are often put on a strict "probation period." If certain volume quotas are not reached within a specified time, the chain's computers will nix reorders—and they will do this with literally an absence of human kindness.

Discount Department Stores

Over the past twenty or even thirty years, this distribution channel has assumed increasing importance. For many products, Kmarts, Wal-Marts, Targets, and similar discount chain stores are the dominant means of distribution. The biggest advantage to you is the sheer volume of merchandise these behemoths can move. Second to this is the discount factor. At lower prices, your product will penetrate the market more deeply and with greater speed. Advertising is typically aggressive, and coverage may be national or regional. And there is all that store traffic! Each day, thousands upon thousands of consumers will see your product.

The disadvantages of distributing through discount department stores are few, but significant: To begin with, this distribution channel pushes you to practice penetration pricing and precludes skimming (these are both discussed in the previous chapter). That's fine, if it suits your product. Just remember that, once you begin selling at a low price, it's almost impossible to raise the price. This also means that distributing through discount chains may inhibit or preclude distribution through other channels, which do not discount or do not discount as aggressively. Discounters also "cherry pick" extensively, going for the "hottest" and fastest-moving items in a line and passing up the rest. Demanding fast turnover, they are rarely willing to give a new product much time to develop market awareness.

Buzzword

Cherry picking is the distributor practice of choosing only certain items in a manufacturer's product line rather than carrying the entire line.

Specialty Outlet Stores

These include hardware, drug, appliance, sporting goods, automotive stores, and so on. Nowadays, specialty superstores abound and offer many of the same advantages as department stores and discount department stores with regard to centralized buying, national or regional coverage, and extensive advertising. Within their areas of specialty, they tend to look for the broadest possible selection, so it's relatively easy to get a trial for a new product. In many cases, salespeople are well trained and have considerable expertise in the store's specialty. This means that your product may benefit from enthusiastic and knowledgeable customer assistance. The benefit to you is accelerated market acceptance.

Although superstores offer discounts, many of the smaller specialty stores are expensive (*not* necessarily bad if you're using a skimming price strategy) and less conveniently located than the department and discount stores (though shopping malls have helped here). Customer traffic—except in superstores—tends to be relatively low, and, in smaller outlets, advertising support may be spotty or nonexistent.

Direct Marketing Distribution

This channel is a great way to test and develop customer interest. If you've done your targeting homework, you can contact only the best prospects, make your pitch to them, and get relatively quick momentum behind the new product. Geographic coverage is

unlimited, because you're using the mail or the telephone (or both), perhaps supplemented by PI advertising. Best of all, because you eliminate the traditional distribution middleman, you can make your margins fatter or your prices lower (and, therefore, your volume greater). You're also no longer at the mercy of retailers who are quick to pull the plug on new products that fail to gain immediate market acceptance.

Direct marketing does have its drawbacks: It can be costly to reach a large market, and startup costs are substantial, including such items as creating, printing, and mailing sales materials. More daunting is the fact that you're on your own—without retailer advertising to back you up—and the customer cannot walk into a store, see the product attractively displayed, and touch and feel it.

Buzzword
PI stands for "per inquiry," and *PI advertising* includes some means for a customer to respond directly to the advertiser. In print ads, this is usually a tear-out reply postcard. In TV ads, an 800 number is usually given.

Limited Distribution Channels

If you're selling non-consumer goods—industrial, professional, business-to-business products—your distribution channels are more limited. In fact, you have essentially two choices (and a third alternative).

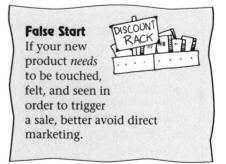

False Start
If your new product *needs* to be touched, felt, and seen in order to trigger a sale, better avoid direct marketing.

First, you can distribute factory-direct, using your own sales force—if you have a sales force. If you don't have one, you'll have to hire one, and that can be expensive.

Second, industrial distributors can provide your product with effective geographic coverage as well as coverage by SIC category, greatly extending your outreach. Some distributors add value to your product, such as local inventory and service, financing, installation service, and so on. An industrial distributor is a *distributor*, however, which means he'll want a bite out of your revenue. Depending on the market for your particular line of products, the distributor may be slow to adopt new merchandise or may adopt it without promoting it. If the distributor already carries a competitive line, it may be quite difficult to get him to adopt yours.

False Start
Don't assume that it's automatically easier to motivate an in-house sales force than, say, retail distributors. Where new products are concerned, it can sometimes be difficult to tear sales people away from their tried-and-true, bread-and-butter merchandise and get them to focus on the new items.

Jump Start
Some companies sell into multiple distribution channels and routes. For example—You have fifteen national accounts and an account with an industrial distributor. It's possible that the industrial distributor will sell your product or another product in your line to some of the fifteen national accounts you service.

Finally, there's a third route some industrial goods may take, especially those that function as components of systems (such as personal computer peripherals, add-on boards, hard drives, and so on). You might simply avoid the distribution function altogether and sell directly to another company or companies that perform the distribution, perhaps under their own label. Options include:

➤ Joint ventures—in which you partner with another firm; you make the product, and the other guy sells it

➤ OEM (original equipment manufacturer) programs—in which you supply components for another manufacturer's system (the Your Company hard drive that is included inside the Acme personal computer)

➤ Private branding programs—in which you manufacture a product to be branded with a (usually nationally known) label

➤ National account programs through one or a handful of distributors—in which you supply goods under contract

The advantage of OEM, private branding, and national account programs is the stability of relatively high-volume, long-term commitments. This takes a lot of the risk burden off of your shoulders. However, such arrangements tend to submerge your identity, screening you from consumers and end users. Not only does this reduce your distribution potential—should you ever decide to go it on your own—but it removes you from direct consumer feedback, which can be important in the evolution of a product. You also lose the ability to add value to the product through distribution, and you may soon find yourself overly dependent on one or a handful of accounts.

Selling the Distributor

Different as the various distribution channels are, they share at least one characteristic: All, in varying degrees, resist change. The innovation *you* see as a boon, the *distributor* may perceive as a problem. Professional buyers are trained and encouraged to be skeptical and suspicious. With time, many add the quality of apathy to the mix. In some organizations, you also have to contend with the sludge of an entrenched bureaucracy. For you, a new product means potential riches. For the distributor, it may mean setting up new stock numbers, scrambling to get the advertising department in gear, making a last-minute change in the catalog, arranging warehouse space, meeting with store managers, and so on. Why do all this if you're already hitting your monthly quotas?

Okay. Don't pull out the hemlock yet. My point is that buyers—in one key respect—are no different from consumers. Before you get anywhere with them, you've got to *sell* them.

Now, in *another* key respect, buyers *are* quite different from consumers. To consumers, you sell a *product*. To buyers, you sell, first and foremost, a *business opportunity*, not just product benefits, features, and technology. Appeal to the buyer by demonstrating how the product will draw large numbers of customers, why consumers will want the product—no, will *have* to have it. If you've got figures that show how other retailers or distributors have already increased their business and profit by selling your product, use this information to sell the present prospect.

In fact, convince the prospect that the risk is greater in *not* carrying than in carrying your product. And if others are not yet carrying your product, persuade this prospect that he's taking a grave risk if he fails to be the *first* to carry it.

Beyond an opportunity for raw profit, buyers look for:

➤ Product quality

➤ Competitive price

➤ Merchandising and advertising support

➤ Sales rep support

➤ Financial stability (A distributor doesn't want to commit to a line from a company that threatens to be a flickering bulb.)

False Start
Don't think that just because you have statistical "proof" that your product outperforms a competing product, a buyer will be swayed. Sometimes a buyer just has a gut feeling about a certain product and can't be budged.

➤ A full line (It's often more cost-effective for a distributor to offer a full line of related products than a single item. Full-line offerings leverage every aspect of the marketing effort, from display space to advertising, to repeat business.)

In addition, buyers typically report the following issues as decisive for them:

➤ The honesty and integrity of the salesperson is vital.

➤ Turnover is becoming increasingly important to distributors, who have come to fear slow-moving inventory more than denizens of the Dark Ages feared the Plague. If at all possible, sell the promise of rapid turnover.

Jump Start
Timing and seasonal stocking can also play a role in a buyer's purchase decision. For example—let's say you and a competitor are selling a similar toy. If your toy can be in the store by September, and your competitor can't get theirs ready until November, you are more than likely to get the sale because you can meet stocking levels for the holiday season.

Jump Start
Many retailers have "rules" about cooperative advertising, as to what products, when, and how they are promoted. Your sales or account representatives should be aware of each retailer's guidelines, if any.

➤ ROI is return on investment, and it's closely related to turnover. Increasingly, retail buyers are evaluated based on their department's ROI, which is linked not only to turnover, but to the product's attractiveness and its cost. Sell a high ROI.

➤ Linked to ROI is the product's available markup. This is not rocket science: The fatter the margin (difference between what you charge him and he charges his customers) you can offer a retailer or a wholesaler, the more eager he'll be to buy.

➤ Consumer advertising is always attractive to buyers.

➤ Co-op advertising can be important to many retailers.

➤ The availability of factory displays—special counter displays, dumps, and the like—can be attractive to buyers for certain products. However, retailers sometimes spurn display offers because they're unwilling to devote valuable store "real estate" to a big aisle display.

➤ Most buyers are impressed by good support material, such as brochures and other helpful literature.

➤ Finally, there's the old-fashioned virtue of company reputation. Buyers know that consumers value this highly.

Old Channels or New?

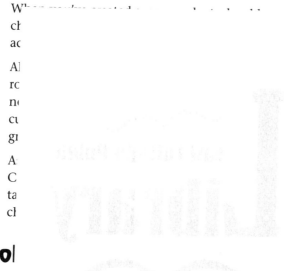

W   :o sell it through the same *old*
cl   you time and lowers your costs. In
ac

Al   mpatible with the new product—a
rc   nnels of distribution tailored to the
n   e, and you risk alienating your
cι   e you need it, you risk something far
gı

A   often the most attractive alternative.
C   ent distribution channel, but set a
ta   fall short of the target, secure new
cl

Loo| |on Channel Analysis

B   product? Well, you do something
tl   el analysis. Actually, this mouthful
st   ɔns you should have been asking all
al   *customers:*

ırs?

;?

what types?

purchase decision is made?

➤ How many competitive products do they consider?

➤ *How* much information do they need to motivate a decision?

➤ *How* important is product demonstration to making the decision?

➤ *How* important is retailer service?

➤ *How* important is location convenience?

➤ *How* important is delivery and installation service?

➤ *How* important is general service and support?

➤ *How* important is availability of financing?

➤ *How* important are accessories and options?

➤ *How* important are retailer guarantee, reputation, and credibility?

Answer these questions, and you'll have a profile of the ideal distribution channel for your product. Perhaps the answers have already emerged as part of your market research. If not, consider doing quantitative research now to profile your target customers.

The customer's perspective is only half of the distribution picture. You also need to understand the current structure of your industry in terms of the channels that exist within the industry. Often, these channels are complex, with various progressions and branches. You need to determine at what point—or points—your product should enter the distribution stream.

Choose the Right Way

Once you identify target customer shopping habits and needs, and you've come to an understanding of the existing structure of distribution channels within the industry, you can arrive at a distribution strategy that is most appropriate to your product. Think in terms of five dimensions:

1. *Profit/volume objectives:* You may set high-volume goals for a new product, and attaining them will probably require broad distribution across more than one channel. At the other end of the spectrum, your premium, high-end, or niche product should be distributed through intensely focused specialty channels.

2. *Geographic objectives:* If it's important to gain quick national exposure, you'll need to concentrate on chain stores. However, depending on the product, another approach is to "hand-sell," store by store, buyer by buyer, to achieve local and regional penetration first.

3. *Timing:* If you're under high ROI pressure and must meet formidable sales goals in year one, you'll need to get aggressive. Consider a blitz of chain stores, but make certain they don't bog you down in the inertia of a buyer's bureaucracy that will cost you time.

4. *Market share:* If you want dominance in the market or market segment, you'll need to operate like Napoleon, attacking and displacing competitors. A kinder, gentler approach is more appropriate for products that appeal to a small but unique position in the product category. In this case, approach distribution channels and retail outlets that don't currently handle the category. Carve out a niche.

5. *Product risk:* You may actually want to *restrict* distribution in the case of products that are so new that they represent a high risk of consumer rejection. The market may need to catch up with technology, or you may be uncertain of market

acceptance. In this case, initial distribution may be concentrated in a relatively small market, which you can "coddle" with extra customer support and assistance. Once the product "catches on" here, you'll be ready to supply a broader array of retailers—and *they* will be more receptive to you as well.

Prototype

The computer modem is a marvelous invention that allows computers to communicate with one another and gives individuals and companies access to a vast store of information. Despite all that a modem can do, it's a compromise. Its purpose is to translate the digital data computers generate and use into the analog (audible sound) data the current telephone communications system can transmit, and then to translate the analog data back into digital form. Although modems have become capable of increasingly rapid transmission speeds, there is a practical limit to what analog phone lines can handle. Normally, that's about 28,800 to 33,600 bits per second (bps)—though special software can push this somewhat higher, to 56,000 bps. A number of modem manufacturers are beginning to market ISDN (Integrated Services Digital Network) modems, which make use of newer digital telecommunications networks and have pushed speeds to 128,000 bps. This is a great advance in data communications; however, until recently, ISDN modems have been deliberately restricted in distribution because the ISDN telecommunications technology is still limited in its availability and requires a substantial investment in the installation of ISDN lines. Doubtless, the market for ISDN modems will be huge—as soon as the telecommunications infrastructure catches up with the product.

The final word here is to balance realistic expectations with a willingness to innovate, not only in the area of product development proper, but in distribution as well. Remain flexible to compromise approaches that start out through traditional and time-tested channels, but move on to uncharted territory if necessary.

The Least You Need to Know

➤ Think of the distributor(s) as your first customer(s). Do not stint on efforts to sell the distributor(s) on your product.

➤ A distribution channel strategy should be formulated early in the product development process.

➤ Devote careful thought and, if necessary, study to selecting the right distributors for your product. Distribution is the connection to your customer.

Part 5
Made in the Shade

The creators of new products are sometimes accused of having their heads in the clouds. That's not necessarily a bad thing, as long as somebody's watching out for you from the neck down. Here are four chapters that deal with the nitty-grittiest issues of developing new products: protecting your intellectual property with patents, copyrights, and trademarks; finding money to develop and market your new product; and ensuring that the product will embody the high degree of quality that, when all is said and done, is the principal source of new product success.

The Fine Print

Folks who have front porches and who are inclined to sit out on them, rocking on the high-backed rocker, maybe whittling away on a nice piece of white pine, like to talk about the good old days, when everybody would leave their front door unlocked.

"Can't do that anymore!" says a whittler.

"Ay-yup," responds his rocking friend.

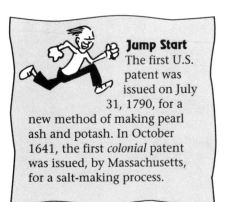

Maybe things were different once. Maybe not. But one thing is for sure: Nowadays you lock up your property. And what's true of your personal property should be true of your *intellectual* property as well. But this is really nothing new. Inventors and manufacturers have been locking up their intellectual property with patents since at least 1421, when history's first recorded patent for an industrial invention was granted in Florence to the architect and engineer Filippo Brunelleschi. The idea of patents is not new, and this chapter will talk about how you fit into this long and glorious history.

Talk to My Lawyers, Not Me

The first question most people have about patents is *Do I need a lawyer?* And because that's the first question, I'll discuss it before I even say anything about just what a patent is.

Do you need a lawyer?

There is no law in the United States requiring you to use an attorney to secure a valid patent. In fact, the patent office is required by its own regulations to give specific assistance to those who bring to them *pro se* (no lawyer) cases. The law notwithstanding, the fact is that if you're working as part of a corporation of any size, over which you do not have complete control, you will almost certainly be required to use the services of a patent attorney. *Really* big companies retain one or more patent attorneys on staff. But if you are a private inventor or you operate a closely held, small company, you may file a perfectly good patent on your own.

But should you?

The principal reason for doing it yourself is to save costs. If that's important to you, you may want to invest a modest sum in such books as David Pressman's *Patent It Yourself,* 4th Edition (Nolo Press, 1995) and do it yourself.

Just remember that *cost* is not solely a function of cash spent. Preparing a patent application takes time and effort. You must be able to accomplish the following:

➤ Prepare a full, clear, and accurate description of the invention. This document tells how the invention is made and how it is used.

➤ Do an effective patent search to ensure that your invention doesn't already exist.

➤ Sell—that's right, *sell*—the PTO on the advantages of your invention. You cannot patent something that is worthless.

Even if you can afford to invest the time and effort, consider the cost of a significant error, which ranges from patent infringement litigation against you to filing an imperfect patent that is insufficiently broad to give you adequate protection.

Now, if you have decided to use a patent attorney, does that mean you should skip this chapter?

Nope.

Buzzword
The official name of the patent office is the *Patent and Trademark Office*, or *PTO*.

Just as the chapters on market research are intended to help you do your own research or work more effectively with consultants, so this chapter is useful even if you leave most of the work in professional legal hands. As usual, too, there is a compromise course. You may decide to do a certain amount of the work yourself—say, the patent search and perhaps the first draft of the description—then have a lawyer finish the job and double-check it.

Ins and Outs of Patents

A patent is a right granted by the U.S. government to an individual or a legal entity (usually a corporation). This is a right to *exclude* others from making, using, or selling the invention that is "claimed" in the "patent deed" for a certain period defined by statute. The patent gives you what lawyers (in their charmingly poetic way) call "offensive rights," chiefly the right to enforce exclusion by filing a patent infringement lawsuit in federal court.

Anyone can apply for a patent—including non-U.S. citizens and foreign corporations—as long as he or she is the true inventor of the invention. A legal entity, such as a corporation, can also apply. Although it covers a form of intellectual property, the patent itself becomes an article of personal property and can be sold outright or licensed in return for royalty payments.

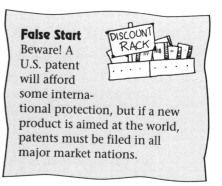

False Start
Beware! A U.S. patent will afford some international protection, but if a new product is aimed at the world, patents must be filed in all major market nations.

The PTO recognizes three broad categories of patents:

1. *Utility patent:* This, the principal type of patent, covers inventions that function in some unique manner to produce a useful result. These patents cover just about anything a human being can make, from apple corers to zippers. Until recently, a utility patent was granted for a period of seventeen years. For patents filed as of June 7, 1995 (and later), the period of coverage is twenty years.

2. *Design patent:* This applies to the unique visible shape or design of an object, provided that the unique shape is purely ornamental or aesthetic. If the shape is utilitarian, then a utility patent must be secured. Design patents are good for fourteen years.

3. *Plant patent:* You can use this to protect your right to a unique asexually reproducible plant (that is, a plant that is produced by means of grafting or cuttings). (Other laws and PTO regulations allow monopolization of sexually reproducible plants, too.) Plant patents are granted for the same duration as utility patents.

Jump Start
To keep a utility or plant patent in force for its full duration, you must pay three "maintenance fees": at 3 ½ years after issuance, at 7 ½ years after issuance, and at 11 ½ years after issuance. Design patents require no maintenance fees.

While just about anything is *potentially* patentable, it is the adverb "potentially" that carries all the weight. In the case of all three types of patents, the patent examiner, before he or she will authorize a patent, must conclude that:

➤ The invention is "novel"—new; that is, different from what is already known to the public.

➤ The invention is "unobvious"; that is, at the time you or your company created the invention, it would have been considered unobvious to a person skilled in the technology used in the invention.

The Patent Process

Providing complete instructions on how to patent-it-yourself is well beyond the scope of this book; however, I can provide a map of the process. But before you even begin the application process, you (or somebody you or your company hires) must undertake a patent search in order to assess "prior art."

Following the review, you prepare an application, which consists of:

➤ A self-addressed receipt postcard

➤ A check for the filing fee

➤ A transmittal letter

➤ A set of drawings of the invention. These drawings, which may be formal or informal, must show every aspect of the invention. The parts of the invention must be labeled.

➤ The heart of the application is the "specification," which fully describes the invention.

Let's pause here to take apart the "specification." There are twelve parts to it:

1. The title of the invention.

2. The background of the invention—specifically, a cross-reference to any related applications.

3. The background as it defines the field of the invention.

4. The background in terms of prior art. This section should discuss and criticize previous developments in the technological area relevant to your invention.

5. List of objects and advantages of your invention.

6. List of drawing figures.

7. List of reference numerals—in essence, a key to your drawings ("6 = pulley," "7 = main gear," etc.).

8. A summary of the invention.

9. The Description—Main Embodiment (i.e., version). This is a narrative description of the structure of the main embodiment of the invention.

10. Operation—Main Embodiment. How does the invention work?

11. Description of Operation—Alternative Embodiments. This narrative description discusses the structure and operation of any alternative embodiments of this invention.

12. Conclusion, ramifications, and scope. This final statement summarizes the invention's advantages and the alternative physical forms ("embodiments") it can take.

Buzzword
Prior art is the state of knowledge existing or publicly available either before your invention in question or more than a year prior to your earliest patent application.

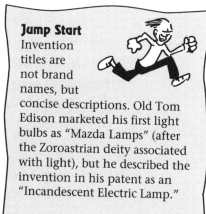

Jump Start
Invention titles are not brand names, but concise descriptions. Old Tom Edison marketed his first light bulbs as "Mazda Lamps" (after the Zoroastrian deity associated with light), but he described the invention in his patent as an "Incandescent Electric Lamp."

In addition to the specification, the application includes:

➤ The "Claims" section. This is a precise non-narrative listing of what you "claim" for your invention—what it is, what it does, how it is advantageous, etc.

➤ The "Abstract." The Abstract briefly summarizes what the invention is and how it works.

➤ The "Patent Application Declaration Form." This form affirms under penalty of perjury that you are the "true inventor" and that you have not and will not withhold from the PTO any information relevant to the invention.

➤ Additional declarations may be necessary, depending on whether you are applying as an individual or an organization.

Several months to a year after the PTO receives your application, a patent examiner will review it. Rarely, the application will sail through to the grant of a patent. Far more often, you will be asked to respond to various objections by making changes, additions, or deletions to drawings, the specification, and/or the claims. It's also possible that the entire application will be rejected as unpatentable. You do have the option of attempting to convince the examiner that the objection(s) or rejection was in error.

The Search

Whether you go it alone or involve patent attorneys and other professionals, preparing a patent application is hard work, and your best insurance against rejection *after* all that work is to devote adequate time and effort to the search. The search will not only allow you to assess the patentability of your invention—and, should the invention prove unpatentable, save you from the time and expense of going through the application process—it also provides the following benefits:

➤ It will provide information that will help you write the application and determine which components to draw and which ones to describe.

➤ It will help you avoid reinventing the wheel by turning up existing components and technologies you may combine into novel forms.

➤ It may provide information that will help you improve the invention.

➤ It may provide commercial information that will allow you to analyze past successes and failures relevant to what you propose.

➤ It may provide proof of your invention's unobviousness—*if* you find references that explicitly state or suggest that your approach will not work.

➤ It should turn up information that will allow you clearly to define the prior art.

➤ It should help you define your invention's novel features.

➤ It should provide information to help you sell and market your invention.

➤ It will allow you to determine if your invention will infringe any patents.

> **Jump Start**
> Should you ever skip the patent search? Possibly. If you are working in a field so new or so arcane—and a field with which you are thoroughly familiar—common sense may suggest that a search will be fruitless.

Getting Down to It

Inventors may do the search themselves or may hire professional researchers. In either case, there are three ways to get at the necessary information:

1. Go to the PTO in Arlington, Virginia. This is the best place to search, since it is the most complete repository of patent information.

2. Search a local Patent and Trademark Depository Library (these may be affiliated with universities or may be public libraries in larger cities). Even non-depository libraries often carry the PTO's *Official Gazettes*, in which patents are published.

3. Use your personal computer and log on to the PTO's World Wide Web site on the Internet: **www.uspto.gov/other.html**. Other *private* patent-related sites are also available.

> **False Start**
> Computer patent searches will not uncover information about patents that are more than twenty years old. The computer is best used for preliminary search work only.

The techniques of executing a patent search are beyond the scope of this book. You'll find an excellent discussion in David Pressman's *Patent It Yourself,* 4th edition (Nolo Press, 1995). As to hiring a professional researcher, you have three choices:

1. Look in the Yellow Pages under "Patent Searchers." This will lead you to lay searchers. You may also consult such periodicals as *Journal of the Patent and Trademark Office Society* or *Dream Merchant,* a magazine for inventors (phone 310-328-1925).

> **Buzzword**
> *Lay patent searchers* are researchers who are not lawyers. No professional certification is required to hang out a shingle as a lay searcher.

2. You may hire a patent agent. The patent agent is licensed by the PTO to prepare and prosecute patent applications, and he may also conduct searches.

3. You may use a patent attorney, who is licensed by the PTO as well as by the state bar association or other authority.

Patent agents and patent attorneys can be located by consulting *Attorneys and Agents Registered to Practice by the U.S. Patent and Trademark Office* ("A&ARTP"), an official publication available in the reference departments of most medium-size public libraries.

Vital Documentation

Whatever else you do during the invention and patenting process, be certain to create adequate documentation. This is vital not only as good engineering practice—allowing you and others to analyze the invention, with an eye toward improving it now or later—but also to establish proof of your ownership of the invention. Do the following:

Buzzword
A *patent agent* is licensed by the PTO to prepare and prosecute patent applications. He or she may also be hired to carry out patent searches. Whereas a lay searcher may or may not have qualifications relevant to the job, the patent agent is certified to have some technical training.

1. Write a clear description of the concept as early as possible and before you discuss it with outsiders.

2. Sign and date the document.

3. Secure the signatures of two persons who will affirm that they have "witnessed and understood" your concept.

Beyond this, if at all possible, build the invention as soon as you can, retaining full written records of the process. Secure the signatures of two persons who affirm that they have "witnessed and understood" your building and testing the invention.

Patent Pending

Jump Start
In larger organizations, where invention is a day-to-day activity, documentation and witnessing policies should always be a matter of strict policy, always in force, and rigorously practiced.

If the patenting process seems daunting…well, it is. But don't be discouraged. There *is* good news. While it can take a matter of years (at least two) to secure a patent, you do not have to wait for a patent to be granted in order to commercialize a product. Pick up any brand-new product, and you're likely to see the phrase "patent pending" somewhere on it. This means that a patent application has been duly and properly filed, and it warns would-be copycats and knock-off artists to stay away, because a patent may be granted at any minute.

Copyright

Like a patent, a copyright is an "offensive right" given by law. Whereas a patent protects an idea—provided the idea is embodied in hardware form—a copyright protects the *manner* in which an author, artist, composer, or software programmer expresses the idea. You cannot copyright an idea per se, but you can copyright the manner of its expression (the arrangement of the words in a novel, for example, or the arrangement of code in a software product).

Buzzword
A *knock-off* is a blatant imitation of an existing product, usually at a cut-rate price.

Why Obtain a Copyright?

If the new products you create are books (or other published "literary" material), musical compositions, artworks, illustrations, or computer software, a copyright does for you what a patent does for an inventor or the corporation that owns the patent. It excludes others from exploiting your work.

You will also want to obtain a copyright on any documentation—user's manuals, maintenance manuals, instruction booklets, and the like—that may accompany a product you create. Special illustrations used on product packaging can also be copyrighted.

How do you know when to obtain a copyright instead of a patent? The two usually apply in mutually exclusive cases. Patents protect ideas embodied in hardware; a copyright cannot protect ideas (or facts), but does protect the expression of ideas (or facts); therefore, things entitled to copyright protection are not entitled to patent protection, and vice versa.

Usually.

In the case of computer software, you may be able to obtain patent and/or copyright coverage. Now, as you will see in a minute, it is much easier and far less expensive to obtain a copyright than it is to secure a patent. So why would you want to patent something that is copyrightable? The answer is that patent protection is much broader. In the case of a software program, a copyright will cover only the form of the program, not what the program actually does, whereas a patent covers *how* and, to a significant degree, *what* the software does.

Copyright and *utility* (not design) patent protection also overlap in the area of shapes and designs. If the design or shape of the invention serves both aesthetic and utilitarian purposes, you may either copyright or patent it. Perhaps you've created a new form of shorthand alphabet that is both aesthetically pleasing and eminently practical. A copyright will protect the specific shapes of the shorthand symbols, whereas a patent will protect the underlying principles—the system.

The Process

Obtaining a copyright is child's play compared to securing a patent. In fact, since 1978, copyright protection begins *automatically* the moment a work is set on paper or otherwise fixed in tangible form. You don't even have to register it. However, registering the copyright with the U.S. Copyright Office deters infringement and is a prerequisite to filing an infringement suit.

The process is straightforward:

Jump Start
Copyright fees are not carved in stone. They rise periodically. Call the Copyright Office at 202-707-3000 to confirm the latest fees.

Jump Start
Copyright on works created after 1977 by individuals lasts for the life of the author plus 50 years. Copyright for works created before 1978 lasts 75 years from the date of publication—though it may be renewed.

1. You obtain the appropriate form by calling the Copyright Office's Forms Hotline at 202-707-9100. The number is available twenty-four hours a day. Form TX, the most commonly used form, is for "nondramatic literary works" (which ranges from advertising copy to the Great American Novel). Form PA is for plays and screenplays; musical compositions and multimedia works are also registered with this form. Form SE is for newspapers, magazines, and other periodicals. Form GR/CP provides special protection for a group of contributions to serial publications by a single author.

2. Fill out the form.

3. Determine how to satisfy the copyright office's deposit requirements. If you are registering an unpublished work, submit ("deposit") one copy of the work. If you are submitting a published work, deposit two copies.

4. Mail your application, along with the appropriate fee.

In contrast to patents, copyrights are readily granted, as long as the work is legally copyrightable. Also in contrast to patents, copyright registration takes effect as soon as the Copyright Office receives your application.

Trade Secrets

Finally, there is a third type of new product protection. A trade secret is any information, design, device, process, composition, technique, or formula that is not generally known and that confers on the owner of the trade secret a competitive business advantage.

Examples of trade secrets include:

➤ Chemical formulas

➤ Manufacturing processes

➤ Certain "magical" techniques, such as those used to produce some theatrical or exhibition effects (for example, special laser light show techniques)

Trade secret rights can be acquired without doing much of anything beyond taking reasonable steps to keep the "trade secret" confidential. Employees should sign an agreement to keep trade secrets secret. If you can document that you have taken reasonable precautions, you have the legal grounds to defend infringement of a trade secret.

If trade secret protection costs nothing to acquire and almost nothing to maintain, if it requires no application process, if the duration of the protection is indefinite (it will last until it is publicly discovered), if it can be established without identifying an inventor—if, in short, it is so *easy*, why bother with patents? The answer is that trade secret protection is weak and unreliable. It lasts only until the trade secret becomes known to the public, provided it becomes known by legitimate means—such as disassembly, reverse engineering, chemical analysis, etc. Trade secret protection *does* confer offensive rights in cases where the secret is made known through illegitimate means, such as employee theft and industrial espionage. Because trade secrets are so easy—and inexpensive—to establish, they are worth acquiring and maintaining. But they are no substitute for full patent protection.

The Least You Need to Know

➤ Patents protect *ideas* embodied in some physical form, whereas copyrights protect the *form* of expression of ideas.

➤ In addition to avoiding patent infringement, you can determine much about consumer wants and needs by doing a thorough patent search.

➤ You cannot protect an invention until it is embodied in some physical form.

➤ A trade secret is a possible alternative to a patent or a copyright; while it is easy to claim a trade secret, it can be difficult to prosecute alleged infringement.

Chapter 20

What's In a Name

In This Chapter

➤ What a trademark is

➤ Naming your new product (or new business)

➤ Creating a legally strong trademark

➤ Relation of trademarks to patents and copyrights

➤ Researching and registering a trademark

I'm sure most of you can identify with my grade-school experience of beginning each day by rising from my desk, facing Old Glory, putting my right hand over my heart, and reciting "I pledge allegiance to the flag...". A full thirteen words into the "Pledge" finally came a reference to "the republic," but, first and foremost, we pledged our allegiance *to the flag*—a symbol.

If you need evidence of the power of symbols and names, think of the Stars and Stripes, think of the Cross, think of the Star of David, think of the Crescent—or think, too, alas, of the Nazi swastika. Then think of the sea of trademark names and symbols in which we all swim: Ford, Westinghouse, IBM, the rain-slicker girl on Morton Salt, the arm and hammer of Arm and Hammer, the fancy calligraphy spelling out GE in a circle. Naming a new product—and perhaps the new business that produces the product—is a key step in innovation and not one to be taken lightly. Read on for more.

Breaking the Bottle Across the Bow

Trademarks are names and symbols—a word or words, picture, symbol, shape, color scheme, color, container, logo, phrase, or song—used to market products. By law, a properly registered trademark is exclusive to the company that holds the trademark. The idea behind this is to prevent competing businesses from stealing the goodwill another business has generated for itself. Also, trademark protection prevents consumers from being misled by duplicate or similar trademarks. I will get into the legal requirements for a trademark shortly, but, for the moment, let's move beyond the basic purpose of a trademark and talk about naming your product.

Buzzword
A *trademark* is a word, phrase, design, slogan, or symbol that serves to identify a specific product brand. A *service mark* serves the same purpose for a specific brand of service. The two are legally equivalent. Often the word *mark* is used to refer to either interchangeably.

Jump Start
For marketing reasons, a trademark should be distinctive. But good marketing practice isn't the only reason for this. Only distinctive trademarks can be legally copyrighted.

Since the late nineteenth century, one of the world's best-known trademarks has been Kodak. This is an amazing thing, considering that the word means absolutely nothing. But that was precisely Kodak founder George Eastman's purpose. He believed that a great trademark should be short, vigorous, easily spelled, and should—in and of itself—mean nothing. "Kodak" fits these criteria perfectly (although many people have noted that the sound of the word suggests the sound of a clicking camera shutter, so it is not *entirely* meaningless).

Most trademark and product-naming specialists would no longer insist on the meaninglessness of the word, but they *would* tell you that a good trademark name should be

➤ Easily pronounced

➤ Memorable

➤ Graphically attractive as a word (not hyphenated, for example)

Recipe for a Great Name

The name of your new product—its mark—is a form of advertising, and that means that you should think about your mark in much the same way as you think about other aspects of your advertising plan for a new product. Consider the following:

➤ Who are your customers?

➤ What are your customers' demographics? A trademark that works for the young and trendy may fail miserably if your target customers are the over-55 crowd.

➤ What are your customers' buying habits? If they make their purchases in a jam-packed discount store, better pick a simple, bold name with graphics to match. If they buy in a setting that invites contemplation, perhaps a longer, more thought-provoking name and more complex graphics are appropriate.

➤ What features or benefits are most important to your customers? If, for example, ease of use is a paramount issue, choose a name and graphic that convey simplicity.

➤ Can your product be nailed with a single word or phrase? A popular varnish and paint remover is called *Kutz It*. A nationally advertised toilet-bowl cleaner is *Vanish*.

➤ What image do you want to create? The brand name "Obsession" creates a very different image from "White Linen." Both are names of perfumes.

➤ Is your product unique or especially distinctive and set apart from the competition? A good name and graphic can help convey this.

➤ Other than on the product package, where will the name and graphic be advertised—on TV or in print ads? And if in print ads, will it be advertised mainly in slick full-color magazines or in black-and-white on coarse newsprint? A bold word and simple logo work best for newsprint ads, in which a complex logo may reproduce as nothing more than a murky blob of ink.

The realm of words is, of course, very wide. But you can focus your creativity by thinking of trademarks in terms of categories:

➤ *Coined words* are like "Kodak." They are completely made-up words without any meaning. Such words should be easy to pronounce and should appeal to the eye and the ear.

➤ *Suggestive words* often make powerful marks, as, for example, Obsession perfume or Comet cleanser or the Jaguar automobile. The idea is to create a strong image that prompts the customer to think positively about the product. Suggestive marks describe a desirable feeling or idea about the product, but they do not *literally* describe the product.

➤ *Arbitrary or fanciful words* can make delightful and memorable trademarks. Arm and Hammer—as a phrase and a logo—has served the maker of this baking soda well for more than a hundred

False Start
Beware of ambiguous or hard-to-pronounce made-up trademarks and product names. These can be eminently forgettable. Also avoid novel or trick spellings that no one can figure out how to say. In Tom Hanks's 1996 movie *That Thing You Do*, an aspiring rock 'n' roll group calls itself "The Oneders." When everyone pronounced it "o-needers," the group dropped the trick spelling and called itself "The Wonders."

False Start
Combining words can result in some pretty clumsy, even comical and old-fashioned–sounding names. Be careful.

False Start
We've all heard about cases in which (for example) a man who happened to be named Henry Ford opened an auto repair shop, but was prevented by legal action from advertising it as Ford Motor Company. You have the right to use your own name for a company or product, provided that it does not confuse or mislead consumers. If, in the future, another Mr. or Ms. Hilton decides to open a hotel, he or she can call it anything but a Hilton hotel.

Jump Start
Sometimes unpleasant trademarks work well. There is a hair-care product called "Grease." The name is so bad, it actually helps sell the product. Rules are made to be broken.

years—though neither the words nor the symbol has any intrinsic connection with the product. And what does a camel have to do with a cigarette?

> ➤ *Novel combinations of existing words* can make fine trademarks, as in Palmolive soap. You don't have to combine entire words, but might use word roots, as in *Soloflex*.

> ➤ *Foreign words* can make good marks, especially if you're looking for an exotic image. "Sirocco" is an Italian word for a Mediterranean wind from North Africa. It made for an exotic name for a fairly ordinary automobile.

It will also help you to focus your trademark invention process by knowing what to avoid:

> ➤ *Words with "o" on the end of them* tend to sound dated and trite. "Brighto" is not a very exciting name for a polishing product, for example. However, many established products have used the "o" ending successfully, as in Rinso bleach, for example.

> ➤ *Names incorporating "o-matic"* have pretty well died out and, applied to new products, would seem tongue-in-cheek at best. (Of course, with some products, that may be a fun effect that is actually desirable.)

> ➤ *Personal names* are usually poor because they are insufficiently distinctive either to be memorable or, in many cases, to be trademarkable.

> ➤ *Generic marks* suffer from the same defects as personal names. Avoid bland marks that describe attributes of the service or product.

> ➤ *Avoid names with unintended or unpleasant connotations.*

> ➤ *Avoid soundalike or lookalike trademarks.* Let's say you've invented a fast, simple, and inexpensive word-processing program. You decide to call it

"McWord." Now, sit back, relax, and wait for the process server to knock on your door with a McLawsuit from McDonald's, who will see you in McCourt.

➤ *Be careful to avoid words that may have negative meanings in a foreign language.* This is especially important, of course, for internationally distributed products.

The Process

One of the best ways of starting the name-generating process is to *brainstorm*, a technique discussed (in connection with new product ideas) in Chapter 4. You can also brainstorm on your own by drawing up lists of names.

Other methods include:

➤ Holding a festive name-brainstorm party.

➤ Offering a prize in a company-wide naming contest.

➤ Using special computer software to generate names. NameStormers (214-350-6214) offers *Namer* and *NamePro* software, and IdeaFisher Systems (800-289-4332) offers *IdeaFisher*.

➤ Consulting a book on naming products. One of the best is Henri Charmasson's *The Name's the Thing* (Dow Jones-Irwin).

➤ Hiring a professional naming consultant, such as Alias Product and Corporate Name Laboratory (619-294-2924) or Name-It (800-776-0530, 800-550-520, 800-340-2010).

Many large advertising agencies also provide product naming consultant services, and consultants often combine name invention with trademark search services (which will be discussed shortly).

Legal Strength

In addition to creating a strong mark in terms of selling your goods, you need to create a legally strong mark. Of the three basic categories of trademark—coined, arbitrary-fanciful, and suggestive—coined and arbitrary-fanciful have inherently more legal strength than suggestive marks.

A Trademark Primer

Trademark law protects marks that are "memorable," which means marks that are arbitrary, unusual, unique, evocative, unobvious, surprising. In effect, trademark law makes a value judgment about the mark. Marks that are *not* memorable do not deserve—or receive—protection.

Jump Start
Trademark law also protects marks that have become familiar over time. Certainly, there is nothing very memorable about the phrase "General Electric," but, over time, it has become so intimately identified with a certain company and its products that it is protected. For obvious reasons (the "over time" part), this won't apply to names of new products.

False Start
At the office, do you ask for a "photocopy" or a "xerox"? If you feel a sneeze coming on, do you ask for a "tissue" or a "kleenex"? Some trademarks get so familiar that they become transformed into generic terms. If a company does not take vigorous action to counter this (as, for example, Xerox did in a long series of ads), it runs the risk of losing its trademark protection.

What kinds of product names and marks *fail* to be memorable?

➤ Marks that incorporate commonly used words or words that many similar businesses might normally and reasonably use to describe their products fail to be memorable. It would be difficult or impossible, for example, to trademark Tasty Ice Cream. (However, combining this common word with another common word in a novel way *can* be trademarked: "Tasty Freeze.")

➤ Generic terms cannot be trademarked—"aspirin," for example.

The key rule is this: If your mark fails to distinguish your products or services from those of others who compete directly with yours, it is a weak mark and probably is not protectable.

The Trademark: An Exploded Diagram

It will help you to think of a trademark as having two distinct parts:

Part 1 of the trademark specifies the company's "version" of the product or service: *Subaru* vs. *Mercedes*, for example. (The first letter of Part 1 is always capitalized, since it is a proper adjective. Used alone—"There goes a Subaru!"—it is a proper noun.)

Part 2 specifies the kind of product or service: Ford *Motor Company*. "Ford" is a protected trademark. The "Motor Company" part of it cannot be protected.

Trademark vs. Copyright and Patent

Like patents and copyrights, trademarks are in the domain of intellectual property law. However, patents generally have nothing to do with protecting trademarks—except that it is possible to obtain a design patent (see Chapter 19) on the ornamental aspects of a functional device if the design is inseparable from the device. If this design is also your trademark, the design patent may afford a degree of protection.

Copyright does not protect names, titles, or short phrases—the very stuff of trademarks. In an ad for your new product, you will probably want two kinds of protection: trademark registration to protect any trademarks and logos, and copyright protection to protect the text and illustrations used in the body of the ad.

There *is* more overlap between trademark and copyright protection than between trademark and patent protection. You may create a logo treatment so distinctive that you not only register it as your trademark, but also copyright the design. This means that no competitor can use the logo to promote his product (under trademark law) *and*, even if no promotion is involved, the logo design cannot be used without your permission (copyright law). This is particularly important in the case of companies that exploit their popular logos to market a variety of goods. For example, the Coca-Cola logo design—a time-honored piece of Americana—appears on everything from t-shirts to key chains. Such use *must* be licensed from Coca-Cola, even though a t-shirt product does not directly compete with a soft drink product.

False Start
Did you know that a book *title* cannot be copyrighted? However, in some cases, a title or part of a title can be trademarked. A series title can also be trademarked; for example, Abbeville Press publishes a series of miniature art books collectively called Tiny Folios™.

Certification Marks and Collective Marks

In addition to the trademark, federal law also protects two other types of marks: certification marks and collective marks. You should know a bit about these.

Certification marks are used exclusively to certify that products or services have certain qualities associated with the mark. The "Good Housekeeping Seal of Approval" is one famous certification mark. So is "Harris Tweed"— which is a mark that may be applied only to tweeds from a specifically defined area of Scotland.

A collective mark identifies goods or services produced by members of a specific group or organization. For example, clothes manufactured by XYZ Corporation might carry the XYZ trademark, but they may also be further distinguished by the collective mark of the ILGWU, denoting that the individuals who actually made the clothing are members of the International Ladies' Garment Workers' Union.

False Start
You cannot simply invent your own certification mark, apply it to your own product, and expect legal protection for the certification mark. The mark must be owned by a third party, and it must represent such qualities as regional origin, method of manufacture, or quality level.

Protect and Register

Well, here's where I let you know that providing complete instructions on how to register your trademark is beyond the scope of this book. Go out and buy *Trademark: How to Name a Business and Product* (Second Edition) by Kate McGrath and Stephen Elias, with Sarah Shena (Nolo Press, 1996). But I can provide an overview of the process:

1. First, you will need to conduct a trademark search, to ensure that your mark is not already in use. I'll say a bit more about this in a minute.

Jump Start
You do *not* have to register a trademark before you begin to use it. However, you do run the risk of someone else seeing it, liking it, and using it (though that person will not be able to register it, either, because you have already used it). Also, if you start using the mark without attempting to discover whether or not it is already registered to someone else, you run the risk of a trademark infringement suit. If you wish, you may file an "Intent to Use" application with the PTO *before* actually using the mark.

2. You obtain from the Patent and Trademark Office (PTO) an application, which you complete and return along with specimens showing the actual use of the mark and a drawing of the mark itself. You'll also have to send in a filing fee with your application.

3. The PTO sorts and classifies your application according to the type of product or service you are asking to trademark.

4. The PTO sends you a filing receipt, advising you that you will not hear further from them for about 90 days.

5. The application is examined by a trademark examiner, who determines whether your mark qualifies for registration.

Let's pause here. The trademark examination is not nearly as rigorous as the patent examination. However, the examiner must answer the following to his satisfaction:

False Start
Be careful. In some countries, registration, not use, is primary. In such areas, be sure to register the mark right away.

➤ Is the mark distinctive? (Favorable answer = yes)

➤ Does the mark conflict with any existing registered—or unregistered—mark? (Favorable answer = no)

➤ Will the product or service be used in commerce? (Favorable answer = yes)

➤ Is the trademark obscene, scandalous, immoral, or deceptive? (Favorable answer = no)

Now, let's go on to step #6:

6. Once the trademark application passes muster with the examiner, it is published in the PTO's *Official Gazette* for the purpose of giving others an opportunity to raise objections to the proposed mark.

7. If no one objects (and no one usually does), the mark is either registered (if you are already using it) or, if you filed an "Intent to Use," it will be registered once you actually begin to use it.

If your mark does meet with an objection, you'll have to hire an attorney if you wish to pursue the registration.

Do I Have to Do Any of This?

You may not want to go through the trouble of registering your trademark if your business and the new product or service associated with it is small and local. If your product or service does not extend beyond the borders of your state or does not affect interstate or international commerce, you cannot register the mark federally. However, it is always wise to conduct a trademark search to ensure that your unregistered product or business name does not conflict with a registered mark.

The Search

A trademark search is similar to a patent search, although it is not nearly as time consuming or as complex. If you employ a search firm to do the work, you will not pay as much as you would for a patent search, because the level of expertise required is not as great.

You have a choice of four kinds of trademark searches:

Buzzword
Commerce, as it applies to trademark law, is any business or trade that the federal government may control. Trademark protection extends *only* to products and services used in commerce.

False Start
If your product is not used in commerce, it cannot be protected by a federally registered trademark. This is not *all* bad news. Most products *are* used in commerce because they cross state lines (or even national borders) or can be shown to affect commerce across these lines and borders. Even if your product is strictly local, you may be able to obtain *state* registration of your trademark.

False Start
Incorporating—and thereby registering a corporate name with your state—does not establish trademark rights in that name.

➤ The *direct hit* search compares your mark with identical or similar marks in one or more of the classes set up by the PTO. It's a quick, easy, and superficial method, which you can do yourself or which a search firm will do for as little as $50 to $100 per trademark.

➤ An *analytical trademark register search* compares your mark with all registered marks (federal and state) that sound or look like your mark, plus any other marks that might cause confusion among consumers. This is a deeper and more extensive search and is much more time consuming. If you hire a professional firm, expect to pay as much as $300 per trademark.

➤ A *common law* search uses Yellow Pages, trade directories, trade journals, and the like to turn up any possible conflicts. Professional searchers charge $100 to $150 for such a search.

➤ A *full* search combines all three methods and, if handled by a professional, costs as much as $500 per mark.

You can find professional search services in the Yellow Pages. Some of the better-known firms include XL Corporate Service (800-221-2972), Thomson & Thomson/Compu-Mark (800-692-8833), Trademark Express (800-776-0530, 800-550-1520, 800-340-2010), Derwent (800-336-5010), Government Liaison Services (800-642-6564, 703-524-8200), and NaPatco, Ltd. (800-221-6275).

Jump Start
A number of software firms publish nationwide Yellow Pages on CD-ROM. Pop one of these in your computer, and you have access to virtually every business listing in the nation. Many of these software packages allow you to search by business type, business name, and even SIC Codes. Visit your local software dealer.

If you want to do the job yourself, you should locate a public library that has been designated as a Patent and Trademark Depository Library (PTDL). If such a library is not near you, you'll undoubtedly *save* money by hiring a professional search firm. However, you can forgo the library experience and use your computer to run a search. The CompuServe online service (800-848-8990) offers (for a fee in addition to CompuServe subscription costs) access to TrademarkScan, which contains extensive federal and even international trademark databases. Dialog Information Retrieval Service (800-3-DIALOG) also offers access to TrademarkScan, as well as to other databases useful in finding trademark information. Dow Jones News/Retrieval (800-522-3567) and Lexis-Nexus (800-227-4908) offer databases that are useful for common law searches.

Care and Feeding of Your Trademark—A Word

Since this is a book about *new* products, I won't delve into everything you must do to protect your trademark over time. Just be aware that, since November 16, 1989, trademark registration must be renewed every ten years or you will lose your protection. But that's not all. If you do not continuously use the mark—even if its registration is in force—it may be deemed to have been abandoned. The PTO considers a mark to have been abandoned after two years of non-use.

To protect your mark, you must control your mark. If someone makes unauthorized use of your mark, you must respond through negotiation or litigation with the offending party. If you just "let the fella go," you risk relinquishing your rights to the mark. Finally, avoid committing "genericide" by vigorously protesting the generic association of your mark with products you did not create. ("I gotta sneeze. Hand me a kleenex before you make a xerox of that report, would ya?")

The Least You Need to Know

➤ Trademarks must be distinctive and memorable in order to receive legal protection.

➤ Focus your creativity by thinking of trademarks in a few categories: coined words, suggestive words, arbitrary or fanciful words, novel combinations, or foreign words.

➤ Knowing what types or combinations of words to avoid can keep you from trademarking a name no one will remember.

➤ No law compels you to register a trademark, but, to avoid possible infringement litigation, you should do a trademark search before committing to a name for your new product, even if you don't register the mark.

Get Out That Bed and Get Some Bread

This chapter is a brief look at how to get the money you need to make and market your new product. It is primarily intended for the small businessperson or for the independent inventor. But folks working in a corporate setting should find the chapter useful as well. You know who you are, and you may think that, as a denizen of corporate America, you don't have to worry about raising money to support your ideas. The money is simply *there*, part of the whole corporate deal. And the fact is that what you do is not *called* "raising money." It's "obtaining funding," or getting "funding allocated," or getting the "green light from Financial," or something of the kind. But the fact also is that, whatever it's called, it smells and feels a lot like "raising money." So even corporate types should find this chapter useful.

Now You Tell Me!

Here's a pair of *ifs* to ponder. If you are a small businessperson or an inventor, and if you are not independently wealthy, you're going to have to find money to get your new product manufactured and marketed. Unless you sell your invention or innovation outright to another firm, then pocket the money and run, there are essentially two ways to raise the money you need:

Buzzword
Venturing is creating a new company to manufacture and market your new product.

1. You can *license* your invention or new product to an established firm.

2. You can *venture*.

Licensing

I will leave the complex subject of the ins and outs of licensing to whoever gets around to writing *The Complete Idiot's Guide to Inventing*. Until that book gets written, you might consult the latest publications of the Licensing Executives Society (71 East Avenue, Suite S, Norwalk, CT 06851). However, let me stress here the importance of not merely unloading a license on the first company that happens to come along. If you want to use licensing as the primary means of commercializing your new product, make an effort to negotiate the license with a company that offers a synergistic fit. This means finding a company that

Buzzword
Licensing is granting the right to manufacture and market a product, usually for a specified period of time, in a geographically defined area, and usually in return for a royalty payment based on sales. Customarily, an up-front "guarantee" is paid as an advance against anticipated royalties.

➤ Is familiar with your type of product

➤ Can manufacture the product in a high-quality fashion

➤ Can manufacture the product without extensive retooling or retraining

➤ Can market the product effectively

Venturing

Licensing can be a most attractive option. It offers an up-front "advance" or "guarantee" as well as subsequent royalty payments based on a percentage of sales. Think about it: If you can find a truly synergistic company to make and market your work, why reinvent the wheel? You've already devoted time, effort, and cash to creating a new product. Why devote *more* time, effort, and cash to creating a new company—*if* an appropriate company already exists?

So why even *think* about venturing? There are at least four reasons:

1. You can find no synergistic company to make and market the product.

2. You can find *no* company—synergistic or otherwise—to make and market the product.

3. You realize that, if all goes well (no, if all goes phenomenally great), you can earn more money exploiting your new product with your own company than you can by licensing it to another company.

4. Rationality aside, you feel that it is part and parcel of the "American Dream" to invent a product and then start your own company to make and sell it.

False Start
Thomas Alva Edison died a wealthy man. But, considering that he had been responsible for so much of what makes the modern world modern, he did not die as wealthy as he should have. Much of his fortune was plowed into "inventing" one new company after another and fighting legal battles associated with them. Somebody should have talked to him about licensing.

"Rationality Aside"

Before you take the venturing plunge, ask yourself some questions about what it means to start your own business in order to make and market your own new product:

➤ Do you want to be an inventor or the owner of a business?

➤ Can you run a business (manage people, fire people, dun delinquent accounts, keep books, endlessly juggle funds from one account to another, etc., etc., etc.)?

➤ Can you write an effective and convincing business plan?

➤ Just how much money can you—personally—afford to lose?

➤ How much can your family afford for you to lose?

➤ Can you put in 60+ hour work weeks every week?

➤ Can your family deal with 60+ hour work weeks every week?

Jump Start
How much does the "average" independent inventor risk on a venture? Hard to say. But the rule of thumb is that you should go into the project *able to sustain* a $20,000 loss.

➤ Do you have reliable investors on tap?

➤ Is there really no other way to bring this new product to market?

You Know, It Really Doesn't Grow on Trees

What do you do when you need backing? The answer is really simple: find money. You will get money only by persuading others that, by investing in your enterprise, they will make more money.

The principal *tool* of persuasion is your business plan, which we will discuss under "Venture Capitalists and What They Want" later in this chapter, but the principal *user* of that tool is *you*—and how you use it depends on your level of confidence, your level of expertise, your level of communication skill.

Sources of Money

The traditional source of funding for almost anything is a bank or other lending institution. While many of these traditional institutions are willing to lend money to small *established* businesses, fewer will risk a start-up business, and fewer still, a start-up business based on a new product or invention.

The bank probably won't boot you out the door. More likely, the loan officer will refer you to the Small Business Administration, an agency of the federal government. The SBA does not make loans, but it guarantees up to 85 percent of a loan that a bank makes. With 85 percent of his risk eliminated, the banker is usually in a much more receptive mood.

The SBA...Maybe

The SBA offers a variety of loan programs. Most popular is the SBA 7(A) loan. Funds may be used for working capital, the purchase of equipment, and the purchase or modification of buildings. Hey! This is great. One problem: a start-up company may be required to have from 30 to 50 percent equity already in the company, and, usually, this type of SBA loan is given to companies with more than two years of operating history. The SBA 504 loan is aimed more directly at developing start-up firms and offers a 100 percent guarantee for the financing of land, buildings, machinery, and equipment. The catch? You can't use any of the money as working capital.

In addition to the SBA, there is the Business and Industrial Loan Program administered by the Farmers Home Administration, another federal agency. The chief restriction here is that your business must exist in a community of 50,000 people or less—and the administration *really* likes businesses in rural communities of 25,000 or less. If you pass that test, you can get a 90 percent guarantee on loans for working capital as well as buildings, equipment, and the like. Still, you need a 20 to 25 percent equity in the new business.

More Government Money...Possibly

George Gobel, sad-sack comic of the "golden age" of 1950s TV, used to say that he felt as if the whole world wore nothing but tuxedos and he was a pair of brown shoes. That's the way most small business folk feel about government grants. They have a vague sense that *everybody* is getting free government money—except them.

Well, it just isn't so.

The government offers very few grant programs for independent inventors or creators of new products. You should be aware that the U.S. Department of Energy (DOE) does give grants for energy-conserving inventions that meet two rigorous criteria (in addition to being energy conserving):

1. It must pass muster with the National Institute of Science and Technology (NIST).

2. Even if it does get NIST's approval, it must vie with many other inventions for an award.

The Small Business Innovation Research (SBIR) grant has similar limitations. A number of government agencies participate in the SIBR program by identifying areas of research worthy of funding. Grants of up to $50,000 are available for preliminary research, and as much as a half-million dollars may be awarded for advanced research leading to prototype development. Again, requirements are rigorous and competition is stiff, but if you're looking for research seed money in areas of potential interest to the Department of Defense, NASA, the Environmental Protection Agency, the DOE, the Department of Health and Human Services, the National Science Foundation, the U.S. Department of Agriculture, the Department of Transportation, the Nuclear Regulatory Commission, the Department of the Interior, or the Department of Education, it could be worth writing for more information: Office of Innovation, SBIR, 1441 L Street, NW, Washington, DC 20416.

False Start
You cannot *launch* a new product with SBIR grants. They are for research only.

Jump Start
The Small Business Administration oversees more than $450 million in SBIR grant money.

Looking Beyond the Feds

Let's go back to the banks and other lending institutions. Just because they may be reluctant to lend money on start-ups, inventions, and new products doesn't mean they won't lend money secured by such tangible collateral as inventory and receivables. If you haven't got inventory and receivables, you may have other property to post as collateral. Could you end up losing your house? You bet.

The good news is that a growing number of states offer programs to help finance small businesses. Go to the phone book and look up the Small Business Development Center (SBDC) nearest you. This agency should be able to provide information about state sources of funding.

Jump Start
Bankers often speak of the "Four Cs" by which they decide whether or not to make a loan: Character, Credit, Cashflow, Collateral. Most lenders, not just banks, base judgments on these criteria.

Accounts Receivable Specialists

The great strangler of start-up businesses is cashflow. You may have a stack of receivables (money owed to you), but little cash to show for it. A viable alternative to bank financing may be a firm that specializes in short-term financing of your unpaid invoices. Your banker may be able to steer you to such a firm, or you can consult the local phone directory. Your banker may also be able to identify a "factor" for you. This is a business that actually purchases your receivables, taking on the risk of payment and giving you immediate cash. Obviously, the factor expects a deep discount.

Venture Capitalists and What They Want

Okay, so there is a limited amount of money available from banks, lending institutions, and federal and state agencies. The operative word, however, is "limited." In a capitalist society like ours, the mother lode of new product development funding for the small businessperson or independent inventor comes from—guess who?—capitalists. Specifically, it comes from that breed of capitalist entrepreneur known as the venture capitalist. These are individuals or corporations that specialize in investing in high-risk, high-reward propositions such as new products from small companies.

Jump Start
Right now, the following states offer *some* type of seed-money or product-development finance program that may be helpful to the creator of a new product: Alaska, Arkansas, Connecticut, Florida, Hawaii, Illinois, Indiana, Iowa, Kansas, Louisiana, Massachusetts, Michigan, Minnesota, Missouri, Montana, Nebraska, New Mexico, North Carolina, Ohio, Oklahoma, Oregon, Pennsylvania, Rhode Island, Tennessee, Texas, Utah, and Wisconsin. Other states may also have useful programs.

Finding a Venture Capitalist

You can network and develop contacts over time. This method, nebulous as it is, can create very strong and productive relationships. Potential venture capitalist partners include:

➤ Former employers and sometimes even current employers

➤ Wealthy friends and friends of friends

➤ Rich relations and relations of relations

➤ General business associates

There are also a great many firms that either advertise themselves as sources of venture capital or that offer assistance in connecting small businesspeople with venture capitalists. Publications such as *Venture Magazine* and *Entrepreneur* publish periodic lists of venture capitalists and also offer information on particular individuals and corporations. You might also contact local venture capitalist associations or such publications as *Pratt's Guide to Venture Capital Sources* (contact Venture Economics at 212-765-5311). Software databases are also available. Try calling Datamerge (800-228-1372) or tap into the online database of Venture Capital Exchange at 503-220-8535 (set your modem to 8,1,N, VT100 terminal emulation; if you don't know what this means, chances are that your modem is already set this way—*if* you have a modem). You can make a voice call to Venture Capital Exchange at 503-695-5701.

Finding an Angel

The word *angel* means one thing to the spiritually devout and quite another to the financially pressed. "Angels" are small investors looking for "private placement"—that is, promising small firms in which to put their excess cash. You might turn up small investment groups by checking in with your local Small Business Development Center (SBDC) or the local office of the SBA.

Buzzword
Venture capitalists are companies or individuals who seek high-risk, high-reward investments, especially cutting-edge start-up companies and the commercialization of new products.

Jump Start
Small Business Development Centers, funded by the SBA, are very helpful. All states have at least one office. Usually, the SBDC office is located at a state university.

Buzzword
Angels are private, part-time investors looking for promising start-up companies. They are also called "doctors-and-dentists" for the simple reason that many of them are doctors and dentists.

Selling a Venture Capitalist

Of course, finding a venture capitalist is one thing. *Selling* your project to one is another. According to a national survey of 102 venture capitalists quoted by Thomas E. Mosley, Jr., in *Marketing Your Invention* (Upstart Publishing, 1992), venture capitalists look for the following qualities before they invest in you and your new product:

➤ Capability of sustained intense effort (64 percent say this is key)

➤ Familiarity with the market (62 percent)

➤ Prospect of at least 10 times return within 5–10 years (50 percent)

➤ Demonstrated leadership (50 percent)

➤ Ability to evaluate and react to risk (48 percent)

➤ Investment can be made liquid (44 percent)

➤ Prospect of significant market growth (43 percent)

➤ Track record relevant to venture (37 percent)

➤ Ability to articulate the venture effectively (31 percent)

➤ Availability of proprietary protection (patents, etc.) (29 percent)

Jump Start Successful venture capitalists know that great *people* make things happen. They invest in people, not technologies and not products.

Take a look at that list. Do you see anything about "technology"? Don't bother squinting. It's not there. What lights a venture capitalist's fire is the promise of *great management*, not the invention itself.

No! What Can I Do For You?

I've looked at a lot of job applications in my career. Many of the people who ask for jobs are really talented and quite capable. Most of the application letters, however, are just terrible. Oh, they're written in good English, and they're polite, and they're neatly word processed. But their message is all wrong: *I want a job. I want an opportunity. I want a challenge. I want more money. I want to grow. I want. I want. I want.*

Jump Start Instead of *asking* for money, *offer* money. Appeal to the venture capitalist's self interest.

Speaking from the point of view of a sometime employer, I feel like answering, *Who cares?*

A job application should not say what *you want*, but should anticipate what the *employer wants* and should therefore tell him what you are prepared to *give*. Communicating with a venture capitalist is no different. Believe me, he is far less concerned with what you want or what you need than with what you and your new product will do for him. Focus your communication accordingly.

The First Demand: A Business Plan

Maybe your impulse is to call on the venture capitalist, not hat in hand, but prototype in hand. He'll look at it, and, at some point, he'll probably have a lot of questions about it. But what the venture capitalist wants to *examine* before anything else is your business plan.

Now, writing a business plan is yet another one of those subjects that warrants book-length treatment. You might take a look at James B. Arkebauer's *McGraw-Hill Guide to Writing a High-Impact Business Plan* (McGraw-Hill, 1994) or Joseph Covello and Brian Hazelgrans' *Your First Business Plan* (Small Business Source Books, 1993). If you like to work with software, Tim Berry's *Business Plan Pro* (Palo Alto Software) is a good choice. However, there are many business plan books and several software packages on the market. I suggest you take a trip to the Business or Small Business section of your favorite bookstore or software supplier. Just remember that whatever any of these aids may tell you, there is also no sovereign prescription for writing a business plan. Many options are viable, and one size definitely does *not* fit all. However, any business plan presented to a venture capitalist should serve four basic purposes:

1. It is a tool to pry loose money.

2. It should be clearly usable as a guide to running the business once the funding is in place.

3. It is a useful means of discovering and addressing issues that might otherwise lie in ambush, ready to pounce when it is too late for you to act.

4. It is manifest evidence of your ability to think, to organize, to plan, to anticipate, and to create.

While the business plan incorporates elements of the business evaluation discussed in Chapter 16, it should be at once more concise and more comprehensive, focusing not just on a particular product, but on the business—specifically, on how the new product will generate around itself a new, highly productive business.

False Start
Don't skimp on the business plan, but try to create one concise enough to be read in a single sitting. Twenty or thirty pages is about right.

You've Got Another Plan to Write

The business plan should provide an overview of a marketing plan, but it is no substitute for a fully formed marketing plan. If you've read Chapter 17, you know the drill. The idea is to create a document that will cover, at bare minimum, ten key issues:

1. The customer

2. The product

3. The market: Size? Growth potential?

4. A strategy for distribution

5. A strategy for pricing

6. A strategy for promotion

7. How your company and product relate to the established industry

8. How you propose to compete—and win

9. The environment: political and regulatory, legal, cultural, economic

10. The technological context

Jump Start
Consider hiring a consultant to help you prepare your business plan. If it saves time and speeds your proposal to venture capitalists, it's worth it.

Depressed Yet?

Venturing is the hardest way for an inventor or small businessperson to launch a new product. Licensing to a synergistic company is much easier. These two sentences are statements of fact. If they depress you, if you can't rid your heart and mind of the desire to venture, if soup-to-nuts ownership of *your* product and *your* business is that important to you, then at least pledge to yourself that you will go into venturing with eyes wide open.

The Least You Need to Know

➤ Always consider licensing as a low-risk alternative to venturing.

➤ Venture capitalists are likely sources for new-product funding; however, they tend to specialize in cutting-edge technologies, with an emphasis on commercializing inventions rather than marketing innovations.

➤ A business plan is an important tool, but it is only a tool. Investors don't invest in your business plan. They invest in you and what you convey about your ability to make money for them.

Execution's the Thing

If you didn't skip Chapter 21, you just heard me say that venture capitalists care less about your new product than about how you manage your company. That may be true for somebody investing in your business at the front end, but it's not the case for your back-end investors: your customers. To them, the product—or service—you offer is paramount. Study after study has made a stab at defining the 10, 23, 27, 38, or more "key factors" that spell new product success. Whatever differing factors these studies identify, they invariably come to at least one commonsense conclusion: The quality of the product *really* matters. And it doesn't take a rocket scientist to understand that the quality of the product is the sum of the quality of each step in its creation and marketing. Plans are fine. Plans are important. But they mean nothing without quality of execution. Here's a chapter about that.

A Really Good Product

In 1990, new product and marketing guru R. G. Cooper and Professor Elko J. Kleinschmidt published a monograph called *New Products: The Key Factors in Success* (American Marketing Association). Of the ten key factors they identified, four were directly related to quality. The number-one factor was the "superiority" of a product that "delivers unique benefits to the user." In a world awash in marketing schemes and gimmicks, this old-fashioned home truth may seem more than a trifle shocking.

Q: What sells?

A: A really good product.

In the Cooper-Kleinschmidt study, superior products enjoyed a 98.0 percent success rate, whereas products not identified as superior had an 18.4 percent success rate. Market share for superior products averaged 53.5 percent versus 11.6 percent for undifferentiated products. On a scale from 1 to 10, superior products rated an 8.4 for profitability, as opposed to a 2.6 for undifferentiated products.

Jump Start
Every step of the pre-development and development process should be given a quality execution—not just because this is the "right" thing to do, but because it is more likely to produce a successful product.

Beyond this, quality of execution of technological activities, quality of execution of predevelopment activities (marketing studies and the like), and the quality of execution of marketing itself all had significant bearing on new product success.

The great American jurist Learned Hand once bewailed the absence of "justice in the streets or in the courts." Surprisingly, however, there *is* justice in the marketplace. Products that are the result of quality execution tend to attract buyers, provided that the quality pervades not only the physical product, but its marketing, its distribution, and its pricing.

At the intersection of perceived quality and price is *value*. This is the very bull's-eye of the new product target. High quality alone won't ensure success. Low price alone won't ensure success. Your best chance materializes when quality is delivered at a fair (or better than fair) price. Nothing more consistently motivates consumer spending than the perception of value.

Validation and Fine-Tuning

Quality assurance is largely a matter of listening—of asking the right questions and of listening to the answers—and then acting on the responses. Within your organization, you ensure a quality development process by listening to everyone involved in the process. Then you make adjustments and corrections as necessary.

You also listen to consumers and customers. Early in the game, you ask questions, perhaps you do full-scale studies. During Stage 3—the actual development of the product—you may test and refine in the lab. Now, at Stage 4, it's time to test a prototype or a pilot production run in field trials, test markets, or a limited distribution.

Hearing the Voice of the Customer

I'm about to discuss some techniques for late-stage testing of the new product. But before I do, you might want to take a moment to give yourself a hearing test. Do you suffer from any of the "auditory" problems listed below?

➤ *Are you overanxious about consumer reception of the product?* If you are, and you are doing the testing, you may communicate this anxiety to the customers, who, being kind and generous human beings, will tell you how much they just *love* the new product. (Later, when you put your merchandise on store shelves, they won't *buy* it, but at least your feelings weren't hurt earlier.) If you are interpreting the results, your anxiety may tend to color your interpretation in roseate hues.

➤ *Are you a great salesperson?* If so, you might oversell the product to the customer and thereby contaminate any test results.

➤ *Are you so concerned with "letting the product speak for itself" that you don't tell the customer what he needs to know?* Be certain that your customers understand the product, how it is used, and what benefits it offers. Test subjects don't want to appear stupid. They will be reluctant to ask you to explain what they don't understand. It's up to you to provide adequate information as part of the test.

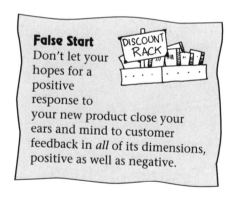

False Start
Don't let your hopes for a positive response to your new product close your ears and mind to customer feedback in *all* of its dimensions, positive as well as negative.

➤ *Do you regard your test customers as price-o-meters?* Pricing is critical, and it can be hard to do. For that reason, many researchers ask graduated intent-to-purchase questions. "Would you buy this for $25?" The response is duly noted. "Would you still buy it for $30?" Fewer people say yes. (Big surprise.) "How about $40?" Fewer still. (Well, thank *you*, Paul Revere.) This is neither news, nor surprising. Yes, purchase resistance climbs as the price gets higher. But a graduated test like this is inherently tainted. Whatever price you begin at establishes a reference price that will almost certainly bias subsequent responses. Your only hope is to try *one* price on *one* test group and *another* price on *another* test group. "This is what it costs. Will you buy it?" Period.

➤ *Do "preference" and "intent-to-purchase" responses make you deaf to reality?* The fact that six out of ten test customers tell you they intend to buy your new product doesn't mean you'll capture 60 percent of the market in the real world. See Chapter 13.

Jump Start
Products involving new and unfamiliar technology require informed test customers. How do you get informed test customers? You inform them.

Buzzword
A *field trial*, also called an *extended user trial*, allows customers to use a product over a certain time period, usually at their own site.

➤ *Can anyone hear the results of the finest of fine-tuning?* Be careful when you interpret test-customer responses to last-minute product tweaking. If the differences between version A and version B are subtle and difficult to distinguish, you are apt to obtain misleading preference results. To "please" you, test customers will tend to fabricate a preference where, in fact, they have none.

In addition to the pitfalls of late-stage test *interpretation*, it is also possible to create test *conditions* that may contaminate the results:

➤ Beware of picking "friendly" customers for your late-stage tests. If they like you, they will probably deliver positively biased responses.

➤ You—or whoever is leading the project—should be present at major field-trial sites. You need to *see* the conditions under which testing is taking place. Blind faith has no place in late-stage testing.

Testing, Testing...1, 2, 3

Market testing has been covered in chapters 10 through 14, but, at this stage of the development game, you've got a prototype or even early production samples to work with. Depending on the type of product you're testing, you may use qualitative or quantitative methods. If you have a limited number of prototypes to work with, your approach must be qualitative, probably based primarily on conversations with a few test users. If, however, you're dealing with packaged goods, you may be able to distribute a sufficient quantity of samples to run a meaningful quantitative test, in which users respond on questionnaires, which are tabulated and analyzed.

Product

Prior to late-stage testing, all of the key personnel who have been involved in the product's development should meet to draw up a list of concerns, potential problem areas to be addressed, and development assumptions to be validated. It should also be made clear at this point what aspects of the product can and cannot be modified. Unless you're willing to scrap a product at this late stage and go back to the drawing board, there is no reason to probe deeply into issues about which you can do nothing. You will need to have confidence that earlier testing and earlier judgments are valid on the main points.

It is most likely that late-stage testing will be monadic; that is, only one product—the prototype or pilot production model—will be tested. In a sense, this is a very realistic test method, because the real world is monadic. People don't usually buy two brands at a time in order to test one against the other.

With some products, it may be practical and desirable to create more than one kind of prototype or limited-production sample and then test in order to decide which version to put into full production. It's also possible to test your product against that of a competitor, using one of the following techniques:

➤ A *paired comparison* tests two products, either simultaneously or one after the other.

➤ *Repeat pairs* is a more sophisticated version of the paired comparison. It is designed to eliminate the possibility that, in expressing preference, consumers are really doing nothing more than making random choices. Two side-by-side (simultaneous) paired comparisons are conducted, one after the other, on the same group of consumers. The first set of comparisons offers a pair of code-labeled products, which the consumer uses; he is then interviewed. The second set offers the same pair of products, but coded with different labels. The two are used,

Jump Start
Ideally, late-stage testing is about making relatively minor product adjustments. It should not be the "final exam" on which the grade for the entire "course" depends.

Buzzword
Monadic testing offers consumers a single product to test.

Jump Start
A sequential paired comparison—in which Product A is used and the consumer is interviewed, then Product B is used and the consumer is interviewed again—is often more reliable than simultaneous paired comparison. It more closely simulates the conditions of real-world use.

False Start
Paired comparisons can get very unwieldy and tedious if multiple pairs are involved. This may skew your results.

and the consumer is interviewed again. If consumer choices are random, one quarter of the respondents will pick one product twice in a row by chance, and one quarter will pick the other product twice in row by chance. If such results turn up, you know that consumers have no real preference in the case of these two products. If substantially different results show up, you can be confident that your test group is expressing a genuine preference, which might well have significance for what product version you put into full production.

➤ *BIB ("balanced incomplete block")* is a method for testing larger numbers of products. It is not usually applicable in late-stage testing, because it is unlikely that *many* different prototypes will be available. However, the method is worth explaining. Two or three of several products are tested at a time, the order and the products rotated in a balanced way. Although not every product is tested in every possible position against every other product (hence the "incomplete" block), the sampling variety is sufficient to create a quick, practical, reliable test.

Package

Packaging should be thought of as integral to the product. More than just a container, it serves as:

➤ A consumer grabber

➤ Advertising

➤ A carrier of information (including ingredients, instructions, cautions, appropriate uses, and applications)

➤ A messenger of value

➤ A conveyor of special deals and promotions

➤ An incentive to purchase—*if* the package builds consumer expectations effectively

In addition, a physically convenient package may make a critical difference in a purchasing decision. (For example, a resealable package for perishable food products should reseal effectively and be easy to use.) A well-constructed package will help prevent damage to the product.

Package testing *should* be done early in the process of developing a marketing strategy. However, in the later stages, you may have more than one packaging option still to test or you may simply want to do last-minute validation of a single packaging option. In either case, you will want to get responses to at least some of the following:

➤ Product name

➤ Color scheme

➤ Illustrations/photos

➤ Logo

➤ Package style and material

➤ Shape and size

➤ Informational panels

Generally, effective packaging is highly *visible*. It can be found readily on a store shelf, and its essential elements can be read easily. You can test these key aspects of packaging using three methods:

1. A tachistoscope, eye camera, or pupil meter can be used to obtain precise, objective information on what areas of the packaging catch consumers' eyes.

2. "Find-time" can be measured by bringing respondents into a simulated retail display stocked with various product packages, including the package for your new product. The respondent is asked to find the product, and his effort is timed.

3. Visual impact can also be measured by showing slides of a store display that includes your product, among others. The image is shown for a set number of seconds, then the respondent is asked to describe what he remembers.

False Start
It is usually impractical to test *every* aspect of the packaging. Marketers, not consumers, give thought to packaging details.

Buzzword
Find-time is the amount of time it takes shoppers to locate a given product on a store shelf. One objective of packaging is to minimize find-time.

After sheer visibility, the *image* the package conveys is of key importance. Consumers can be asked what they like and don't like about the overall look of the package. They can be asked specifically to talk about what messages the packaging delivers about the product inside. This kind of testing may or may not be very helpful in adjusting package nuances, but it can uncover hidden problems and consumer turn-offs.

Finally, the package should be observed in use. Is it easy to handle? Easy to grasp? Sturdy enough? Convenient enough? Is the resealable function really and truly functional? Are all instructions easy to find, easy to read, complete, and clear?

Advertising

Advertising is perhaps the most difficult ingredient in the marketing mix to evaluate. This may surprise you, since common sense tells us that the purpose of advertising is to generate sales; therefore, you have only to measure the effect of a particular advertising campaign on sales volume in order to ascertain whether or not the campaign is effective. The problem is that it's not so easy to correlate advertising and sales.

It is difficult to isolate advertising from other ingredients in the marketing mix:

➤ Measuring the effect of *your* advertising when competitors may vary *their* advertising. That up-tick you see in sales for November—is it due to *your* new ads, or is it because competing *Brand X* did not advertise heavily that month?

➤ It may be difficult to calculate the time lag between the introduction of new ads and their impact on sales.

➤ Advertising is not like a light switch—flip it and the bulb burns. Advertising tends to work cumulatively, building up consumer awareness not just of a particular product, but of an entire company over a period of months and even years.

➤ Your mode of distribution (for example, if you are an OEM; see "And How Ya Gonna Reach 'Em?" in Chapter 18, "Distribution, Distribution, Distribution") may insulate you from consumers, making it difficult to see or to interpret minor variations in sales.

The point is that late-stage or post-launch testing of advertising may be too complicated to be truly effective. Nevertheless, you have three options:

1. Draw on the expertise of a good advertising agency to create what promises to be an effective ad, launch the product, and watch sales for a time. If sales meet or exceed projections, don't bother testing the advertising.

2. If sales prove significantly disappointing, advertising is one ingredient of the marketing mix that you should review. Just remember that it is only *one* of many ingredients.

3. Test advertising earlier in the new product development process, perhaps as soon as you have mock-ups or early prototypes.

Because there are so many obstacles to correlating sales with ad campaigns, it is generally more effective to define relatively modest and specific objectives to test. For example, does the ad/campaign effectively:

➤ Create consumer awareness of the product, brand, or company?

➤ Communicate the product benefits and features that make it unique, that show it as clearly superior to the competition?

➤ Create favorable consumer attitudes?

➤ Motivate purchase or create a predisposition to purchase?

➤ Help to generate repeat business by reinforcing satisfaction with the purchase?

Specific research techniques also isolate different aspects of the advertising. You might try out advertising copy on focus groups or through consumer interviews. Usually, research on advertising copy must be qualitative; however, it is possible to introduce a quantitative element by creating a questionnaire that asks respondents to indicate on a grade scale (1 to 5, perhaps) the degree to which a particular piece of copy is persuasive, humorous, informative, exciting, and so on.

With print ads, it is possible to show test groups a number of ads and simply ask them to choose the one they like best. A variation on this is to show each respondent a portfolio of several ads, including the specific ad that's being tested, then close the portfolio and ask the respondent to name as many brands and products as he can remember. If your brand is consistently *not* among these, it's probably time to rethink the ad.

It is also possible to actually publish a test ad by inserting it into selected quantities of certain magazines (this is called "tipping in"). A sample consumer group is recruited—usually through shopping mall intercepts—to take the magazine home and read it. At the time each respondent is recruited, a telephone callback time is arranged. During the callback, the respondent is asked to recall the test ad. A number of established professional consulting firms are prepared to carry out this and similar kinds of research. The best known are Gallup & Robinson Inc. (609-924-3400) and Mapes & Ross Inc. (609-924-8600).

Like print ads, radio ads are relatively inexpensive to test in multiple versions, and they can be tested in similar ways, using a simple tape recorder and without having to pay for broadcast time. Television ads, however, are much more expensive to test, especially if you insist on showing test groups fully produced, finished commercials. Usually, it's more practical to show storyboards or other rough-and-ready material.

A number of consulting firms specialize in the measurement of aspects of television advertising.

Jump Start
Do you think that you are in business to sell products and services? Think again. Your primary goal should be to create satisfied customers. Satisfaction leverages a single customer into multiple sales.

Two of the best-known firms are ASI Market Research Inc. (818-637-5600) and Research Systems Corporation (812-425-4562), but there are many others. They specialize in such techniques as "day-after recall," in which respondents are recruited to watch a certain television program during which your ad will be broadcast. After the broadcast, the respondents are questioned—by phone—about their recall of the ad. The results are analyzed against historical data concerning ads for products in similar categories. Another method is "theater persuasion measures," in which test groups are invited to a theater to watch what is usually described as a television pilot. Commercials are inserted into the pilot. Before the show, the test group is questioned about their preference among certain brands of products. After the show, the test group is again asked about their interest in the products. The idea is to gauge the effectiveness of the ad in influencing intent-to-purchase decisions.

Satisfaction

New product development should not stop after the product is launched. One way or another, you need to stay in contact with your customers, who will tell you how satisfied—or dissatisfied—they are with your new product. This does not necessarily require sophisticated research. A good customer service program can gather a great deal of response information. So can your sales, distributor, and dealer networks. Listen to them. You may also find it useful to send letters to customers, soliciting their opinions, comments, and feedback. This is an especially useful technique to use for non-consumer—business-to-business, industrial, and professional—products. Alternatively, you can prepare (or have a consulting firm prepare) full-scale tests.

Buzzword
Regression analysis is a multivariate statistical technique that relates a dependent variable (the thing you're trying to predict) to one or more independent variables (the predictors, the things—such as demographics, attitudes, etc.—that explain or predict the differences in the dependent variables).

However you go about tapping into customer response, be aware that satisfaction has three key dimensions:

1. The product meets the *customer's* priorities.

2. The product meets the *customer's* performance expectations.

3. The product exceeds what the *customer* perceives as the performance of competitors' products.

Create and ask your questions accordingly.

What Do Customers Want?

You could just ask. Present customers with a list of product performance criteria, benefits, and/or features, and ask them to rank or rate these in order of importance. You can also perform a regression analysis to identify the product factors most highly correlated with overall satisfaction.

What Do Customers Expect?

Again, you could ask customers what they expect from the product or service you offer. Then you can see just where you exceed expectations, where you meet them, and where you fail to measure up. This technique can be ratcheted up to a higher level of sophistication through gap analysis:

1. Create a profile of an excellent product or excellent supplier.

2. Ask customers to rate your product's (and/or your company's) performance in areas that correspond to elements of the profile.

3. Look for gaps between the profile and your performance ratings.

Act on the gaps by trying to fill them.

False Start
In looking at the competition, don't lose your focus on the customer. Regardless of where you seem to stack up against competitors, it is the degree of *customer satisfaction* that is the more critical key to success.

Stacking Up Against the Competition

To obtain a subjective picture of how you stack up against the competition, ask your customers. However, you should also look for objective criteria, such as price, performance, features, benefits, and value, as well as product or service elements that are specific to the kind of product or service you're selling (for example, your mountain bike includes a kick-stand and a gel-foam padded seat, which are extra-cost options on other brands). You can then plot out graphically where you're meeting, beating, or lagging behind the competition.

Jump Start
Late-phase and post-launch testing serve no purpose if they aren't "actionable"—that is, capable of being acted on. Create tests that will yield answers you can actually use to improve the new product, generate more sales, and create greater satisfaction.

The Least You Need to Know

➤ Quality is critical in every phase of product development, as well as in the product itself.

➤ Don't limit late-stage testing to the product, but also include packaging and advertising.

➤ Late-stage testing should address issues that can be acted on, adjusted, tweaked, and improved.

Part 6
Can You Do It Again?

Think you'll have it made with one new product success under your belt? Think again. These days, new products typically account for one-third of sales revenue. That means that developing new products has to become a way of life for you and your business. I offer in this final section some strategies for making innovation the rule rather than the exception. The dimensions of these strategies include ways of staying in touch with marketplace trends and marketplace needs, techniques for "keeping score" in order to measure the success of what you do, and some guidelines to help you flex your "risk muscle" and keep a sharp edge on your creative attitude.

Chapter 23

From Flash in the Pan to Eternal Flame

In This Chapter

➤ Why you need a new product strategy

➤ The five basic strategies

➤ Choosing your new product arenas

Let's just suppose your new product is a smash hit—takes the market by storm. What then? A comfortable retirement? Well, maybe, if it's a *really* great product....

More likely, though, you'll come to work the day after launch, and the day after that, and the day after that. The fact is that very few wars are won in a single battle, and even fewer wars are won without a plan that anticipates battle after battle, fighting toward some overall goal. The same thing is true for creating and marketing new products. You need a plan, and this chapter will suggest ways of making one in order to repeat new product triumphs.

Making Customers vs. Making a Sale

The stupidest thing a salesperson can do is set his or her sights on *making the sale*. Unless you really don't care about tomorrow, the goal of a sales department is not to make *a sale* here and *a* sale there, but to make customers *everywhere*. A good salesperson needs an overall plan to leverage each single sale into a satisfied customer who will be the source of many sales—now and over the years.

Buzzword
Marketing experts call a firm's new product strategy its *product innovation charter (PIC)*—a written statement of the goals and processes of new product development within the company.

Paint the Big Picture

To leverage similarly a single new product success into one success after another requires a well-defined new product strategy. Your strategy should answer three very large, very key questions:

1. What markets should we be in?

2. What products should we create?

3. What technologies should we work?

Pyrrhic Victory

If you're tempted even to *consider* innovating without a strategy, give thought to the fate of Pyrrhus, who ascended the throne of Epirus (northwestern Greece) in 307 B.C. In 280—remember, this is B.C., so count backwards—Pyrrhus led 25,000 men and 20 elephants against the Roman legions at the Battle of Heraclea. He had not planned very well, but he and his men fought bravely, and they won, albeit at great cost. Congratulated on the victory, Pyrrhus replied, "One more such victory and I shall be lost."

Without a sound strategy, even a *successful* new product launch can ultimately lead to disaster. It can strangle cashflow. It can lead you into an area of technology you cannot afford to develop sufficiently to remain competitive. It can lead you into distribution channels that prove dead ends. It can cause you to compete with yourself, to deal knockout blows to your existing product line.

And that's a *successful* new product launch! If, however, your new baby falls on his face, and you are without a plan, well, the disaster will just come a lot more quickly and be a lot messier.

Developing a New Product Strategy

To answer the three major questions that will guide your new product program, develop two major *whats* and a single *how:*

1. In the long term, what role will new products play in your firm? (The answer might include a projected percentage of income to be generated by new products. Of course, it will also have to include projected costs and acceptable risks.)

2. Into what arenas do you want to enter? ("Arenas" include markets, market segments, products, technologies, and so on. Which ones will you define as fair game? Why? Which ones will remain off limits? Why?)

Now for the *how*. You need an overall plan for implementing your innovation goals. *How will we achieve our goals?* The *how* should always be formulated with reference to the *whats*. Review Chapter 2 for a list of possible new-product innovation options.

Choose Your Strategy Scenario

Open the window—not to jump, but to take a nice, bracing breath of fresh air. The good news is that, in most established corporations, a majority of new products do succeed, and they are generally responsible for somewhat more than a third of sales revenue. Many firms have a deliberate, consciously conceived innovation strategy. In even more firms, however, the "strategy" is accidental and inconsistent—a strategy by default. So maybe it shouldn't be called a strategy, but simply "the way we do things." But, often, "the way we do things" can be improved.

Marketing professor Robert G. Cooper identified five distinct innovation strategies among 120 corporations he studied. Remember, the "strategies" aren't always consciously chosen, but may just be "the way we do things."

Type A is the technologically driven strategy. More than a quarter of Cooper's firms followed it, which suggests that this is the most popular innovation strategy around. Basically, R&D runs the show in these firms, and the philosophy—"hope" is a better word for it—is that "If we build it, they will come." In fact, this popular strategy is inefficient. While it may produce some exciting products, the lack of market focus often results in a low rate of success and poor profitability.

Buzzword
An *entry strategy* is the official-sounding term for *how* you plan to implement innovation goals in order to enter new arenas.

Jump Start
The PIC—product innovation charter—does not exist in a vacuum. It should be part and parcel of an overall corporate strategy.

Jump Start
A study by Robert G. Cooper (published in the second edition of his *Winning at New Products*) found that, among 120 firms he looked at, the average success rate for new products was 67 percent. Seventeen percent of new products failed after launch, and 16 percent were killed prior to launch. Among the 120 firms Cooper studied, new products represented an average of 36.5 percent of current sales.

Type B is the balanced strategy, which 15.6 percent of Cooper's 120 firms followed. This approach balances technological factors against market orientation, with results that are significantly better than the average. Whereas the average new product success rate is about 66 percent, "Type B" firms enjoyed a 72 percent success rate, and while new products, on average, account for a little more than a third of sales, for "Type B" firms, they account for 47 percent. Since "Type B" is the clear winner among innovation strategies, we'll return to it in a moment.

Type C strategy is technologically deficient. This is essentially a "me-too" approach to new products and was followed by 15.6 percent of the Cooper study's firms. Results are well below average. The "me-too" new product strategy does not guarantee failure, but it does yield a relatively low rate of success with new products. You're better off innovating.

Type D is a low-budget, conservative innovation strategy. A high percentage of Cooper's companies—23.8 percent—followed this strategy, and it's not a bad approach, although it isn't as generally successful as the Type B strategy. For Type D companies, innovation is incremental and stays close to home. Typically, the new products are line extensions rather than out-and-out innovations. Impact on sales revenue is unspectacular, but steady.

Type E companies seem to take a *ready, fire, aim!* approach to innovation, allocating a high budget to a diverse new-product program. Almost 19 percent of Cooper's firms followed this practice, with results about as disappointing as the "me-too" folks in Type C firms.

Anatomy of a Winning Strategy

Let's look at the Type B balanced strategy a bit more closely, since it yielded the most impressive results. Here are some of the salient guidelines that make up this strategy:

➤ Seeks markets with high potential growth.

➤ Avoids competitive markets.

➤ Avoids markets new to the firm.

➤ Technologically sophisticated and innovative, but always market oriented.

➤ NOT afraid to embrace a skimming (premium) pricing strategy.

Set Objectives

Whatever strategy you choose, define a destination, a set of objectives for new product development. This should not be some vague idea in your head or in the corporation's collective unconscious, but a clearly stated part of a written plan. Viable role objectives for new product development include (among many others):

➤ Percentage of company sales derived from new products by a certain time.

➤ Percentage of corporate profits derived from new products by a certain time.

➤ Dollar figure of revenue to be derived from new products by a certain time.

➤ Percentage of growth derived from new products over a stated period.

➤ Proportion of new, innovative products versus updates, line extensions, and so forth.

➤ The role of the new products—for example, to hold a market share, to expand a market share, to exploit company strengths, etc.

Once role objectives are defined, you should also operate from stated—and budgeted—performance objectives. Set realistic targets for:

➤ New product success rates

➤ New product kill rates (prior to launch)

➤ Number of new products entering development

➤ Minimum financial goals for any new project

Obviously, you cannot meaningfully formulate performance objectives until you have set role objectives for new products.

Jump Start
Objectives should be measurable. Metrics—the art and science of keeping score—will be discussed in the next chapter.

Enter the Right Arenas

What business are you in?

As we saw back in Chapter 2, this isn't all that easy to answer. Instead of thinking in terms of specific products or services, you might try thinking in terms of arenas—combinations of product, market, and technology areas. An arena should define an area of synergy.

For example, a publisher of reference books may decide that its arena is not reference *book* publishing, but information gathering, processing, and distribution. Printed books play a role in this arena, of course, but so do online technology and CD-ROM publishing. Perhaps the company's information-gathering assets can be leveraged not just to create materials for general publication, but to create custom publications tailored to specific users—to create publications on demand. An outsider, looking at the reference book publisher, might suggest that the company expand simply by publishing other kinds of books—novels, say. But those inside the company recognize that this area lies outside of any appropriate arena; that is, the company's synergies have less to do with publishing *books* per se than with gathering and exploiting information.

Thinking of Dimensions

Try thinking of arenas in at least three basic dimensions:

> *Who:* What customer groups do you serve? (For example, does our reference book publisher serve the book-buying public? Or does it serve people who need information on certain topics?)

Prototype

Who: Rubbermaid Corporation has long been admired as an example of corporate management at its best. For years, housewares industry mavens called it the "new product machine." In his privately printed memoir, *Like Only Yesterday*, Donald E. Noble, Rubbermaid's chief executive officer emeritus, describes how new product development began humbly in the 1920s with director James R. Caldwell's flair for working in the kitchen (and thinking up new kitchen gadgets in the process), then progressed to the creation of a formal Product Review Committee. The committee met monthly, submitting ideas for further development to a semi-annual review. Ideas came from every conceivable source—customers, buyers, store clerks, salespeople, factory employees, executives—and were added to what Noble called the "Laundry List."

> *What:* What applications are created? What customer needs are served? (In the case of our reference book publisher, do its customers need *books,* or do they need *information*—which, traditionally, has just happened to come in book form?)

Prototype

What: Typically, some 300 ideas were reviewed semi-annually. Of these, 20 would be more intensively studied, and perhaps three would go on to actual development. At first, opinions were solicited informally from corporate wives, but, starting in 1955, Rubbermaid invented its own version of the focus group, taking the product ideas to groups of "church women" and "band mothers" for their (modestly paid) opinions.

How: What technology, processes, and raw materials are required to create the company's products? Can these be profitably manipulated to create other products? (The reference book publisher's raw material is information, which he decides to use to create a line of CD-ROMs, a dial-up subscriber online information service, and a custom research service.)

Prototype

How: By the 1960s, Noble established a goal of 30 percent of annual sales to be derived from products introduced within the past five years. (The company's present goal is 33 percent.) "Me-too" products were banned. A new product "had to be totally new or had to have an improvement making it demonstrably better than anything currently being sold." Furthermore, the company developed a strategy allowing the development of a new product "if we knew either the manufacturing processes or the marketing requirements involved.... Although we could overcome one hurdle, two would constitute an unacceptable risk. So we never entered into a new product development project where we neither knew how to manufacture the product nor how to market it."

Thinking in these three dimensions should simultaneously open up new arenas for new product development, yet should also define these arenas and products in a way that makes sense for your company by exploiting current synergies, current markets, and current levels of technological expertise.

Where's the Entrance?

Once you decide that a particular new arena is appropriate for your company, you must figure out a way to enter it. E. B. Roberts and C. A. Berry, in an article published in *Sloan Management Review* (Spring 1983), put together a four-dimensional framework to help think through entry strategies. Relative to a company's "base business" (the arena in which a company currently competes), a new arena may be evaluated according to:

➤ *Newness of a technology:* This is the degree to which the new arena involves technologies new to the company; its current products do not embody the technology represented by the new arena.

➤ *Newness of a market:* This is the degree to which the new arena involves markets not currently targeted by the company.

➤ *Familiarity with a technology:* This is the degree to which knowledge of the new arena's technology exists within the company. This may range from some knowledge (even though the technology is not embodied in current company products) to expertise (the knowledge is currently exploited in the company's products).

➤ *Familiarity with a market:* This is the degree to which the new arena's market is known to the company. However, the company may or may not currently be selling to this market.

How can you put this framework to use? The answer is simple. Your greatest chances of new product success tend to be in arenas that involve technologies and markets already familiar to your company. You are taking a bigger leap if you venture into an area of unfamiliar technology but familiar market, or familiar technology but unfamiliar market. And you are taking a giant leap if both the technology and the market are unfamiliar. Will the longest leaps prove fatal? Maybe not. Maybe they will lead to great things. But the risks are probably substantial, and it will be very difficult to build a new product strategy on wholly unfamiliar ground.

From the Inside

It is possible to enter an arena from within your current company, by developing your in-house resources and acquiring, for in-house use, the resources you don't currently possess. Sometimes, it will be most effective to create new entrepreneurial companies—wholly owned subsidiaries—within the current company.

Buzzword

Strategic partnering is usually an alliance of a large firm with a small firm for the purpose of creating a specialized new product. Typically, the larger firm supplies venture capital and the necessary marketing and distribution muscle, while the small firm furnishes the specialized creative expertise.

From the Outside

Another way to enter new arenas is to acquire a company. Corel, a maker of graphics-related and desktop-publishing software, wanted to get into the related arena of word processing. Instead of spending a fortune of time and cash on reinventing word processing, then trying to compete in a market dominated by two or three software suppliers, the firm acquired an established leader, WordPerfect.

But you don't *have* to acquire a company in order to enter an arena from the outside. Often, you can license various technologies for use in your new product. You may even be able to license entire products to sell under your name.

Beyond acquisition and licensing, there are joint ventures, in which two or more companies pool their separate strengths to create a new product that requires multiple expertise. The most common forms of joint venture are strategic partnering and mutual pursuit joint ventures.

Best-Laid Plans

Of the many satisfactions and rewards new product development brings, a guarantee of success is not one of them. Being told that better than two-thirds of new products that are actually launched succeed— and that an additional 16 percent are killed in development before they can do much harm—is

> **Buzzword**
> *Mutual pursuit* joint ventures are informal alliances, often between a smaller and a larger firm, to create specific products. No third "joint venture" corporation is formally created.

little comfort if you happen to hang your career on one of the 17 percent of new products that fail. ("I'm going to shoot you out of this cannon. There is only a 17 percent chance that the experience will prove fatal. Relax! Enjoy!") But we've already seen that innovating can be rewarding and, in any case, is probably *necessary* for long-term survival. These being the facts of life, it is wise to do everything you can to stack the odds in your favor, and that means refusing to rely on one-shot successes. New product strategies pay off.

The Least You Need to Know

➤ There are many new-product development risks you can do little to control, but you *can* choose to operate with a conscious, considered strategy—and that alone will help you manage some of the risks.

➤ It is helpful to think of your business in terms of "arenas," which unite considerations of *who*, *what*, and *how*, thereby defining your business in three dimensions.

➤ If you are committed to innovating, the most consistently successful strategy is one that balances advanced technology against a current knowledge of the marketplace.

Chapter 24

What the World Needs Now

In This Chapter

➤ Metrics: what, why, and how

➤ Keeping in touch with trends and needs

➤ The creative beat: problem-solution rhythm

➤ Managing new product development by managing people

The chapter you just left suggested some approaches to creating a new product strategy. That chapter was about strategy. This one is about attitude—about creating and maintaining a business orientation that fosters new product development and helps to ensure its success.

Creating a business orientation friendly to new product development involves staying in touch with your "babies" after they leave the nest—tracking how new products fare in the marketplace—as well as staying in touch with the world as a whole. It also involves a commitment to innovative people and a willingness to reinvent yourself or your department or your entire company as may be necessary to achieve the goal of excellence or even plain old survival.

Keeping Score

To the half of the nation that does not spend "Superbowl Sunday" transfixed before the tube, the fact that the other half does is a source of mystery and wonder. What is *so* appealing about *watching* people play a game? Why does life grind to a halt come the Superbowl? Why, in some parts of the world, do riots and even entire wars erupt over soccer games? I suppose there are a lot of reasons, many of them I won't mention. But let me suggest that at least *one* source of attraction and gratification in competitive sports is that, whatever else the play generates, it produces a score. It's easy to see who won and who lost. It's easy to see how well "your" team did.

Or is it?

Just how much does a score tell you? What does it measure? Basically, it measures certain goals achieved— home runs, baskets, whatever—but the score hardly tells the whole story of just exactly how well or how poorly the team played. Casual sports fans are interested only in scores, but true fanatics are into *statistics*—the "stats." Baseball fans, for example, pore over the figures that report a player's hits, runs, errors, RBIs, and earned-run average as solemnly as a serious investor examines the tables in an annual report.

How do you keep score on a new product? Obviously, you look at sales. The raw numbers say something—like whether you made money or not. But just as the final score in a ball game doesn't tell the whole tale of that game, so sales figures alone do not supply sufficient information for measuring the performance of new products. I touched on evaluating customer satisfaction in Chapter 22, and satisfaction is usually the most important factor—actually, it's a cluster of factors—to measure. Marketing professionals call the process of measuring product performance "metrics."

Buzzword
Metrics is the art and science of measuring product performance in the marketplace.

Metrics are a way of making a process visible, of identifying those elements of a new product that are working well in the marketplace and those that are faltering. Metrics provide a basis for making post-launch decisions about the product.

What Do You Measure?

Business folk *speak* many languages—all the languages of the world, in fact—but they *hear* one language more clearly than any other. It's called the language of business, and its nouns, verbs, adjectives, and adverbs are dollars (or *lire, yen, francs, marks, pesetas, pesos,* whatever). To measure is to quantify, and, in business, anything quantified ultimately gets translated into units of dough. Now, when businesspeople hear about *dollars,* they act. So whatever you decide to measure—to express a numerical score—is what will likely get acted on. Measure it, and it may be done. So you'd better be sure you're *measuring* what you want to *do.*

Maybe you already know what aspects of new product performance you want to measure. But if you aren't sure, a foolproof place to start is with the concept of customer satisfaction. Now you may begin to quantify customer satisfaction by translating it into terms of customer value. But what, exactly, are the elements—the *measurable* elements—of customer value? A good way to ferret these out is to create a tree diagram of customer value. This is a graphical, hierarchical representation of what constitutes customer value. Here is a very simple customer value tree:

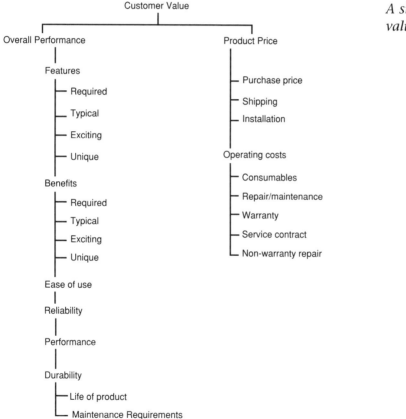

A simple "customer value" tree.

The tree should be the work of key R&D, engineering, production, marketing, sales, and finance people with, if possible, input from actual customers. What they produce may be very complex, with hundreds of elements, or it may be relatively simple. Just what goes

False Start
Quantifying priorities can be a chicken-and-egg dilemma. You can't quantify the elements of the equation without measuring (that is, conducting a survey), but you don't want to conduct a survey without first determining priorities. One answer is to conduct studies—or use published studies—to determine the value factors consumers deem most important. Another solution is to extrapolate from previous launch experiences.

into your tree depends on the product or service you create and the customers you serve. But it is usually impractical to measure *every* element on even the simplest tree.

The next step, after you've drawn up the tree diagram, is to decide which *few* elements are worth measuring. These should be the factors you identify as most strongly contributing to customer value. You might determine these factors subjectively, by making some commonsense leap-of-faith assumptions about your product and your customers. If, however, you have research data from previous new product launches, you may be able to extrapolate that information to this case.

You may find it helpful to quantify the components of priority. The *PDMA Handbook of New Product Development* (John Wiley, 1996) suggests two equations for establishing the priority of each attribute of customer value:

priority = importance × performance gap

where: performance gap = desired level of performance ÷ current level of performance

➤ *Importance* is the degree to which a change in the attribute under investigation will influence the customer's perception of product value. *Importance* is quantified as a percentage of the entire customer value.

➤ *Current level of performance* is how well the product under investigation is performing with respect to the attribute under investigation. It is usually expressed as a rating figure on a scale you establish (for example, 1 to 5, 1 to 10, etc.).

➤ *Desired level of performance* is a quantification (on whatever scale you establish for evaluating the current level of performance) of where you want the new product to be.

➤ The *performance gap* should be a point spread between the current and desired levels of performance.

More Numbers

Even after you put numbers to key value attributes, you're not done counting yet. Let's say you're marketing a new high-end CD player. "High accuracy" has emerged from your market research as something your customers *really* want from a great CD player. How do you measure accuracy? Well, *you're* building the product, so it's up to *you* to decide. Probably, accuracy can be quantified in terms of figures for audio distortion, which engineers call wow and flutter. Similarly, you are marketing a new, inexpensive, high-capacity hard disk drive for personal computers. Market studies show that "reliability" is a key attribute of perceived value. For critical high-use components such as hard drives, "mean time between failures" (MTBF), expressed in hours, is a standard measure of reliability, which predicts how long the component will operate without error or breakdown.

In the absence of engineering or industry standards, you may have to be inventive. Let's go back to the issue of reliability. What if MTBF figures for your product don't exist? You might instead count up repair calls over a certain period and compare the frequency of repairs on the new product with averages for your established products. If there is a gap, you'd better modify the product to close that gap—especially if customers have identified "reliability" as a key value issue.

> **Jump Start**
> Good metrics are objective, accurate, and informative. To whatever degree possible, they should have reference to accepted industry standards. This makes the metrics easy to communicate and understand.

It Don't Mean a Thing if You Let Go the String

The key to a meaningful program of metrics is consistency and longevity. That means a string of tests over time. Consistently monitor new product performance over a long period—if possible, over the life of the product. Then be certain that you express the measurements in a meaningful way and for meaningful reasons. Here are three important considerations to take into account before embarking on a metrics program:

> ➤ Is the purpose of the measurement to improve performance? If it is, you must set an improvement goal. Express it as a number, a measured gap that can, degree by degree, be closed.

> ➤ If you are satisfied with the current level of performance, and the measurement is part of a program to maintain performance levels, set a minimum performance threshold. Should performance numbers dip below this threshold, action must be taken.

> ➤ Are the goals achievable? Do you have the resources? Do you have commitment from the staff?

Collect data regularly, and report the results regularly. Share the results with everyone responsible for the product. Results should be reported as straightforward, vivid graphs, not just rows of numbers.

> **Buzzword**
> Whereas the Internet can link your organization to the outside world, an *intranet*, built on the model of the Internet, networks the people within your organization. More than an e-mail system, it is a sophisticated, interactive electronic bulletin board, characteristically with a strong graphical orientation.

Don't Just Sit There...Analyze the Data

Begin your analysis by identifying the greatest performance gap, then use this as the focus of new-product group discussions aimed at discovering the causes of the gap. This important exercise can be a fixture of periodic reviews of the product. Once causes have been identified, steps should be agreed on to correct the problems and close the gap. The next scheduled measurement session should tell you how well you've done. Of course, it's possible that you will never be able to close the performance gap. In this case, your measurements may be telling you to resume innovating and come up with an entirely new product.

Tune In and Turn On

Metrics are hardly the only way of staying in touch with the world and what it wants. Many would-be innovators look for trends and, in fact, try to anticipate them in order to "ride the crest of the wave." This can be a most inexact and risky business, to say the least, albeit a fascinating and seductive pursuit—and that is why the books of futurists like Alvin Toffler and Joel Arthur Barker and trend gurus like Faith Popcorn sell so well.

False Start
By the time most of us pick up on a trend, it is often too late to catch the crest of that fabled wave. On the other hand, make your assumptions too soon, and the trend may prove a fluke. Trend marketing is a matter of critical timing and lots of good luck.

But there is another, far less exotic approach to tuning into consumer needs and wants: Innovate by *recognizing problems* and *finding solutions*. Problems have certain key advantages over trends:

➤ Problems are almost always easier to identify than trends.

➤ Problems are often more "real," more "substantial," more "enduring" than trends. They make a more solid foundation on which to build a new product.

➤ Problems are almost always more urgent than trends. Consumers *may* buy a product because they want it. However, they *must* buy a product if they *need* it. Problems generate needs rather than wants.

Keeping Up with Change

Make it a part of your ongoing program of new product development to look for problems and to look for ways in which you and your company can solve them. Look, too, at how others solve them. I once had a music teacher who explained the essence of classical composition in very simple and vivid terms that have stayed with me ever since. She said that even the most magnificent Mozart symphony is, at the most basic level, a series of musical questions and answers. If three inquiring notes ascend the scale, you can be sure that another three descending notes will answer. In this way, the music moves forward, with a graceful urgency no one has ever achieved more wonderfully than old Wolfgang Amadeus.

This question-and-answer analogy is not limited to classical music. In fact, most meaningful change can be seen in terms of a rhythm of questions and answers, of problems and solutions. Back in Chapter 10, I discussed some methods of staying in touch with customer needs, technological developments, and developments in your field. Let me suggest now that you shouldn't settle for merely keeping abreast of change, but that you should actively *engage* change by learning to see it in terms of problems and solutions, questions and answers.

Kicking the Wheel

It is not always necessary to respond to each perceived problem with an invention or a new product. Look at your current products on an ongoing basis with an eye toward modifying, improving, and evolving them to answer newly emerging needs.

Inventors talk about "ramifying" their basic inventions. This is a process of modifying it in order to make it faster, cheaper, better, bigger, smaller, stronger, lighter—whatever. One viable ramification strategy is to exploit the *basic* invention commercially, let it pioneer or even create a market for itself, then introduce the *ramified* product ("New and Improved!") into this prepared market. Instead of a single sale to a given customer, you may make two—the basic product and, later, its ramification. Software developers have institutionalized this approach and, typically, even offer consumers the incentive of special "upgrade" pricing as they introduce each ramified iteration of their original product.

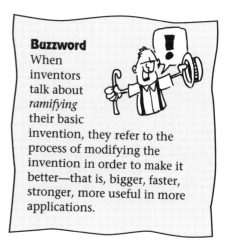

Buzzword
When inventors talk about *ramifying* their basic invention, they refer to the process of modifying the invention in order to make it better—that is, bigger, faster, stronger, more useful in more applications.

Eternal Values: The Human Element

You launch the product. It's out the door, and you watch with breath held, waiting to see how the market will respond. It's a big deal, a very big deal. Not something that happens every day.

Well, the truth is that something like this *does* happen every day. I mean, at the *end* of every day, your company's real assets walk out the door. Fortunately, the next morning, they walk back in. Your greatest new product assets are not embodied within the metal or plastic or silicon of your new product. They are the flesh, bone, heads, and hearts of the human beings who work with you. New product development is distinctive, demanding, challenging, and rewarding as a business activity because it cuts across every function of a business. At minimum, it requires skillful communication management to avoid breakdowns and errors. Optimally, it requires cross-training in a variety of functions. Certainly, it requires the cooperation, coordination, and active synergy of professionals with a broad range of skills. It requires teamwork—often in spite of corporate departmental structures that foster conflicting goals and private agendas. Examples of such conflicting agendas include the following:

➤ R&D wants to reach technological nirvana—fast.

➤ Engineering wants long, orderly phases of development—not because they're slow-witted, but because they want to produce a masterpiece of performance and reliability.

➤ Manufacturing wants to minimize the number of parts; wants to use standard, off-the-shelf components.

➤ Finance wants an 80 percent gross margin. That means minimal tooling, minimal development time, and minimal investment in people and equipment.

➤ Sales and marketing are already complaining that the product is late.

Prototype

You want to make and market a brand new kind of plastic widget. One thing all departments agree on is that the widget has to *look* great. Now, to the injection mold maker, "looking good" means that parting lines are perfectly matched, that cavities are perfectly polished, that gates and ejectors are absent from outside surfaces. To the plastic processor, "looking good" means an absence of flash, sink marks, and warpage. To the design engineer, achieving a good appearance means added complications: more difficult contours to calculate and draw in order to hide assembly devices; more parts to squeeze into tighter places; more fasteners to design so that they won't appear intrusive, yet will not fatigue and fail. To the industrial designer, "looking good" is a matter of beautiful form, color, balance, and proportion. He'd like to win a design award—set a new standard of elegance. Finance, of course, wants a good-looking design that's cheap to produce. Sales and marketing want a good-looking design that's trendy so that it is guaranteed to generate sales.

All departments agree that appearance is important in this widget. But within that area of agreement, there is a vast wilderness of potential conflict and cross purposes.

Try a Little Tenderness

When you bring a new product development team together, begin by recognizing that everybody wants the product to succeed, but, to each team member, success has a different meaning. Sometimes the differences work well together. Sometimes they conflict. The new product manager needs to understand that these differences are the result of training and perception, as well as of personality—not just personality in the sense of "Mary is a nice person, but Jack can be pretty testy," but *professional* personality. Here's what I mean:

➤ R&D people tend to be inquisitive, they crave variety, they may be hypersensitive and moody, they may seem (or, indeed, be) maddeningly disorganized. A manager must nurture *and* nudge, keeping R&D on course without slamming the lid shut and suffocating the ferment of ideas.

➤ Market researchers tend to be analytical types, with a remarkable affinity for detail. Let loose, they can bury a project in numbers. The skillful project manager will keep key questions in the forefront, and will gently but relentlessly probe researchers for interpretation rather than more numbers.

➤ Engineers (and their equivalent in various industries), so essential to the development of a new product, frustrate other members of the team because they often seem reluctant to release the product to the market. Engineers labor under a built-in personality conflict. Their *profession* aims at 100 percent accuracy with 0 tolerance. Their *jobs* require them to deal with the utter uncertainty of new products. Moreover, their *profession* also poses such goals as lifetime durability and an MTBF of hundreds of thousands of hours. The realities of the marketplace—i.e., no one (the Department of Defense aside) will fork out $1,000 even for a *really good* monkey wrench— seldom permit the full exercise of the engineer's profession, and he is therefore under the continual stress of compromise. Sensitive— that is, *effective*—project managers will recognize the engineer's dilemma and will deliberately expose engineering to marketing. If possible, engineering personnel should be involved in market research, field testing, and marketing decisions.

> **Jump Start**
> The effective project manager strictly controls research costs, establishing a firm research budget from day one.

➤ Manufacturing—production—professionals tend to be like Henry Ford. You remember his infamous marketing pronunciamento regarding the Model T: *You can have any color you want, as long as it's black.* Manufacturing professionals crave standardization, minimal tooling, and turnkey solutions. It's not because they're lazy or unimaginative. It's not because they're inherently inflexible. It's because, in their

Buzzword
Ownership means giving project team members a tangible stake in, and responsibility for, the success of the project. People care most about what they "own."

Jump Start
If your sales force has regular sales meetings, why not ask them for a half hour of their time to listen to a talk about something pertinent to your product. For example, if you're going to be featuring a new technology in your product, why not give them a brief presentation on the technology? This will, in turn, help them sell the product better or even pose a question to you that you didn't think of.

profession, the discipline of simplicity and economy is highly prized. The most effective way of addressing the needs of manufacturing people is to create for new product development a separate "advanced manufacturing planning" group, which is accustomed to retooling and doing other things that are out of the ordinary.

➤ Financial people can be especially frustrating because they tend to be uninvolved during the early phases of development—when expenditures are relatively modest—then "suddenly" descend like a pack of Scrooges when tooling requires investment, materials have to be purchased, and advertising has to be budgeted. The answer is to welcome finance people early in the development stage. Give them a voice—*early*. Get them to make an ownership commitment to the project from day one.

➤ Marketing and sales may be overly optimistic, setting unrealistic expectations for the product, or they may be deliberately conservative, setting "safe" goals to ensure success in "making their numbers." Often, sales and marketing will try to provoke the other team members into rushing a product to market prematurely. The effective manager recognizes that sales and marketing are being asked to take ownership of a product they did not create. This puts special pressures on them.

The solution, as might be expected, is to get sales and marketing involved in the *creative* process as early as possible.

Products and People

To sustain new product development, you need to manage people at least as well as you manage products. Invest in people. Recruit the best you can—intelligent, inquisitive, creative, persistent, and willing and able to work in concert with others. Create a team.

➤ Give the team authority within prescribed strategic guidelines.

➤ Foster project ownership by giving team members a sense of participation from the earliest stages of development.

➤ Short-circuit formal reporting channels by creating an informal working relationship within the project team.

➤ Staff the new project team with self-starters whose judgment can be trusted. Give team members as much autonomy as possible, within strategic guidelines.

➤ Granting autonomy does not mean simply cutting the team loose and hoping for the best. Top management must stay in touch with the team, continuously communicating what is expected of the new product effort in terms of timing, technology, quality, and performance.

➤ Recognize and reward the performance of the new product development team.

> **Jump Start**
>
> If you skipped Chapter 21, maybe you should give it a second shot. Look at the section on "What Venture Capitalists Want." Try putting yourself, for a moment, in the role of a venture capitalist. Apply the venture capitalist's criteria to the process of putting together a new product development team. Believe in your people as much as in your research and your products.

Never Lose a Good Idea

If you make new product development a part of your regular way of doing business, you will have to accept the homely proposition that you'll win some and you'll lose some. Some products will succeed, some will fail, and some will result in a wash. But what you cannot tolerate losing is a good idea. A product is a product—done, finished, for better or worse. In contrast, an idea is the potential of any number of new products. It is a beginning. It is, in fact, many beginnings.

However you choose to manage the development of new products and, even more important, however you manage the people who manage the development of new products, work to create an environment in which ideas are nurtured and rewarded. To be sure, not all ideas will find embodiment in a new product. But create a space in which even those apparently non-productive ideas will never be lost. Given time, given an ever-changing marketplace, given an ever-evolving technological environment, you can never be sure just when you will need a good idea. But you can be sure that you will, sooner or later, need one.

The Least You Need to Know

➤ Key to integrating innovation into your overall business strategy is staying in touch—with your products (through, for example, metrics) and with your customer base.

➤ Instead of making vague stabs at reading "trends," take deliberate steps to identify problems and formulate solutions (that is, create new products).

➤ Become sensitive to the "human element" in the development process. Remember, without people, there *are* no new products.

Chapter 25

On Taking Risks and Being First

In This Chapter

➤ Developing the innovation habit

➤ Redefining the measure of success

➤ Managing risk—for your firm and for yourself

This will be brief. I want to write an epilogue to my book that's really a prologue for you: some thoughts about what it means and what it takes to make new product development a way of life for you and your business.

The 1980s taught us, I hope once and for all, the folly of failing to innovate. Fortunes were made on junk bonds used to finance not research and development (the creation of products) but mergers and acquisitions (the shifting of funds). Fortunes were made, and they were lost. In fact, it's probably more accurate to say simply that money changed hands. That was the characteristic activity of business in the 1980s. One memorable result of this was "Black Monday," October 19, 1987, when the junk hit the fan and the Dow plunged 508 points. A more enduring—and positive—result, however, was a kick-in-the-head recognition that America had slipped as the world's chief creator and innovator. The land of Bell and Edison had become the province of arbitrageurs and leveragers. The epilogue/prologue that follows assumes that the reader is duly grateful for that kick in the head.

Cutting Through the Thicket of Portfolios

When you've decided that it's time to stop moving money around and start making products, you need to develop a special set of habits and a special set of values. Here's what I mean:

➤ We are all raised to avoid problems, to "let sleeping dogs lie." But problems are manna from heaven to anyone developing new products. Learn to look *for* problems, and then to look *at* them as opportunities.

Jump Start Nothing creates a market more thoroughly, rapidly, and efficiently than a problem.

➤ Don't set out to tear down the organization in which you work. Study the corporate culture in which you and your colleagues swim. Figure out how to work within the organization, to create change "with the flow." Avoid adversarial tactics.

➤ Pile up corporate and collegial credits. Do unto others. Go the extra mile. Soon you will have created a climate surprisingly open to the innovations you sponsor.

➤ Never put projects before people. Everything you and your company does is incidental to the people who do it. Hone your people skills.

➤ Cross-train your staff and yourself. Are you a marketer by profession? Start exploring the world of the engineer, the researcher, and the customer service rep.

➤ Develop your "risk muscle." Use it or lose it.

➤ Be a hunter. Ideas are everywhere. Find them. Save them. Develop them. Don't lose them.

➤ Realize that you will make mistakes. Go ahead, make them. Then learn from them, but don't dwell on them. Get them over with—fast.

Commitment

If you're bracing for another bulleted list of avuncular advice, relax. I've got a five-part prescription for commitment that's not a matter of personal virtues, but of changing the way corporations keep score. Traditionally, American business has looked at earnings, profit margins, dividends, and debt ratios, toting each of these up every quarter. Instead, why not make a commitment to a new set of indicators? Measure success by:

➤ Customer base and rate of growth

➤ Revenue from products introduced in the last five years as a percent of total revenue

➤ IQ—innovation quotient: number of patents awarded each year

➤ New markets developed (keep score using SIC codes)

➤ Investment in R&D compared to industry and to foreign averages

False Start
Don't measure your firm's "innovation quotient" with a strictly American yardstick. Have you noticed that Sony is not a U.S. corporation?

Managing Risk

If you decide to become the person who creates change and growth inside your company—that is, if you decide to become an intrapreneur—the rewards can be great, in financial terms and in personal satisfaction. There is, of course, no reward without risk, but you can learn to manage risk.

For Your Company

You will have to decide what level of risk is acceptable for your business. In large part, this is a judgment that must be made on a project-by-project basis. However, here are some general guidelines to help you evaluate risk:

➤ *Is yours a developing or a mature business?* Developing businesses require—and tolerate—more risk than mature businesses.

➤ *Relatively speaking, is your business more capital intensive or more people intensive?* If large capital investments are routinely required, the constraints on innovation are greater and the level of acceptable risk generally lower than in people-intensive businesses.

➤ *What are the goals of your business?* If you aim at maintenance of market share rather than expansion into new markets, your business will accept relatively little risk.

False Start
Don't be tempted to evaluate risk by somebody else's standards. Take into account the type of company producing the product, the nature of the product itself, and—not least—the personalities of the principals involved. Each situation is unique.

➤ *Is yours a low-tech or high-tech business?* Low-tech businesses tend to operate on familiar territory, whereas high-tech businesses continually push the envelope. For them, risk is the name of the game.

➤ *What motivates your management team?* Tune into risk patterns by taking the pulse of top management.

For Yourself

By "personal risk," I mean risk to your survival within the company and within the industry or profession. The first step in evaluating degrees of personal risk is to take the measure of your company, using the guidelines I've just suggested. These aren't rules, of course, but they are rules of thumb.

Then you must answer a frank question: "Why should I stick my neck out to be first on the market with a new product?"

To be sure, there are a host of spiritual and philosophical reasons to do this. Louis Armstrong once responded to a woman who asked him to define jazz. "Lady," he said, "if you need me to tell you, you'll *never* know." The realm of spirit and philosophy is personal and profound and, in any case, beyond the writer of this particular *Complete Idiot's Guide*. So let's look at some more immediate reasons to stick your neck out:

Jump Start
Successful executives tend to be motivated more by a need to make their own decisions than by a desire for a steady paycheck.

➤ It is the people who innovate, create change, and build new ideas who get noticed—and who get rewarded.

➤ It is the innovators who are most frequently recognized as the most effective managers.

➤ Innovating is the best way to learn a business—bottom to top, top to bottom—because innovating requires cross-training and exposure to the entire spectrum of the business.

I Lift My Lamp Beside the Golden Door

Being first is sometimes a harrowing experience, but it is a liberating one. It expands horizons. It frees you from outworn ideas and rules. Done right, being first expands existing markets and creates new ones—for your company, and for you. Creating and developing new products enlarges your world in time as well as space, pushing the horizon out into a future that, in some part, *can* be—*should* be—of your own making. I wish you well, and I look forward to seeing you in *some* form of that future.

The Least You Need to Know

➤ It is possible to make innovation a habit.

➤ If current yardsticks of success in business fail to promote innovation, make a different yardstick.

➤ Risks are not only "taken," they are managed. Base your evaluation of risk on the kind of company you operate or work for and on the type of product you are developing.

Buzzwords Glossary

Active listening   An aid to creative discussion. During a brainstorming session, a moderator writes an ongoing list of key concepts and leading ideas on a flip chart. This *active listening* reinforces the listening process and ensures that nothing important is lost.

Angels   Private, part-time investors looking for promising start-up companies. They are also called *doctors-and-dentists* for the simple reason that many of them are doctors and dentists.

Arena   A way of defining a company's business in terms of a combination of product, market, and technology areas involved.

Attitude and opinion studies   Marketing research that measures consumer psychographics and life-style factors.

Attractive market   A market that offers high potential (is large and growing, consisting of customers who need the product and for whom purchase of it is important) and that is not burdened by intense competition (not crowded with competitors who offer strong products of high quality and low relative price, and whose sales force, distribution, and support services are highly rated).

Beta testing   Field testing of a preproduction version of a product. The beta version of a product is more fully developed and perfected than a prototype (or "alpha version"), but is still subject to user input for modification.

Brainstorming   A method of problem solving in which a small group (usually six to ten persons) focuses on a problem or issue and spontaneously contributes ideas without censorship, inhibition, or critical evaluation.

Buying power   Disposable income factored by retail sales factored by population.

Champion   In the context of new product development, a *champion* is someone willing to fight for a new product, pushing it through, over, and around the many organizational and human obstacles that threaten to mire it in the muck of inertia.

Cherry picking   A retailer buying strategy in which products are chosen from a supplier's product line and selectively purchased. It is an alternative to a retailer's purchasing and stocking an entire product line.

Closed-ended questions   Interview, survey, or questionnaire questions that limit the respondent to a stated choice of answers. *See also* **Open-ended questions.**

Commerce   As it applies to trademark law, any business or trade that the federal government may control. Trademark protection extends *only* to products and services used in commerce.

Concept testing   Procedures for assessing consumer response to new product ideas *before* the new product is put into development.

Consumable goods   Merchandise that is purchased, used up, and must be purchased repeatedly. Toothpaste is an example. *See also* **Durable goods.**

Consumers   Buyers and users of economic goods or goods of a certain class. *See also* **Customers.**

Cooperative advertising   A promotional arrangement in which the supplier and the retailer share the costs of advertising a product or product line. This generally means that both the product and the retailer are featured in the ads or promotions.

Copyright   A grant from the federal government that allows the holder of the copyright the right to exclude others from copying, using, or selling the copyrighted material (fiction and non-fiction texts, music, computer programs, dramatic works) for a fixed period of time.

Creativity   George M. Prince provided a provocative definition of *creativity* in his 1970 book, *The Practice of Creativity*: "an arbitrary harmony, an expected astonishment, a habitual revelation, a familiar surprise, a generous selfishness, an unexpected certainty, a formable stubbornness, a vital triviality, a disciplined freedom, an intoxicating steadiness, a repeated initiation, a difficult delight, a predictable gamble, an ephemeral solidity, a unifying difference, a demanding satisfier, a miraculous expectation, an accustomed amazement."

Cross-tab   In market research, a significant sub-group within a study sample. Typical *cross-tabs* are defined by demographic characteristics (age, sex, etc.), geographical location (city, region, neighborhood), and frequency of usage (those who regularly use a given product, those who do not regularly use it, etc.). A *cross-tab* is sometimes called a *banner* or *break*.

Customers   In the context of marketing, people who have bought products from you. *See also* **Consumers** and **Prospects.**

Cyclical   Demand for a product is said to be cyclical when it rises and falls in recognizable, predictable patterns not necessarily tied to seasons.

Deliverables   Criteria for progress at each stage of development. Usually, planners draw up a list of mandatory deliverables and desirable deliverables.

Demographics   The statistical characteristics of human populations; these may include age, income, gender, and so on. *See also* **Psychographics** and **Life-style.**

Durable goods   Merchandise that is not consumed in use. While toothpaste is a consumable, an electric toothbrush is durable and will not be purchased repeatedly. *See also* **Consumable goods.**

Entrepreneur   Someone who organizes and operates a business venture and assumes the risk for it. Characteristically, the entrepreneur operates in the context of a small, independent business. *See also* **Intrapreneur.**

Entry strategy   How a company plans to implement innovation goals in order to enter a new arena.

Field trial   Also called an *extended user trial.* Allows customers to test a new product over a certain time period, usually at their own site. *See also* **Beta testing.**

Find-time   The amount of time it takes shoppers to locate a given product on a store shelf. One objective of packaging is to minimize find-time.

Focus group   A group of consumers assembled for the purpose of responding to new products or new product concepts. Also commonly called *group interviews, group discussions, group depth interviews,* and, sometimes, *qualitative research.*

Hawthorn effect   The tendency of people under observation to respond more positively than people who are not being observed; the *Hawthorn effect* may distort market research efforts.

Home page   An Internet site, created by an individual or organization, that contains "hypertext links" to data relevant to the individual or organization. A home page is like an electronic table of contents, providing orderly access to whatever the individual or organization has to offer.

Inertia   In physics, the tendency of a body to resist acceleration, to remain at rest (or, if already in motion, to stay in motion in a straight line) unless acted on by an outside force. In business and other human affairs, *inertia* describes resistance or disinclination to motion, action, or change. Whether in physics or business, *inertia* operates with the force of natural law and is difficult to overcome.

Intellectual property   The vast field of commercially exploitable concepts that, as with any other kind of property, entail certain rights and privileges for the owner.

Internet   A group of worldwide information resources linked together in an electronic network of electronic networks and accessible by anyone with a computer and a modem.

Intrapreneur   A person working within a large corporation who takes personal responsibility for turning an idea into a profitable finished product. Like the entrepreneur, he or she does this through assertive risk-taking and a relentless drive toward innovation.

Keyword   In the context of market research, a single word or short phrase, highly relevant to the subject under study, which is typed during a computer database search. A good keyword is the kind of term that would be sought in a book index in order to find the desired topic.

Knock-off   A blatant imitation of an existing product, usually marketed at a cut-rate price.

Lay patent searchers   Patent researchers who are not lawyers. No professional certification is required to become a *lay searcher.*

Licensing   Granting the right to manufacture and market a product, usually for a specified time period and usually in return for a royalty payment based on sales. Customarily, an up-front "guarantee" is paid as an advance against anticipated royalties.

Life-style   In market research, the specific activities, interests, and habits of a particular consumer group.

Line extension   A new product that represents a continuous, logical development of the products a company currently offers. For example, a maker of conventional cameras might introduce a digital camera, designed to feed electronic images into a personal computer.

Market   That portion of a population that is considered buyers or potential buyers of a given product. *See also* **Marketing.**

Market research   The acquisition and analysis of data relevant to consumers, products, buying habits, and purchasing patterns. Market research may be qualitative or quantitative.

Marketing   The art and science of creating a profitable fit between products and consumers.

Metrics   The art and science of measuring product performance in the marketplace.

Milestones   Checkpoints in the development of a product. Milestones are places to pause for review and control, but they are not go/kill points.

Mission   At its simplest, an assigned task. In the context of strategic planning for a business, the mission defines the boundaries of business activity in terms of a specific goal or set of goals.

Monadic testing   A market research study that offers consumers a single product to test rather than a comparison among two or more products.

Multivariate analysis   Any analysis that studies several variables together.

Mutual pursuit joint venture   An informal alliance, usually between a smaller and a larger firm, to create specific products. No third "joint venture" corporation is formally created.

Objective   Describes something you want to achieve in the short term, whereas a *goal* is something you want to achieve over the long term. Usually, it is best to define a goal, and then to define the objectives necessary to reach that goal.

Open-ended questions   Interview, survey, or questionnaire questions that invite and require the respondent to answer in his own words. *See also* **Closed-ended questions.**

Ownership   In the context of new product development, *ownership* means giving project team members a tangible stake in, and responsibility for, the success of the project.

Patent   A grant from the federal government that allows the owner of the patent the right to exclude others from making, using, or selling an invention for a fixed period of time.

Patent agent   An individual licensed by the PTO to prepare and prosecute patent applications. He or she may also be hired to carry out patent searches. Whereas a lay searcher may or may not have qualifications relevant to the job, the patent agent is certified to have some technical training.

Patent pending   After applying for a patent, but before the PTO issues a patent, the applicant may affix the phrase "patent pending" to his product in order to discourage potential competitors from copying the product.

Penetration   The degree to which a product is sold or recognized in a particular market.

PIC   Acronym for Product Innovation Charter. The *PIC* is a firm's new product strategy—a written statement of the goals and processes of new product development within the company.

Pilot production   The trial production of a product; *pilot production* is limited and, therefore, may be more or less feasibly tweaked as necessary.

Positioning   How a product or service (or an entire company) is perceived by the best potential customer for that product or service (or company). *See* **Repositioning.**

Prior art   The state of knowledge existing or publicly available either before a patent is sought on a given invention or more than a year prior to the earliest patent application for that invention.

Product class usage   Describes consumer buying patterns for various types ("product classes") of merchandise.

Prospects   Potential customers.

Psychographics   A word coined specifically for marketing, *psychographics* describes attitudes and beliefs relevant to purchasing habits. *See also* **Demographics** and **Life-style.**

PTO   The U.S. Patent and Trademark Office.

Qualitative research   Market research conducted chiefly through interviews and focus groups, using open-ended questions, in order to access purchasing preferences, carry out concept testing, survey customer satisfaction, and perform other market analysis functions. Statistical samples are usually small.

Quantitative research   Market research conducted chiefly through questionnaires (with closed-ended questions) and such techniques as telephone interviews, as well as the tabulation of product registration cards, store receipts, etc., in order to access purchasing preferences, buying patterns, customer satisfaction, and other market analysis functions. Statistical samples are usually fairly large.

Ramifying   The process of modifying an invention in order to make it better—that is, bigger, faster, stronger, more useful in more applications.

Regression analysis   A multivariate statistical technique that relates a dependent variable (the thing you're trying to predict) to one or more independent variables (the predictors, the things—such as demographics, attitudes, etc.—that explain or predict the differences in the dependent variables).

Repositioning   If the way a product or service (or company) is perceived does not produce satisfactory sales, an effort is made to *reposition* it—that is, to change the way consumers perceive it. *See also* **Positioning.**

Scoping   The quick, low-cost preliminary research that is carried out in the earliest stages of new product development. *Scoping* is primarily a method of screening new product concepts, culling out those that do not seem viable.

Segment   A specialized area within a market. For example, the automotive parts business sells into a market called the automotive aftermarket. Within that market are such *segments* as automotive chain stores, garages, and parts houses.

Serendipity   A faculty for making fortunate discoveries.

Service mark   A name or symbol used to market a service. Registering the trademark with the federal government confers on the owner of the trademark the right to exclude others from using it for a fixed, but renewable, period of time. Often abbreviated as *mark*. *See also* **Trademark.**

SIC code   Acronym for Standard Industrial Classification code. A U.S. Department of Commerce–sanctioned system that breaks business activity into a defined and number-coded set of industrial segments organized by major divisions, industry groups, sub-groups, and, finally, specific industries.

Skimming   A pricing strategy that sets the initial price of a new product high in order to establish high perceived value for the product. Later, the price may be reduced to promote wider sales.

Stage-gate system   A method of reducing the new-product development process into discrete stages. Preceding each stage is a "gate," which is a go/kill decision point that determines whether the project should proceed to the next stage, remain in the present stage for additional work, or be killed so that everyone can get on with something else. The method was created by Robert G. Cooper.

Strategic planning   The process of rationalizing the operation of a business to achieve defined goals in the context of defined strengths, weaknesses, resources, and needs.

Strategic partnering   Usually an alliance of a large firm with a small firm for the purpose of creating a specialized new product. Typically, the larger firm supplies venture capital and the necessary marketing and distribution muscle, while the small firm furnishes the specialized creative expertise.

Superior product   Can be many things in many different contexts to many different customers; however, a *superior product* may always be defined by the following characteristics: offers unique features that differentiate it from other currently available products; satisfies customers more than the competitors' stuff does; is of high quality and represents good value; solves customers' problems with competitive products; reduces customers' costs; is innovative.

Synergy   As applied to a new product, *synergy* describes a product in which two or more known product elements are associated a new way that results in a whole greater than the sum of the parts. For example, concrete is a building material that was known to the ancient Romans. In 1854, an Englishman reinforced concrete with iron bars. The new product, ferroconcrete, is one of the most successful examples of synergy.

Target consumer   A buyer who has (through test results or purchasing history) shown himself *likely* to buy products in a given category.

Tracking   Ongoing consumer testing conducted after a product is introduced into the marketplace.

Trademark   A name or symbol used to market a product. Registering the trademark with the federal government confers on the owner of the trademark the right to exclude others from using it for a fixed, but renewable, period of time. Often abbreviated as *mark*. *See also* **Service mark**.

Value   The perceived ratio between product features, benefits, and quality versus product price.

Venture capital   Money made available for innovative enterprises, especially where the reward and the risk are high.

Venture group   A unit established to handle a firm's new ventures. In contrast to the ad hoc venture team, the *venture group* is an established and permanent unit.

Venture team   Usually, an *ad hoc* group organized within a corporate context to take charge of a specific project. *See also* **Venture group.**

Venturing   Creating a new company to manufacture and market a new product.

Vision   An act of imagination that is guided and informed by discernment and foresight. In developing new products, *vision* should both reveal possibilities and focus on practical limits.

World Wide Web   On the Internet, a graphical system of presenting information in easily retrievable, heavily cross-referenced form. Also called "the Web."

Index

D

303

When You're Smart Enough to Know That You Don't Know It All

For all the ups and downs you're sure to encounter in life, The Complete Idiot's Guides give you down-to-earth answers and practical solutions.

Personal Business

The Complete Idiot's Guide to Terrific Business Writing
ISBN: 0-02-861097-0 ▪ $16.95

The Complete Idiot's Guide to Winning Through Negotiation
ISBN: 0-02-861037-7 ▪ $16.95

The Complete Idiot's Guide to Managing People
ISBN: 0-02-861036-9 ▪ $18.95

The Complete Idiot's Guide to a Great Retirement
ISBN: 1-56761-601-1 ▪ $16.95

The Complete Idiot's Guide to Protecting Yourself From Everyday Legal Hassles
ISBN: 1-56761-602-X ▪ $16.99

The Complete Idiot's Guide to Surviving Divorce
ISBN: 0-02-861101-2 ▪ $16.95

The Complete Idiot's Guide to Getting the Job You Want
ISBN: 1-56761-608-9 ▪ $24.95

The Complete Idiot's Guide to Managing Your Time
ISBN: 0-02-861039-3 ▪ $14.95

The Complete Idiot's Guide to Speaking in Public with Confidence
ISBN: 0-02-861038-5 ▪ $16.95

The Complete Idiot's Guide to Starting Your Own Business
ISBN: 1-56761-529-5 ▪ $16.99

You can handle it!